ChALLeNged

A Tribute

chALLeNged

A Tribute

*One man's true story of caring for, laughing with
and learning from people with special needs*

Steve Grieger

Copyright © 2012 by Steve Grieger.

ISBN: Softcover   978-1-4797-0527-6
              Ebook   978-1-4797-0528-3

All rights reserved. No part of this book may be reproduced or transmitted in any form or by any means, electronic or mechanical, including photocopying, recording, or by any information storage and retrieval system, without permission in writing from the copyright owner.

This book was printed in the United States of America.

Rev. date: 04/29/2014

To order additional copies of this book, contact:
Xlibris LLC
1-888-795-4274
www.Xlibris.com
Orders@Xlibris.com
595497

For Mom, Dad and the real Jim.

AUTHOR'S NOTE

TELLING A STORY which spans twenty years doesn't come without some degree of poetic license. One of the key challenges I found was trying to represent the lives of dozens of different people – and the impressions they made on me – by consolidating them into a minimal number of characters. Therefore, while all the stories and experiences in this book are true, certain characteristics, dates and incidents have been combined for the purpose of dramatic structure, and all the names, except for those of Chris Burke and my own family, have been changed to ensure privacy. Hence, the end result becomes what I like to call a "tribute" as opposed to a strict "memoir."

Contents

A Prologue of Sorts 13

PART I: WELCOME TO ITF VILLAGE
– NOW GO HOME

Chapter 1:   The Rabbit Hole At The End Of The Rainbow 17

Chapter 2:   Knock, Knock. *"Coming In!"* 26

Chapter 3:   Why Are You Here? 34

Chapter 4:   The Cleavers Live Down The Street 43

Chapter 5:   Bloopers, Blunders, Screw Ups And Oops 56

Chapter 6:   5:30-Ish In The Garden Of Good And Evil 65

Chapter 7:   Party Downs 73

PART II: RIDING THE SHORT
ROLLER COASTER

Chapter 8:   Holiday Spirits 83

Chapter 9:   To Mickey Mouse And Carmen Miranda,
             With Much Gratitude 96

Chapter 10: New Faces, Places And Social Graces 106

Chapter 11: Road Trip 112

Chapter 12: The Other Side Of The Fence 128

Chapter 13: School Dazed 134

PART III: WELCOME TO THE CLP – MAKE YOURSELF AT HOME (WILL YOU BE STAYING LONG?)

Chapter 14: 1986– Big Brother Finally Blinks 141

Chapter 15: Normalization Nation..154

Chapter 16: People Like This Shouldn't Be Allowed
To Live On Their Own 160

Chapter 17: True Love Conquers All.. 171

PART IV: NORMAL NOTWITHSTANDING

Chapter 18: The One-Two Gut Punch..181

Chapter 19: Redemption 101 193

PART V: WELCOME HOME – SET A SPELL, TAKE YOUR SHOES OFF. Y'ALL COME BACK NOW, Y'HEAR?

Chapter 20: The Day 10,000 Clients Disappeared.......................................203

Chapter 21: Get Up, Stand Up, Stand Up For Your Rights.......................208

Chapter 22: Hey Kids, Let's Put On A Show! 212

Chapter 23: Acceptance 222

Epilogue...229

Postscript...235

Acknowledgements...237

"This life's hard, man, but it's harder if you're stupid."
– *Jackie Brown*, **The Friends of Eddie Coyle**

A PROLOGUE OF SORTS

I LIKE TO tell people that, for me, the year 2000 didn't actually end until February 10, 2001. The Director of Residential Services asked me to host a tour of one of my group homes for a few of Shepherd Hills' donors, mucky-mucks and higher-ups. Apparently, they wanted to see just where and how the consumers lived – and, more importantly, just where and how their money was being spent. "Dee-lighted," I responded cheerfully. I was always one for showing the world how the other half struggled.

Afterward, I was invited back to the main campus board room to join them for a board-certified luncheon. As we exchanged small talk about the standards of community living, I smiled and nodded and put forth my best efforts to act like I belonged there.

Soon the plates of lightly-herbed chicken, sautéed veggies, sourdough rolls and butterballs gave way to coffee and something cakey drizzled with butterscotch. The Executive Director stepped behind a podium at the head of the room where she coolly slipped into a series of brief speeches recognizing a handful of board members who helped make The Hills' dreams possible. Applause, sip coffee, smile, applaud some more.

Then something happened I didn't see coming. "Each year," began the Executive Director, "Shepherd Hills selects an employee who brings knowledge, commitment and high standards to his or her work as Employee of the Year . . ." For the next few, fleeting seconds, my ears burned and my spine began to tingle. As the Executive Director denoted certain characteristics and achievements of this year's recipient, my hearing fuzzed over and I could only make out remnants of words like *". . . QMRP . . ."; ". . . teaching someone how to . . ."; ". . . career at Shepherd*

13

Hills . . ."; "*. . . volunteered his time . . .*"; and "*. . . Shepherd Hills Famous Players.*" Slowly, the blood returned to my head as she finished with the phrase: "Shepherd Hills Board and Care is honored to recognize Steve Grieger as the 2000 Employee of the Year."

Damn, I thought. I'm Employee of the Year! How the hell did *that* happen?

To the distinct sound of executive applause – and believe me, it *has* its own distinct sound – I somehow found my way to the podium where I was awarded with a plaque and handshakes from both the Executive Director and the Shepherd Hills Board President.

Turn this way, smile – *flash!* – a picture is snapped, congratulations are rendered, and before I knew it I had returned to my seat.

It was irrefutable. I was Employee of the freakin' Year.

Sitting there in silent reflection, I realized that while I'd always been fond of the work I did, and proud of it, this was something very different. I felt validated. I felt genuine. I felt that I mattered.

Gazing down at the plaque, I smiled, and the plaque smiled back with the following epithet:

Leaders build teams with spirit and cohesion
to develop collaborative goals and cooperative relationships

Well, whaddaya know? I guess I belong here after all.

PART I

WELCOME TO ITF VILLAGE – NOW GO HOME

CHAPTER 1

THE RABBIT HOLE AT THE END
OF THE RAINBOW

"How do you know I'm mad?" said Alice.
"You must be," said the Cat, "or you wouldn't have come here."

THAT FACE! THAT face! That hideously gnarled, shockingly repulsive, poop-in-your-pants-inducing face! It was a face unlike any other I'd ever encountered before. So startling in its appearance, so vivid in its delivery, so unanticipated and abrupt on an otherwise picture-perfect afternoon. Huge nose, droopy liver lips, plaque-riddled horse teeth, bright orange hair, and Coke-bottle glasses magnifying a lazy eye. Looking into Sammy's face was like being forced to watch a 3-D horror movie in extreme close-up. It was a disfigured face of swollen, exaggerated proportions, taut, shiny skin, and a port-wine stain birthmark spilled across half of it, which forced me to wonder if maybe he had a twin brother somewhere, and when you put their heads together their faces would complete a map to buried treasure. In short, it was one freaky-looking mug.

Prior to this moment I'd never had much exposure to retarded people, and I found the sight of someone even microscopically disabled unnerving. So it was probably fate that the first individual I encountered on the way to my interview would be little Sammy White. As I sauntered across the courtyard, full of high hopes, that's when I was suddenly and so abruptly accosted nose-to-nose, in-your-face, by Sammy The Face.

"Do you have five dollars?"

Silence.

"I said, do you have five dollars?"

Flustered by this troll-like being before me, I fumbled and fished my pockets. "Uh . . . no, I sure don't."

"I have *one* dollar," The Face proclaimed with childlike pride.

"Oh. Well, isn't that nice –"

"BUT I WANT *FIVE* DOLLARS!" Suddenly, The Face threw its arms around me and burrowed deep into my best shirt, sobbing relentlessly as snot erupted from its nose like tepid green lava. I froze like the victim of a bear attack – a bear with a killer sinus infection, no less. Stunned into submission, I gently patted The Face on the head. I didn't know what to do, how to react. Should I slowly back away and try to walk around it? If I dared so much as twitch would the scary face eat me? Could it smell my fear as clearly as I could smell the tuna fish casserole it had consumed for lunch? I didn't want any trouble. All I wanted was to arrive on time for my interview. But The Face refused to let me pass, clinging tightly, locked in a mortal standoff.

The year was 1982. In my final semester at San Diego State, successful graduation required not only the completion of courses in my declared major, but also a set of "General Ed" classes – including three credits of physical education, which I had conveniently forgotten. I mean, who the hell goes to college to suffer through P.E. all over again? (I mean, really. *Who?*) The only sports I'd ever excelled in were the 50-Meter Muscle Pull and the Lunch Toss. But, alas, if I had any hopes in procuring that coveted piece of parchment, P.E. I must and so P.E. I did.

Perusing the class schedule my options included all the customary hells of Ass Sweating 101: Softball . . . Volleyball . . . Track and Field . . . Weight Lifting . . . what's this? *Ballroom Dancing?* The words shone from the page like a beacon of anti-athletic compassion. No need to look further, the choice was simple. I would undulate my way through higher education, if for nothing more than to spare the world the sight of another chubby collegiate in gym shorts.

It was in this class I met Michelle Montgomery. Michelle was blessed – or, as she might say, cursed – with the kind of beauty that only tends to blind men to her straightforward social-mindedness. And I was no exception. Her hair was like a cascade of champagne you could drown in. When she spoke, her voice was rich and sensual, resonating deep from within her well-filled velveteen vest. On a campus filled with slender tanned legs sprouting from red and black school-color shorts, Michelle's dressy-casual chic put them all to shame. For fifty minutes every Monday, Wednesday and Friday I devoured her with my eyes, taking full advantage of the opportunity to worship her from afar as so many other males must have done over the years. And yet, in spite of my horny hunger, we were still able to strike up a casual friendship because I had the ability to make her laugh and, no doubt, because she considered me "safe." Ah, but sometimes being a funny fat guy does have its advantages, as this enabled me to enjoy eighteen wonderful weeks of arm-in-arm intimacy, all under the guise of the Fox-Trot, the Lindy, the Waltz, the Cha-Cha and, of course, the cheek-to-cheek cunning of the Tango.

It was there I also learned about Michelle the Good Samaritan. In addition to school Michelle worked for Shepherd Hills Board and Care, a non-profit facility that provided residential care for the mentally retarded. The place was located roughly a few dozen miles from where we tripped the light fantastic, safely tucked into the foothills of San Diego's East County. Michelle shared with me her plans to become a psychiatric social worker in the disabilities field, and how Shepherd Hills was a great training ground for just such a goal. I greatly admired this about Michelle, her calling to help others – and never once gave it another thought. The last thing that interested me was the antics of a bunch of belated brains. Not that I had anything against them, mind you, they just weren't a priority on my get-to-know list. I mean, if they wanted to live on their own secluded campus out in the boonies somewhere, then more power to 'em – so long as they didn't bother me. Good for them, I thought. Good for the retarded people. And I meant that sincerely.

By semester's end I graduated *cum laude* from the nation's Number 4 party school, a dubious honor at best. My original dreams when I first entered college to become a novelist and playwright had since evolved into the pursuit of a teaching credential in English and Drama. For me, childhood had been one big, long, reclusive phase. And yet, for some reason, I'd always been fascinated by the tribal relations of school life. School had always offered escape, comfort, and a sense of ritual, if not, at times, refuge. I respected the classroom and all the potential it held. And so, my future was well-mapped. I would continue on, acquire a credential, settle in someplace as a high school English teacher, and foster a nice little writing career on the side. I would become Mr. G., the *cool* educator of radical literature and experimental drama. The teacher with a Muppet beard who wears vintage Hawaiian shirts and Birkenstocks. The mentor who fills young minds with inspiration and ogles the occasional student teacher a la Karen Valentine in *Room 222*. And that would suit me just fine.

Unfortunately, making my way to the head of the class required at least two more years of school, which in my case meant two more years of living with my parents – or, more to the point, with my father. (But more on that fanciful hell later.) What it meant more pressingly was I now needed a summer job to replenish my share of expenses. After a week of procrastinating and moping around the house, the time came to face the inevitable. I dragged myself down to the student center job boards with a belly full of book smarts, a chest full of conceit and a soul full of uncertainty. There, posted on a simple 3"x5" card, I saw the following:

WANTED

SHEPHERD HILLS BOARD AND CARE

Position: Houseparent

Status: Part-Time

Wage: Minimum

NO EXPERIENCE REQUIRED

Contact: Human Resources Dept.

(619) 448-1000

You know those moments when a tiny star shines over your head and you try to shoo it away but it just won't leave until it finishes guiding you to some unknown destination? Me neither. But as I stood there in the warm sunlight, the allure of foamy pitchers of beer calling to me from the on-campus pub nearby, the fact remained that I needed a job – and the prospect of seeing Michelle again was just too keen to pass up. Besides, I thought, how hard could it be to push a few kids around in wheelchairs? Maybe even volunteer for the Special Olympics to help tie shoelaces or some deed equally noble. Who knows? Perhaps I'd even meet some interesting characters and have something colorful to write about. Maybe my own version of *One Flew Over the Cuckoo's Nest*. This was going to be a cinch. A no-brainer, pardon the pun.

Twenty-four hours later, I found myself navigating a series of back roads and cattle crossings in search of Never-Never-Land, tucked within a cluster of Cleaveresque tract homes still awaiting the arrival of modern civilization. At last, I stumbled upon the Shepherd Hills campus. From the street Shepherd Hills Board and Care appeared no more threatening than your average neighborhood elementary school of gated stucco-and-stone, surrounded by adequately trimmed lawns and a sentry of scrubby pine trees. I pulled my trusty little used Honda Civic into the lot and parked.

Applying the final touches to my application at the front desk, I made sure to slip in the fact that I, quote – "make an awesome Santa Claus" – unquote. I thought for sure this would clinch things. Last but not least, I specifically made a notation that I was interested in working in Michelle Montgomery's department – whatever that might incur.

My application was hastily swallowed by Human Resources with unbiased resolve, and I was told that they did indeed have a position available in Ms. Montgomery's department. In fact, if I were interested, they could get me in for an interview with the department's supervisor right away. *Yes!* I thought eagerly. Everything was falling into place. One brief phone call and I would be on my way to interview with a woman named Dawn Barry, head of the "Independent Training Program" – a program for retarded adults.

At that, my eagerness skidded to dead stop.

Adults? Aw, Jeez! I don't wanna work with *adults*. I wanna work with *kids*. Retarded *kids*. You know, the way Hollywood always depicted helping sweet-little-innocent Johnny Mongoloid "find himself." I mean, who in their right mind wants to work with retarded *adults?* But the opening in Michelle's department was with adults, and so adults I would have to bear.

With chin held high, I set out along a series of intertwining walkways toward my destination. The main campus was at once serene and foreboding. What had appeared from the street to be no bigger than a modest grade school was, in fact, a facility that engulfed a full 14 acres, governing an array of administrative offices, a central kitchen, a greenhouse, an auditorium, a small park with a sand lot, and twelve residential dormitories surrounded by an all-encompassing chain link fence. Common areas of deep green lawns were dotted by more pine trees, a few battered picnic tables, a playground-regulation swing set, and a swimming pool securely fashioned with a wheelchair ramp. At last, I arrived at the back gate, which opened onto a sizable off-the-street parking lot for the employees. There, beyond the steaming blacktop, awaited the humble ITF Village; a small, separate apartment complex – and the impending face-to-chest encounter.

After allowing The Face what I concluded was more than ample time for a good long sob, I attempted to steer it away with a sympathetic "there, there." But The Face tightened its clutches. Following several more attempts, I was finally able to peel The Face off me, which in turn yielded a long, elastic stick of viscous goo linking its nose to my shirt. The farther I pushed it away, the longer the wet green rope stretched until it finally snapped – *sss-thwop!* – and recoiled back onto my chest with a milky splash. The Face trotted off. I stood there trembling, dripping with neon green, the bitter taste of bile slowly rising in the back of my throat, my skin virtually crawling from a bad case of What The Fuck Was *That?*

"Don't worry about Sammy. He likes to get up close and personal when he talks to people. It's just his way of being friendly."

The voice I heard belonged to none other than Michelle. Like a guardian angel, she appeared from nowhere to rescue me with a damp wash cloth.

I quickly gathered my wits. "Well, if he's the welcome wagon, I'd sure hate to see his gift basket."

As Michelle laughed I felt the color return to my face – as did my feelings for her. The same college crush, the same horny hunger. Mopping the Sammy stain from my shirt, we briefly re-acquainted over memories from the good old days of Ballroom Dance, and I eventually mustered my cool to explain I was there to interview for a position. Oddly, Michelle didn't seem all that impressed. Still, I had apparently survived the first initiation: I had been snotted on and lived to retch about it. And so, Michelle escorted me onward to Dawn's office. Fool in love that I was, I followed.

Dawn Barry was a silver-haired surfer chick in her early-fifties, dressed in OP shorts and a *Changes in Latitudes, Changes in Attitudes* tank top. She was currently in the middle of a debate with a small gravel-voiced man who was passionately defending the artistic merits of Lawrence Welk. Nevertheless, Dawn greeted me professionally and – after successfully shooing the man out the door – sat with her back to the glare of a large picture window that looked out onto the apartment courtyard.

"Steve . . . Gry-ger, is it?" she said, scanning my application.

"*Gree*-ger," I gently corrected. "Like Robby Krieger from The Doors, only with a G." (Which is where any further comparison of me and a member of The Doors ends.)

As she passively grilled me through the typical applicant Q & A, all I could make out was her silhouette. Though her voice was characteristically surfer-mellow, still, conversing with a shadow was not without some degree of intimidation. I learned that while the other dorms on the main grounds housed residents with varying levels of retardation, Dawn's domain harbored nine "high-functioning" adults who were learning skills to achieve "normalization." For the crux of our interview Dawn focused primarily on two things. On my application under hobbies I had listed cooking and drama. She told me she liked the cooking because one of the job duties was to help teach these people to cook, and she liked the drama because houseparents were often required to teach skills through role playing. (I neglected to mention that despite the Drama degree I had virtually no training in acting; it was hard enough just trying to act like I wanted the job.)

Dawn described her apartment program as different from the basic board and care provided by the main campus. According to Dawn, her Independent Training Facility or "ITF Village" was a radical new concept for 1982. It was a community-based, minimally-restrictive setting designed to help guide each resident into a normal, independent lifestyle. Classes were taught in cooking, cleaning, banking and shopping; the basics needed to survive "out there." By providing everything from verbal demonstration to hand-over-hand assistance, the ultimate goal was for each of the ITF residents to one day move out on their own. Dawn was also forthcoming in that she was looking to hire a male to help handle some of the "occasional aggressive behaviors" that occurred. The only other male staff who worked there had just given notice and was in the middle of his final two weeks. Otherwise, the remaining employees were all female. The hours were part-time, 4 p.m. to 10 p.m., with rotating days off. The pay was cheap, but the benefits were good. She never once commented about my "awesome Santa Claus."

Meanwhile, throughout the entire interview, a stream of voices in the background wafted steadily over the courtyard, each periodically taking turns to yell at someone named Owen:

"– Shut up, Owen, before I slug ya! –"
"– Go away, Owen! Get outta here! –"
"– Cut it out, Owen! I punch your lights! –"
"– Owen did it, not me! –"
"– Your head, Owen! –"

Plodding onward, I began to grow less enthusiastic, despite the draw to make some time with Michelle. I shifted uneasily. My stomach felt queasy. Would this job really be worth it? Didn't I see a sign on my way here that Taco Bell was hiring? Did I really want to spend my summer having to deal with "occasional aggressive behaviors?"

On cue, Frankenstein's monster entered the room. He was brandishing a blood-stained kitchen knife. He was tall and massive-skulled with hands the size of rakes and wild gnarls of streaky gray and white hair, and when he walked his right foot pivoted outward. Eyeing me with contempt, the man and his knife loomed closer . . . *closer* . . . until he towered directly over me. I sat there, paralyzed with fear. What the hell is *this*? First an assault by a deadly mucus and now this one's gonna finish things by slashing my throat?

"Dawn? . . . I think I n-n-need a f-f-first aid," he said.

Timidly, the colossal beast lifted his pinky finger to display a small cut, like a lion with a thorn stuck in its paw. Rather than show concern, Dawn simply looked annoyed. The man continued, "I c-c-couldn't open my C-C-Coke, so I t-t-tried to twist it off with the knife and –"

Dawn sighed wearily. "How many times have I told you not to play with knives? And where's your helmet?"

The large man grinned coyly and tucked his chin into his chest. "I dunno."

Dawn sighed a second time for effect, took the man by the arm, and motioned for me to follow. Our interview continued in the adjoining bathroom, as Dawn cleaned and dressed the man's finger. I offered him a broad, friendly smile, but the man would have no part of it. The kitchen knife was nothing compared to the daggers he was shooting at me; his eyes were fixed and angry – how dare I intrude on *his* territory?

Dawn finished the dressing and patted the man's back. "There! Good as new. Cut down on the sodas, dude. They're hazardous to your health." At this point Dawn noticed the man glaring at me and playfully ruffled his hair. "What's the matter, big guy? You checking him out? Does he pass inspection?"

Taking the initiative, I awkwardly extended my hand and asked the million dollar question. "Hi there, are you Owen?"

I could hear the audible sizzle of a lit fuse.

"OWEN?!" the man shouted. "I NOT OWEN!"

"HEY-Hey-hey-hey-hey . . ." Dawn's voice trailed to calm. "Lighten up. He's just being friendly." Dawn delivered the words with great distinction. "Jackie, this is Steve." Then back to me, the same. "Steve, this is Jackie." Her manner turned impish. "But he and Owen *are* sometimes mistaken for one another because they both have such rotten tempers. Right, Jackie? Huh? Hmm? Huuuhhh? . . ."

I watched with quiet admiration as Dawn masterfully channeled Jackie's anger back into a puppy-like demeanor, complete with him giggling and laying his head on her shoulder. This was Jackie Chuckam, the sleeping giant. Cheerless and distrustful.

Dawn capped off the introduction by informing me, "Jackie and Owen are roommates. They'll be in your group."

Hearing this, I managed an Oscar-worthy smile. "Oh . . . boy." I said. "Isn't that . . ." (*c'mon, you can do it, you can do it*) ". . . sssssswell."

Jackie left Dawn's office without another word. "Don't forget your helmet," she called after him, just as casually as a mother reminds her child to bundle up before going out to play. As the two of us observed him through the window, Jackie walked into the courtyard, mounted a rickety, red and white bicycle, plucked a scuffed, white plastic helmet from atop the handlebars, placed it on his head, and rode off up the driveway, chin straps dangling unclasped.

It was then Dawn asked me if I'd ever had any prior exposure to this population.

"Oh sure," I verified. "Once I lived near a school that had a Special Ed program and me and my friends used to walk by it every day and say hi to the kids wearing football helmets."

"Uh-huh," Dawn replied. "But nothing with retarded adults?"

"Er . . . no, not really," I confessed. "I need more experience, don't I?"

Dawn straightened. "Not necessarily. Tell me . . . why do you *really* want to work here?"

Now, there was no way I was about to tell this woman I was only there to hit on one of her employees. Instead, I began riffing an excuse, a reason, and a justification all rolled into one. I explained that I thought the job could be a blessing in disguise. That I'd always had a certain curiosity about retarded people. A place in my heart. Not a calling, really (no, even I couldn't pull that one off), but a certain interest . . . concern . . . inquisitiveness . . . regard . . . fascination, but in a *good* way . . . thoughtfulness . . . respect . . . reverence . . . self-motivation . . . What was the question again? By this point I had no idea where I was going. I couldn't discern truth from lie from naivete. Ultimately, I trailed off with the first honest words I'd said that day: "I think I just want to help."

Dawn smiled. It was the type of smile I couldn't read. Was it one of sincerity or amusement? Or knowing? "Well, listen," she said, "I realize you came out here today just for the interview, but . . ." her face left the shadows and brightened in the sunlight ". . . how about hanging around for the rest of the shift? See how you like it."

With nothing to lose I decided to give it a try, despite the threat of another mucus attack or a good knifing. "What should I do?" I asked.

"Just observe. Knock on a few doors and say hello. You know . . . '*mingle*.'"

I'm not sure why, but there was something about the way she said "mingle" that didn't sit well. Just what the hell was I getting into?

And the Cheshire Cat vanished quite slowly,
beginning with the end of the tail, and ending with the grin,
which remained some time after the rest of it had gone.

CHAPTER 2

KNOCK, KNOCK. *"COMING IN!"*

I WANDERED SILENTLY from Dawn's office out into the still air of the ITF Village courtyard. A wave of apprehension lapped past my knees, threatening to pull me under. Looking around, I was unimpressed by it all; just a series of modules linked in the shape of a horseshoe, anchored by the staff office at one end, and a small rec room/kitchen with a single pay phone mounted outside at the other. At the open end of the U, a wide driveway led back up to the parking lot and around the main campus, where it ultimately spilled out onto the residential streets and into the community at large. Everything was the color of sunbaked mud trimmed in dried mustard.

As good a place to start as any, I tentatively approached Apartment #1. Inside, I could hear the distinct opening riff to "Spill The Wine" by Eric Burdon and War, mixed with the innocence of giggling children. I gently tapped on the door and waited for a response. No answer. I tapped again. Still nothing.

"You have to do it like this."

Once again, Michelle appeared from nowhere. With a loud, deliberate jingling of her keys, she knocked with two sharp raps, cheerfully announced, *"coming in!,"* unlocked and then whipped open the door, all in swift and familiar succession. Michelle and I entered, and I gazed in wonder at the décor of Day-Glo posters displaying the trippy likes of The Beatles, The Who and Jimi Hendrix. Scarves shrouded lampshades, beads dangled from doorways, and misshapen ceramic bowls accented the furniture which consisted of a couch covered by a multi-colored

26

afghan, a lacquered coffee table crafted from an empty wooden spool of telephone cable, and a whole shitload of psychedelic throw pillows. The place reeked of wild strawberry incense.

"*Am I going crazy . . . or is this just a dream?*" sang Eric Burdon.

In the center of the room a man and a woman, each with Down syndrome, were dancing to the beat of the music – that is, the woman was spinning and twirling skillfully while the man simply stood immobile, giggling non-stop. The woman wore a beribboned square dancing dress and Chuck E. Cheese baseball cap. The man appeared as if he had just recently eaten a large slice of cake, as there were chocolate crumbs conspicuously smeared around the corners of his mouth. He was dressed in nothing but a limp, battleship-gray T-shirt and jockeys, with a mop of brownish-red hair and wet sheepdog bangs covering his eyes. The startling sight of a grown man standing there in just his underwear sent a brief knee-jerk reaction to the pit of my stomach.

"Guys!" Michelle shouted above the music. "I want you to meet Steve. He's visiting us for the day." Michelle introduced the dancing couple as Darlene Beaudine and James Livingston. Both were squat, moon-faced, and adept ambassadors at making me feel welcome as they immediately approached and gave me a hug. Of the two, Darlene was the more outgoing. She also shouldered ample breasts, which she apparently enjoyed using. "Hello, handsome," she chirped. "Do you like to dance?" Before I could answer, she arched her back and added coquettishly, "Maybe I can dance with *you* sometime." Her speech was clear as a bell, but not as clear as her intentions.

James, on the other hand, spoke with a thick speech impairment. The words spilled out of his mouth as if he were mumbling, stammering and mooing all at the same time. Cradling my right hand in both of his – dry, rough, leathery hands that felt like they'd been freshly scrubbed with a wire brush – he gave it a reassuring shake, as if to say "everything's gonna be all right." However, his benevolent greeting sounded more like "bob-bobby-brown" and "muh-muh-muhm." In fact, I would learn most everything James ever said sounded like "bob-bobby-brown" or "muh-muh-muhm."

Michelle continued. "And that fool over there is Cole." A body I hadn't initially noticed rose from the shadows at the far end of the couch. With the distinct *clack-clack* of two metal crutches, a figure with mild cerebral palsy hobbled forward with dirty bare feet. He fashioned a fringed leather vest, peace symbol-patterned shirt, and long, straight blond hair floating behind miniscule John Lennon sunglasses just big enough to cover his pupils. I received a "Hey, man" and staunch power-to-the-people handshake. "You like my pad?"

"Groovy," I said.

"Far out," he replied, and quietly returned to his spot on the couch. This was Cole Petersen, resident hippie, artist, and all-around funkmeister. It would later be explained to me that Cole was obsessed with the '60s, while at the same time fully aware and "cool with it" being 1982. After all, he wasn't a *nut*. Just nutty. But somehow, on him, nutty worked.

Michelle asked Cole and James if she could show me their room. Both said okay (or rather, one "okay" and one "muh-muh"). Their apartment, like every other apartment in the complex, consisted of one cigar-box living room, one pill-box bathroom, a kitchenette with the square footage of a Wheat Thin, and a single bedroom shared by two residents. Cole and James' bedroom was divided in half by their personal decorating tenets. Cole's half continued the '60s motif with a smattering of vintage *Playboy* magazines splayed next to the bed, including a few familiar issues both rare and precious that I myself had been fortunate enough to fish out of the trash bin of a nearby singles complex in my youth. (Ah, memories.)

In contrast, James' side could've won first prize at a *Star Wars* convention. From the *Star Wars* posters, action figures, mugs and bedspread, all the way to the life-sized cardboard standee of Darth Vader brandishing a Pepsi – rescued, no doubt, from some idle 7-Eleven Dumpster. The entire experience within those mere few minutes was eye-opening. For here I'd discovered a minor amalgam hidden in the middle of Cleaverville. And there were still four more apartments left on the tour.

On the way out, Michelle remarked to Darlene, "Better get ready for your outing, they'll be leaving soon."

"I *am* ready," Darlene said.

"You're going dressed like *that?*" Michelle said, arching an eyebrow toward the Chuck E. Cheese-square dancing getup.

"You're not the boss of me. It's my *right*," Darlene said defensively, at which point she turned to me, obviously feeling the need to authenticate herself. "I work at Chuck E. Cheese. Fun for the whole family!"

"Fine, fine," Michelle dismissed, and the subject was hastily dropped.

For the next hour Michelle led me through the ITF complex, answering questions and introducing me to a few of the other residents. It became an afternoon of sticky handshakes, random bear hugs, and broad smiles with dentures that didn't quite fit. Following my interview, Michelle had spoken to Dawn and offered to play tour guide, apparently as an extension of our college friendship. But I was clearly on cloud nine just to be in her presence once again, in spite of any misgivings about actually taking the job.

Next door to Cole and James lived Sammy "The Face" White. Sammy currently resided alone, as the empty bed next to his awaited a new referral. Thankfully, Sammy was not around at the moment; I'm not sure I could've handled another face-to-Face just then. It turned out that Sammy had taken off for the afternoon to catch the bus downtown.

"Seriously?" I said. "You mean they let them go off by themselves, with nobody to watch them?"

Michelle eyed me sideways. "It's not like they're in prison."

I was somewhat surprised to learn from Michelle that, despite a kisser that looked like the entire cast of a Fellini movie, Sammy went out in public all the time. One of his greatest joys was to hang out in coffee shops where he made friends with cashiers, busboys, waitresses, and even the regulars. Apparently, he was quite articulate with a head for current affairs. When I asked if anyone was ever worried he might get picked on, Michelle laughed. Sammy was also a natural-born scrapper, having learned to handle himself in a scuffle or two. So maybe it was because of his appearance – or in defiance of it – that Sammy was his own best champion.

Knock, knock. "*Coming in!*"

Located at the butt end of the horseshoe, Apartment #3 was shared by Darlene and another young woman with Down syndrome, Holly Gross.

"What's that smell?" I asked, following Michelle through the door. "Eggs?" I was promptly educated it was a "potty smell," and I immediately felt stupid for not knowing the difference. Holly was the only person in ITF Village confined to a wheelchair. Because of the extended periods spent in the chair, this led to many a toileting accident, which caused her to endure a perpetual funk. This only made the last name Gross – as in *pew, that girl smells gross!* – all the more ironic, if not cruel. Moving into the apartment further, I was caught off guard to see the bathroom door wide open and Holly sitting on the toilet, naked from the waist down. Like Cole, Holly also had mild cerebral palsy – which made something as simple as perching atop a toilet seat an arduous chore that required the synchronization of several muscles determined not to cooperate.

As Michelle impassively attended to Holly's needs, she pointed to a shelf beyond her reach. "Hand me that roll of toilet paper, will you?" I thought it remarkable that Michelle didn't even ask me to avert my eyes. *I shouldn't be watching this*, I thought. *No one should.* I tossed her the roll and took it upon myself to wait outside.

Once Michelle rejoined me, we continued our way across the courtyard. I looked around disparagingly at the cracked-and-patched cement, meager flower beds, parched ice plant, and a few rusty, wrought-iron patio chairs. Suddenly, a young man burst from the door of Apartment #4 and cut across our path as he bee-lined it for the driveway. He wore black dress slacks, black dress shoes and, for reasons I couldn't fathom, a black tuxedo vest without a shirt, which made him look like a malnutritioned Chippendale's dancer. Michelle called to him. "Billy! . . . BILLY!"

"I *can't*. I going to be *late*."

"Aren't you going to put on a shirt?"

"Fuck off!"

Refusing to look back, the man dismissed us with a swipe of his arm.

Michelle gritted her teeth. "That's Billy Mattila. He's an asshole."

(Excuse me, he's a what *now?)*

Reading the look of surprise on my face, Michelle explained that Billy Mattila was equally hated by all. Staff, residents, even his own family – which was apparently why they never came to visit. In fact, the staff even went so far as to nickname him "Mattila the Hun" behind his back. I nodded as she explained her slur, but still thought it bizarre that Michelle would introduce one of the residents by calling him such a thing. I mean, even *I* know you're not supposed to say something like that about retarded people.

Onward to Apartment #5, the final apartment. As Michelle and I approached, we heard a loud, angry ruckus coming from inside. Flying past me with keys a-janglin', Michelle burst in without a knock-knock or a "*coming in!*" – only to be halted by a blue flash. The place was a wreck. On the living room floor laid an empty birdcage, while on the sofa a small, truculent Down syndrome dwarf hopped up and down, wielding a badminton racket with murder in his eyes.

"DON'T LET HIM OUT!"

Instantly, Michelle slammed the door. Before I could say "what the – ," she grabbed me from behind, poised me like shield, and charged back in, prepared for gladiatorial combat. Inside, the fiery homunculus was scrambling furiously after a simple, innocuous blue parakeet, the kind that could never do anyone any harm.

"I was trying to feed him but he got away," the man cried. "C'mere, damn it!"

Michelle's face was stern. "Owen," she scolded, "we've told you if you can't be responsible for your bird –"

"I can take care of it! Just leave me alone!"

Now, the darn thing couldn't have been any bigger than, well, a parakeet, yet judging by their reaction it might as well have been a literal bat out of hell. As Michelle stumbled to help Owen catch his agitated feathered friend, I hung back to watch the show. *Crash!, bang!, ouch!, look out!* – a broken lamp here, an overturned table there, a badminton racket *every*where. All that was missing was a cream pie and a couple of "nyuck-nyucks." Finally, the bird came to rest on its own, choosing to land – of all places – on my shoulder. (Great. First mucus and now bird shit. I could hear my shirt sarcastically thanking me for pulling it out from the back of the closet just for this.) The room went silent. With great care, the diminutive man tiptoed toward me and gently cupped the bird into his hands.

All of a sudden the man exploded. "I *told* you not to fly away! I *told* you! You want me to put you in a hole?!"

"Owen!" Michelle shouted. "In the cage! Now!"

Immediately, the man complied, slipping the bird back into the cage and replacing it to its stand. "I was just kidding," he muttered. "*Cheez*us."

"One more chance, Owen. One more, that's it."

"Yeah, yeah," he said, turning his back.

Michelle regained her composure. "Okay, then. I want you to meet someone. This is Steve. He's visiting us today. Why don't you show him your room?"

Owen huffed. "Well, I'd like to, but I *can't*."

"Why not?"

Once again the feisty little man began to sizzle. "Because my roommate, Jackie Chuckam, put my tape recorder *on the goddamn roof!* He went, '*Oooo*, Owen, you're *stooo*-pid, you're a *duuuu*-my, I *haaaaate* you,' and he grabbed my tape recorder and he threw it on the *ROOF!*" The man punched his words with dramatic gestures. "That's *MY* tape recorder. *MY* tape recorder! I don't like that word – *stupid! HE'S* the *STUPID* one. *NOT ME!*"

Owen Van Winkle was a surly, scant little man in his mid-fifties with a voice that sounded like a bowl of corn flakes and whisky. The roundish features were there, but otherwise he didn't seem to fit the typical profile of a person with Downs; instead, the skin on his face hung in wrinkles and folds like a dry shower curtain. For the record, he was not a "dwarf" or "midget" or "little person," just small. A crusty fireplug atop stubby legs.

When I'd first arrived for my interview, Owen was the one heatedly debating Dawn about Lawrence Welk. (Not to mention the recipient of everyone else's wrath.) As he and Michelle continued their exchange, I shifted sideways to peek into the bedroom. Though he shared the space with Jackie The Giant Knife-Wielding Maniac, it was obvious the big screen TV and multi-component stereo system belonged to Owen. The entire wall next to his bed was plastered with greeting cards, postcards, family photos, and Special Olympics certificates. On Jackie's side, the wall was completely bare. The only item of note was a small, framed photo next to his bed of two people I assumed must've been his parents, dressed like the picture had been taken in the '50s.

Meanwhile, Michelle and Owen were still going at it.

"I *hate* that stuttering fuck."

"Owen, be nice! Jackie's . . . well, he's working on things."

"Yeah? Well, how would he like it if I wrecked his *bike?*"

"You *know* you don't want to do that."

"But how come he gets away with this shit? *HOW COME?!*"

"All right, enough! I'll get the ladder."

Moments later, Michelle climbed down a ladder against the rear of Apartment #5, carrying a portable cassette tape recorder. Returning it to Owen with what appeared to be a customary promise that she would "speak to Jackie," Owen trudged off, muttering under his breath. *"Everybody here's a fucking dumbshit . . ."*

Michelle turned to me, stone-faced. "You still want this job? C'mon, I need a cigarette."

The ITF Village rec room was a place designated for laundry, daily medication passes, and an endless exhibition of TV reruns resonating from an old Magnavox wooden console still running on diode tubes. Michelle and I plopped onto a threadbare couch, which called to us with Salvation Army goodwill. In the background, a gristmill of classic sitcom fare churned with studio-audience laughter at the sound of Archie Bunker's toilet flushing taboos.

Thinking about the tour, I was struck by how natural, homelike, and downright *unremarkable* everything was. The cast of overzealous residents notwithstanding, each apartment had the smell and feel of every other home in America; not a Norman Rockwellesque home redolent of comfort food and cedar chests, but a *real* home inhabited by the smells of old sneakers and burnt toast, urine stains around the toilet grout, improper lighting, dust bunnies, and clutter, lots of clutter. In other words, the kind of home the rest of us live in.

Michelle lit up a cigarette and I took a beat before breaking the silence.

"You handled him really well."

"Owen?" She shrugged. "Eh, he's a sweetheart, really. Shame the others can't stand him."

"Why's that?"

"'Cause he's got a mouth that won't quit and an ego that won't sleep. Jackie's the only one who'll tolerate him. Sad thing is, it's not his fault. His parents are dead, his brother spoils him rotten, so he expects the same from everyone else. Otherwise, he's a very nice man. Too bad he's retarded. He'd make the perfect game show host."

Was I missing something? It seemed to me if Owen lacked anything it was civilized charm. "So," I said, "is this like one of those progressive schools where everybody accelerates at their own pace?"

Michelle eyeballed me and I could sense her suppressing a smile at my expense. "This isn't a school. It's their home."

I confessed to Michelle I'd never seen anything like it, and asked her if there were many of them around.

"No," she said, not bothering to hide her sarcasm, "we're a privileged few."

"What do the neighbors think?"

"Some think we're great, some treat us like lepers. A few give the guys candy at Halloween. The Shriners come out at Christmastime and sing. That's about it."

"What about the Special Olympics?"

"What about it?"

"Do any of them participate?"

"A couple. Owen. Sammy. Sometimes Darlene."

I tried to impress Michelle by telling her I'd like to volunteer for the Special Olympics, but instead was met by a blasé response, dismissed in a puff of smoke.

"Knock yourself out."

This caused me to pause, a bit humbled. In college I'd adopted a sense of humor that helped me joke my way out of uncomfortable situations; sometimes as a means to avoid confrontation, other times in response to a fear of the unknown, and once in a while simply because you just need to be a smartass. But this sort of aloofness in Michelle was a side of her I'd never envisioned. My own lack of interest in these people aside, I was still taken aback by the way she spoke to them – and *about* them – so casually. She spoke about them like they were ordinary people, not special like they were supposed to be. In a way it almost seemed . . . disrespectful. Finally, I couldn't help myself. "Is it me or do all the staff around here seem a bit . . . jaded?" (By "all the staff" I obviously meant Michelle.)

"Eh." More smoke. "Comes with age."

"But what if somebody got hurt? I mean, hurt bad. Earlier, I saw this one guy, Jackie, cut himself with this *humongous* knife." I sat back to gather my dismay and shook my head. "If I were you I'd be really worried for these people."

This struck a nerve. "Hey!" she snapped. "My whole *life* revolves around this place."

"I didn't mean –"

"Let me give you some advice, Steve. Don't be so quick to judge. Don't wear your heart on your sleeve unless you want it ripped off. Believe me. I know." Michelle snubbed out her butt and moved behind the kitchen counter.

I sat there dumbly, longing for the innocent days of Ballroom Dance, wondering where my dream girl had suddenly disappeared to. Finally, not knowing what else to say, I said what I thought she needed to hear.

"Thanks."

Michelle smiled and shrugged it off, content to change the subject. "So, how'd the interview go with Dawn?"

"Fine." Though I had to add, "a little unsettling. It was kinda like taking a meeting with The Godfather."

"The back to the window thing? The glare in your eyes?"

"Yeah! Exactly."

"Mm. That's Dawn."

"More like Dawn Vito," I quipped. Michelle stared at me deadpan. "You know, as in Don Vito Corleone . . ." I trailed off to no response. (Oh, the jokes were still coming, but they were growing small and weak.) "Anyway, it was nice of her to let me stick around today. I just hope I qualify for the position."

At that, Michelle smirked playfully. "Oh, you qualify all right."

"You think so?"

"I guarantee it."

"How can you be sure?"

"Because . . ." Michelle rocked forward for emphasis ". . . you're the only one who applied for the job."

CHAPTER 3

WHY ARE YOU HERE?

A ND JUST WHAT of that "fanciful hell" I mentioned earlier?

Before there were rabbit holes and sleeping giants, before there were volcanic noses and tape recorders rescued from roof tops, and long before a dormant lust was reawakened by any dream girl, there was already a different destiny in progress. For me it all started when I was born in sunny California, which, in theory, should make anybody happy. Nevertheless, this did nothing more than grant me the dubious privilege of growing up a native of hot, monotonous and ultimately uninspiring atmospheric conditions. (Still, it was a dry heat, so who was I to bitch?)

Trekking our way like nomads across the greater Los Angeles basin, the tribe consisted of me, my older sister, Carolyn, and my parents, Art and Theda. My father never wanted to purchase a place of his own, so we grew up surrounded by a countless array of walls with only one thing in common: they were always painted *white*. Color is verboten in a rental unit, so the psychological color palette of my formative years was fundamentally inspired by eggshell, cream, pearl, bone and Swiss coffee. Moving around also made it difficult to lay the foundation for any lasting friendships, including those within my own family. We never lived in a home – we always lived in a house.

My youth was something that could've easily transpired in one of playwright Eugene O'Neill's rough drafts, with a rageaholic father who loved to scream, curse, and randomly beat his world into submission before there was medication for such things, and a displaced, poor-little-rich-girl for a mother, loving yet hyper-sensitive,

34

also before there was medication for such things. Both were originally from Pittsburgh, Pennsylvania, and both had been extremely spoiled as children in completely different ways.

Dad was a tough little Mama's boy, the youngest of seven, who was allowed to cuss as a toddler and roam the alleys as a child. He grew up big, bad, strong and handsome. As an Army corporal during WWII, he had great aspirations of becoming a Master Drill Sergeant after the war – that is, until his left leg was blown off below the knee by a landmine in France. In a literal flash his entire world screeched to a halt, forever sanctioning a bitterness about God, the French, the war, humanity, and ultimately his family. To him we became a surrogate platoon of grunts. My mother, on the other hand, was a Daddy's princess, an only child of a well-to-do stockbroker and an ex-silent movie actress from Russia who, herself, was bitter about having to give up the silver screen when she got pregnant. Like Dad, Mom also grew up good-looking and proud of it, and married my father just to spite her overbearing mother. Oh, those crazy, impetuous, pathologically self-preoccupied kids.

But whereas Theda was allowed to *have* anything she wanted, Art had always been allowed to *do* anything he wanted.

Dad's disability should have automatically garnered sympathy – if it wasn't for the fact that he demanded it. In the middle of a party or neighborly game of Tripoli, my pop was the kind of joker who, if he didn't feel he was getting enough attention, would sit in a corner, remove his wooden leg, and showcase the empty dangling pant leg. Instantly, all heads would turn and he'd find himself surrounded by a doting, servile audience:

> *"– What's wrong, Art? You feeling okay? –"*
> *"– Can I get you anything, Art? –"*
> *"– You want to lie down awhile? –"*
> *"– You need some help there, Artie? –"*
> *"– Your leg bothering you, buddy? –"*
> *"– Can I get you a drink? –"*
> *"– Can I bring you a snack? –"*
> *"– Is there anything I can do to make your life better, you wonderful old war hero you? –"*

And my father played it to the hilt. Perfectly syncopated with little grunts and groans – not enough to warrant a call for an ambulance, but just enough to get him the attention, if not that snack. This wasn't the conventional kind of parental embarrassment most kids suffer like, say, a dad who retrieves the morning paper from the front lawn in his underwear. This was serious, psychologically-scarring embarrassment. Is it any surprise the neighbors would soon stop asking my parents to their parties and neighborly games of Tripoli? And so, every few years, we'd pull up stakes and move once again. Sometimes because my father got a new job lined up, sometimes because he'd lose a job due to his temper, and sometimes because everything around us had just grown too cold.

All my life my father remained a frustrated soldier, constantly in search of combat that would assure him victory. *"You're lucky to be livin' here!"* was one of Pop's favorite battle cries; a cry uttered so often and determinedly I grew up with no other choice but to surrender to it. Granted, we always had food on the table, clothes on our backs, and the required physical trappings over our heads, I'll give dear old Dad that. But he also never let us forget it.

My dad was always mad. My dad was always, *always* mad. But, alas, this was the Baby Boom and so Father Knew Best. Words like "dysfunctional family," "anger management" and "psychotropic drug therapy" didn't exist in 1960's mainstream lower-middle class America. Instead, we had drugs like *My Three Sons, Leave It To Beaver* and *The Andy Griffith Show* to handle these issues for us. Every night became a two-hour fix of family benevolence in a box, causing me to cling to a headstrong faith that the world – like that on TV – should be, ought to be, why-oh-why can't it be . . . *fair?*

And yet, my old man's explosions continued to be as baffling as they were harrowing; bursting into our rooms as we slept or while sitting on the toilet, isolated amidst desperate cries of *"but I didn't do anything!-I didn't do anything!,"* pounded by a storm of curses and belt-welts, left mystified in a wake of bruises and infinite dismay. And when he got really mad, *bizarro* mad, sometimes he'd actually hurl his wooden leg at us from across the room. Many were the nights my sister and I ran terrified to our beds, only to glance back to see that ghostly pant leg dancing mockingly.

This inevitably led to a defense of utter silence. All the monumental milestones of that swirling, turbulent, amazing time – the Civil Rights movement, the assassinations, the Space Race, the Vietnam War, the peace-love-dove revolution – were lost on me. Instead, I spent the decade a hostage of my own design, imprisoned by my father's daily downpour of ridicule and blame, heightened by the pungency of Old Spice, Kentucky Club pipe tobacco and bourbon. Meanwhile, my mother's answers to most things were sweets. I swallowed a lot of anger and fear chased by my own weight in Ho-Hos.

Heading into the '70s my sister and I now endured a new kind of psychological torment, as my father convinced us all we were good for was costing him money. It was as if he took great delight in saying it, despite being delivered through gritted teeth. As a result, we Children of the Scorn became no strangers to guilt. Not your typical brand of guilt – not traditional Catholic guilt or timeless Jewish guilt – but Atheist guilt. When it came to the fine art of resentment, my father was an equal opportunist. He didn't believe in anything, hence he could hate everything. Ultimately, my sister (whom I'd always considered the smartest member of the family) dropped out of school, left the house at seventeen, and married a slow-witted construction worker, thus forging her own personal – albeit misguided – escape. As for me, like every adolescent, I went on to play the role of wounded child, sullen teen and oppressed youth. The only difference was I played them all inside my head, hidden behind an obedient trance.

Throughout high school I prided myself on being a ghost. Never absent, never got into a fight, never spoke in class so as to call attention to myself. I developed a talent for projecting an aura of anonymity that deflected the glances of peers and passersby. If you remember me in high school, you weren't there. Oh, sure, I had friends, but they were "safe" friends. We ate lunch in the stairwell at the far end of the Humanities Building. Why? Because it was *safe*. I took Drafting instead of Drama. Attended study hall instead of after-school dances. Why? Because they were *safe*. Safe clothes, safe hair, safe pens and Pee Chees. I wasn't a jock, didn't get stoned, wasn't smart enough to be a math or science nerd, couldn't play an instrument, wasn't allowed to date, didn't have a car, didn't streak or moon, was nowhere near the stature of a bully, and didn't come of age until long after graduation. I was strictly middle-of-the-road, straight-as-an-arrow, white bread non-committal. I played it safe because I knew if I stepped out of line at school I'd sure as hell catch hell at home. Thus "Safety First" became this apparition's motto.

When the time came for me to give college a try, this elevated my father to a whole new level of resentment. Dad never went to college. He was a talented wood-worker, but this often left him poor and out of work due to his inability to accept a simple workingman's status. Instead, he preferred to live a martyr's existence on a disabled vet's pension – and insist we live it with him. As a California resident I merited the financial benefits of in-state tuition, but the only way I could afford college was to remain living at home. And so, when my nomadic parents next decided to forage into San Diego, I was left with little choice but to apply to San Diego State University because it was (a) cheap and (b) easy to get into. In exchange for food, rent and text books, I handed my father every penny I'd ever saved from every after-school part-time job – from paperboy to stock boy to ice cream jockey at the local Sav-On Drugs. For the next four years I secretly survived college on a mix of federal grants, student loans, and lots and lots of communal beer.

With an undeclared major I landed in a class called Introduction to Drama taught by a stand-up comedian masquerading as a professor. By the end of the first session I'd had an awakening. I wanted to be part of those brethren. There was just one problem. I couldn't act, sing or dance – a triple threat. And so I decided to become ... a playwright! (Eugene, are you listening?) Two administrative signatures later, I officially became an English major with an emphasis in Creative Writing and a nice little Drama minor tacked on the side.

The day I finally graduated I stood silent and fast, staring boldly into the oncoming headlights of Come What May. For the past twenty-two years I'd listened to a timid voice inside me whispering *"Somebody please tell me things will get better"* – while the stronger, angrier voice of my father fought to suppress all I had struggled to learn. And yet, the point remains ironic that if my old man taught me anything, it was what *not* to do. By his example, by his hand, I inadvertently fostered a desire to challenge him. Not only in fundamental principles, but in lineage. I swore that one day, if I ever had kids, I would teach them all of life's lessons in exact opposition to my father's values. I would be tolerant, cool, respectful, kind – and most of all, un-*fucking*-believably fair.

Just you wait, I told myself. Just you wait.

SO IT BEGINS . . .

To my father's credit, following graduation Dad graciously took it upon himself to submit an application on my behalf for the night janitor position at the company where he currently toiled as a receiving clerk for computer parts. Because, to quote Pop's reassuring sentiment: *"I don't know what else you can do."*

In my father's mind this constituted a show of parental support. This, despite my having earned a Bachelor's degree. This, despite my ability to cover my own living expenses for the last four years. To say the least, the thought of having just endured four years of college only to find work as a custodial engineer – not to mention the aspect of both living *and* working with my father – proved a tad dispiriting. Nevertheless, the gauntlet had been thrown. My old man's lack of faith in me – as usual – proved nothing if not inspiring.

Within seconds I was on the phone to Shepherd Hills, confirming my acceptance of the position.

Monday morning I found myself in a week-long orientation with two other new Shepherd Hills hires destined for positions somewhere on the main campus. As it turned out, the three of us had been the only ones to apply to Shepherd Hills *for the entire month*. Our little trio included a perky and punctual, eighteen-year-old cheerleader slathered in too much make-up, a forty-something biker dressed in a sleeveless denim vest and waffle stompers, and me, a clumsy, chunky, wannabe scribe, lost somewhere between learning and education. Still, Shepherd Hills devoted an entire week's orientation just to the three of us because we were, I suppose, better than nothing.

"*WHY ARE YOU HERE?!*"

The instructor's thunderous voice cleared the room of any other sound. She was thick and mannish, dressed in lumberjack flannel and jeans. As she stood before us, the first question out of her mouth was met by our dim-witted gazes. "It certainly isn't for the money," she continued. "So then, why are you here?" The answer was given for us: "Because you *care.*"

Waffle Stompers raised his hand. "So, uh, when do we get paid?"

(Instantly, I could tell that all the inappropriate things that were going to run through my head, whether by accident or on purpose, *this* guy was gonna say out loud.)

Orientation outfitted us with all the basics required to step gingerly into the field of residential services. Soon we would become "houseparents," otherwise defined as:

> **houseparent** (hous´·pâr´·ënt) *n.* **1.** One employed to look after and ensure adequate care and hygiene for residents on a daily basis. **2.** Surrogate mother, father, sister, brother, advocate, liaison, counselor, translator, mental contortionist, freelance detective, intermittent whipping post, general all-around miracle worker, or any combination of the above. [< L *housparere*] – **houseparenting** *n.*

We were informed that Shepherd Hills was a non-profit, public benefit corporation, built in 1967 by some well-meaning, non-profit Lutherans. Since then, it had provided quality residential support to 150-plus people with special needs.

Now, I had lived in San Diego since the summer of '78 and had absolutely no knowledge of Shepherd Hills. So I asked myself, why have I never heard about this place? Then I answered my own question. *Why* would I have heard about this place? After all, this wasn't the kind of company to run PSAs during primetime, or ads in the *SDSU Daily Aztec* soliciting donations. It was, for all intents and purposes, a private society buried deep in the hills, known only to those who either prospected its good will or saw it as a dumping ground for the secret shame of 150 families. To some it was a place silently doing God's work, to others a godforsaken hideaway.

As houseparents, a.k.a. direct care workers, we were systematically introduced to not just a job but an adventure. We quickly learned the term "mentally retarded" was on its way out, in the process of being replaced by "developmentally disabled." However, that's not to say "retarded" is a dirty word. The term remains a practical and necessary clinical definition. So then, I wondered, why does the phrase "mentally retarded" seem to terrify so many people?

Mental retardation can be caused by any condition that impairs development of the brain before birth, during birth, or in the childhood years. It reflects a person's need for a combination of special, interdisciplinary services, individualized supports, or other forms of assistance that are of lifelong or extended duration. Or, in plain English, all retarded means is that a person's "mental age" hasn't kept up with their "chronological age" and so they need a little extra help. *Booga-booga!*

And so, from that point on, I would make every effort not to use the term "mentally retarded" disrespectfully – while at the same time never once feeling guilty or disparaging about using it when applied appropriately.

The lessons continued.

Our Mission:
To provide *quality of life* for people with special needs through services,
training, advocacy and innovation.

It was here the instructor decided to pull us into the mix. "So just what do you suppose we call these 'people with special needs'?" Her eyes zeroed in on me with laser-like intensity.

"Um . . ." I shifted uncomfortably, ". . . Patients?"

"*Wrong!* Anyone else?"

"Friends?" offered the ever-perky cheerleader.

"Inmates!" shouted Waffle Stompers.

"No!" the instructor said, slamming her hand on the desk. (Clearly she was having too much fun at our expense.) "They're not 'patients' or 'inmates' or 'friends' or 'buddies' or 'loonies' or 'Mongoloids,' and especially not 'kids.' The correct terminology for the people we serve is '*client*' or '*resident*.'"

This made an instant impression on me. Client, I mused. Such an esteemed word. It was a term resounding with respect and I admired its progressive sensibility.

Waffle Stompers nudged me and whispered aside. "Good thing I didn't say 'crazy bastards,' huh?"

The lessons continued.

Shepherd Hills, or "The Hills" as it was casually known, was a place designed to serve all levels of people who were "D.D." Each dorm or "*unit*" had its own group of staff, a house manager, and a nurse consultant. A central kitchen delivered meals to each unit's warming bins, and a maintenance department handled anything that cracked, rusted or sprung a leak. Repair of the clients, however, was up to us.

As the week progressed, we were TB-tested, fingerprinted, CPR efficient and First-Aid qualified. We learned the basic philosophies and history of mental retardation, the evolution of client civil rights, and the groundwork of buzzwords such as "*quality of life*," "*behavior modification*," and "*normalization*."

Orientation also taught us technique. We were told never to "*direct*" a client to do something, but rather to "*re-direct*" them. Bad behavior was never "*punished*," but good behavior was always "*rewarded*." To better illustrate this, the instructor announced we would begin a variety of "role-playing" scenarios. We performed how-tos on Program Implementation, exercises in Emergency Response, and dramatic readings of Universal Precautions. Throughout each scene, Cheerleader chirped with delight. Her incessant pep and positivity was tailor-made for this kind of thing, while all it did was remind me why I wanted to be a playwright and not an actor.

When we got to the section on Managing Seizures, Waffle Stompers eagerly volunteered to be the client while Cheerleader and I acted as staff. With great zeal, Waffle Stompers threw himself on the floor and began to convulse violently, writhing in agony, screaming, spitting and drooling from the mouth. I stepped back, afraid he was going to pee his pants. Suddenly, in the most offensive voice this side of a schoolyard playground, Waffle Stompers screamed, "*Doiy-doiy-doiy! I'm 'tarded and I'm havin' da seizure! Somebody helps me!*"

Cheerleader and I looked at each other, aghast. Then we looked to the instructor.

The instructor stared at Waffle Stompers, expressionless. "Break for lunch," she said flatly.

Next came our training on Medication Administration. The three of us dutifully lined up at our desks with a punch card of sugar pills in one hand and what looked like a soufflé cup for an elf in the other. One by one, we practiced popping pills from their individually numbered bubbles into the cups, taking care not to drop any on the floor.

"Any pills that touch the floor must be returned to the nurse and destroyed," the instructor cautioned.

As we finished, the instructor surveyed the mini soufflé cups for accuracy. Cheerleader and I exchanged proud glances, attesting our dexterity. Then we looked at Waffle Stompers – just in time to see him coolly slip the last of his pills into his mouth.

"What the hell are you doing?" said the instructor. "Why are you eating the sugar pills?"

Waffle Stompers swallowed. "*Sugar?*"

The instructor hung her head and sighed. "Break for lunch."

Then something odd happened. On the next to the last day we began a training in Management of Assaultive Behavior, which was sort of like a crash course in *jujitsu*. The purpose was to effectively foresee, deflect, and ultimately contain any burst of physical client aggression, should it occur. As we began to practice some of the basic moves, I could sense Waffle Stompers becoming increasingly agitated. Suddenly, he stopped. "I can't do this," he mumbled.

"What's the problem here?" asked the instructor.

Waffle Stompers shook his head. "I can't throw down with a retarded guy. That's bad karma." Cheerleader and I exchanged uneasy looks as Waffle Stompers grew more anxious. "Those people have, like, mad, wicked *retard* strength."

I began to edge toward the door, awaiting the instructor's inevitable command to suspend activities for noontime sustenance. Instead, she stared at Waffle Stompers, on the verge of a possible brain aneurism. "Excuse me?"

"C'mon, you know what I mean. It'd be like jumping in the gorilla cage at the zoo. They'll tear your ass apart!"

There was a moment of disbelieving silence. I stopped, fascinated as the instructor and Waffle Stompers faced off. For a split second the room smelled like ozone. Finally, the instructor took a breath and spoke cleanly. "Get. The. Fuck. Out."

Waffle Stompers stiffened. "Fine!" he huffed. "To hell with this shit and to hell with you!" And with that, he waffle-stomped out of the room.

I turned to the instructor in anticipation. Slowly, a beaming smile spread across her face and she clapped her hands brightly. It appeared there was only one thing left for her to say.

"Break for lunch!"

The final day of orientation, Cheerleader and I were the only two new hires left to finish. Waffle Stompers' chair remained empty.

That week we came to the final realization that the more we learned about the field, the less we really knew about it. Fact is, we had no idea how much we didn't know – about *anything*.

CHAPTER 4

THE CLEAVERS LIVE DOWN THE STREET

FOLLOWING ORIENTATION THE *real* education began. Upon closer examination, I took special note of the way ITF Village had been built behind the main Shepherd Hills campus, sandwiched safely between the back parking lot and a dairy farm that afforded the occasional visit from a stray cow, sauntering past the back fence to peek in on its neighbors. By this very virtue, the complex was secured by a natural buffer zone. Perhaps not quite as community-*based* as Dawn liked to think, but rather community *accessible*. And though the ITF residents were allowed to come and go as they pleased, they essentially lived in a world removed. The Cleavers had no cause to worry about neighborhood infestation.

As for the clients themselves, they remained at the mercy of the system that enveloped them. They were disciplined by the schedules placed on them to wake up, toilet, groom, dress, eat, take meds, and catch the bus in time to attend some sort of day activities program or sheltered workshop, where tasks such as packaging confetti and shrink-wrapping Chia Pets were assumed in earnest. Upon returning home their schedules then quickly resumed to bathe, eat, learn new skills, take *more* meds, and go to bed so they could get up to do it all over again the next day. Weekends, on the other hand, were "free days"; unfettered to wander the courtyard and beyond.

All full-time employees came and went in three distinct shifts: Mornings 6 a.m.-2 p.m., Evenings 2 p.m.-10 p.m., and Overnight or "Third Shift" 10 p.m.-6 a.m. Working the evening shift put me in league with Michelle and three other staff. At first Dawn instructed me to simply coattail the other houseparents and observe them for a few days before assigning me my permanent group. Having already had a taste of Michelle's tutelage, I nibbled what morsels of wisdom I could from my other co-workers:

> *"Get ready because they're going to test you. The clients are masters, absolute masters, of manipulation. If you let them, they'll lead you down the path and push you off the cliff. Consider it 'initiation.'"*
> *– Anita Rodriguez, Full-time houseparent.*

Anita was a young, pretty Hispanic girl with big brown eyes and bigger brown hair, so fondly styled in the '80s. Having grown up with an autistic brother, she had a personal interest in the field and took her duties in stride. Still, she made no bones she was only there until something better came along – preferably a rich husband.

> *"Just remember, your job is to be perfect. That's all. We're role models. We show no feelings, no emotions, no mistakes. Only 'appropriate behavior.' Personally, I like to lock myself in the office when Dawn's not around and scream my ass off into one of her throw pillows."*
> *– Dot Lindberg, Part-time houseparent.*

Dot was fat, fifty and feeling it; a separated-at-birth twin to Ralph Kramden. She was a mouthy empty-nester who had returned to the workplace with no experience in the field, but a knowledge of how to raise kids – or so she liked to boast. In fact, Dot was representative of many of The Hills' employees who believed themselves to be more insightful than they actually were; the perfect storm of sourpuss, sarcasm and know-it-all.

The final houseparent on my shift was Paul, the male staff I was replacing. Paul was the designated "primary counselor" for Jackie The Giant Knife-Wielding Maniac, Owen The Crusty Fireplug, and Sammy The Face. Hence, they were earmarked to become my group.

Fresh out of junior college, Paul was a laid-back baseball jock who'd been accepted to train with the San Diego Padres pitching staff. This fact alone made him an instant all-American hero in the eyes of the local community. He'd only been with The Hills for a short time, but had already captured the hearts of both the clients and his co-workers. I could see why. Paul reminded me of a summer school counselor I'd worshipped when I was eight. Broad shoulders, lantern jaw, voice like molasses, a pillar of cool. Whenever he entered the room, everyone naturally lit up, sat up, and listened. It quickly became apparent that once "Baseball" Paul left, I would have enormous cleats to fill.

As I followed behind Paul in the hopes that some of his fortitude would rub off on me, I admired his natural "aw shucks" approach to training. For instance,

Paul had a habit of always ending each session with the phrase "very good," which inevitably left the client feeling upbeat and inspired. His approach was subtle and his execution clean. It was little details like this that fed the clients the motivation they needed to succeed.

Case in point, each ITF resident was expected to do their own grocery shopping and cook their own meals. I scrutinized Paul's technique as he casually planned a weekly menu with Jackie just as wholesome and well-balanced as could be. Yet, when I tried to do the same with Owen, it went a little differently.

THE MENUS OF OWEN VAN WINKLE

A play in One Act

Scene: Owen Van Winkle's kitchenette.

Time: 7:23 p.m.

(*Owen Van Winkle and his houseparent, Steve Grieger, are sitting at the kitchen table. Owen is alert and chipper. Steve appears harried and frustrated. Steve sits hovering over a piece of paper, a tooth-marked pencil clasped in his sweaty hand.*)

STEVE (*exasperated*): *Fine*, Owen, if you say so. Lawrence Welk is a musical genius. Now can we *please* finish this menu? For the last time, what do you want to cook on Thursday night?

OWEN (*long pause*): What's that thing called on the commercial? For McDonald's. Two all-beef patties, special sauce, lettuce, cheese, pickles, onions on a sesame seed bun.

STEVE: A Big Mac?

OWEN: Yeah! I want to make that.

STEVE: Fine. (*writing quickly*) Hamburgers on Thursday.

OWEN: No, not hamburgers. Two all-beef patties, special sauce, lettuce, cheese, pickles, onions on a sesame seed –

STEVE: That's a hamburger!

OWEN: It is?

STEVE: *Yes!*

OWEN: Oh. (*long pause*) I don't want that.

(*Steve snaps his pencil in half.*)

CURTAIN

And that was just the *first* hour.

When Paul's last day arrived, the entire village gathered in the courtyard. Countless hugs later, Paul eventually waved good-bye and started up the driveway, off into the smog-friendly sunset of orange and purple. Immediately, Jackie ran after him. I had seen this run once before. When I was sixteen a bunch of us had helped a neighbor move following his divorce. Just as we finished loading the truck and he turned to walk away, the man's son, a little boy no more than six years old who'd been watching from the front porch by his mother's side, scampered after his daddy, down the asphalt in stocking feet, with that look of flushed desperation a child gets just before he's about to cry. It was the same look on Jackie's face as he ran after Paul, following him all the way to his car. And though Paul had invested good, honest effort in preparing Jackie for his departure – as I'm sure the father had with his son – neither the boy nor Jackie could hold back their tears. It didn't matter one was six and the other was forty-six. Both were forced to watch the most important person in their lives drive away without them. And in Jackie's case I realized not only was I now burdened with big cleats to fill, but also the empty heart of a man-child who wanted nothing to do with me.

It was also within those inaugural days I was finally able to meet the last few ITF clients I'd missed on my initial tour. Apartment #4 was home to the resident odd couple: Hughie Lamb and the aforementioned "asshole," Billy Mattila. Hughie and Billy were considered an odd couple not because one was neat and the other was messy, not because one was stout and the other was skinny, not even because one was black and the other was white. They were an odd pair because one was a pacifist and the other an apparent hole of an ass. (As Cole put it, "bad mojo" came from that apartment.)

Unlike Jackie who turned a cold shoulder to me and me alone, Billy looked upon *all* the staff as a waste of time, as if we were just passing through a revolving door marked "Personnel." His disregard for us was generated by a deliberate indifference if not superiority. This quickly became apparent the night I passed him in the courtyard and playfully greeted him.

"Hiya, Mr. Bill."

Billy stopped dead in his tracks. He shot a bony index finger in the air, never once bothering to look at me. "My name not *Bill*," he admonished. "It Billy . . ." (*pause for effect*) ". . . Joseph . . ." (*pause for effect*) ". . . Mattila. You got dat? *Good!*" He then unclogged his nose at my feet and snapped his fingers curtly, as if summoning a busboy to clean up after him before swaggering off. At that precise moment the only thing that came to my mind was: *You know . . . this guy really IS an asshole.* And I didn't feel all that bad for thinking it.

Then I had to laugh. The fact that Billy corrected me by using all three of his names seemed only fitting. Isn't that the prerequisite for achieving infamous notoriety? Leastwise the assassins: John Wilkes Booth, Lee Harvey Oswald, Mark David Chapman, John David Stutts, the list was potentially endless. In fact, I think one of Billy's personal goals may have been to one day own his own bell tower. Michelle was right – Mattila the Hun had been fittingly nicknamed.

Nevertheless, duty called.

Thrust to the head of the rec room forthwith, I found myself teaching the fundamentals of independent living to a Notorious Nine of confused faces and wandering attention spans. There were cooking demonstrations and lessons in nutrition. (*Who am I to teach nutrition?* I thought. *I drink strawberry Margaritas with a slice of pecan pie – for breakfast.*) There were lectures on the virtues of proper mass transit etiquette. (*How am I supposed to teach etiquette when I can barely decipher a damn bus schedule?*) There were even group sessions on how to "appropriately" express one's feelings in social situations. (*What the hell do I know about "appropriate" behavior? – I went to a* state *college, for crissake.*) I was at once home economist, Miss Manners and shrink.

Meanwhile, this left the gaps of basic board and care to be filled. Everyday drudgery such as ensuring the clients were properly groomed, fed and dressed became a series of "programs" to teach ADL skills ("Activities of Daily Living"). Between class time and direct care responsibilities, my job became a frenzied mix of one-to-one supervision, hands-on intervention, and verbal re-direction. And because bathing and grooming were part of the job, this meant I had to get used to the sight of a grown man naked – fast.

Am I being immature or is it difficult to look at another man's winkie? I'd never had to wash someone before, let alone an adult male. I didn't even like showering in high school gym class – and had, up to this point, successfully avoided no more than a mere glimpse of another living penis. The first time I was treated to a gander at Jackie's body was jolting. His physique was unmistakably middle-aged, covered in moles and back hair, with a scrotum like the wrinkled jowls of a feeble old man, and a shriveled penis that dangled sadly below a wad of gray pubic hair. It was a penis that blazed like a signal fire, forcing me to look at it. *No, no, don't! Don't look!* But it was no use. No matter how hard I struggled to avert my eyes or pivot my head in another direction, the old gray weenie followed me like the eyes of Emmett Kelly on Tijuana velvet. *No, no don't! Don't look!* But alas, once I saw the man naked, I was left with no choice but to resign myself to the fact that I would have to continue seeing him naked five nights a week.

And it didn't stop there.

Nudity and casual sex between the clients were concepts I was introduced to all too quickly. As it turned out, Darlene Beaudine was not merely content to play the sassy village flirt with dance partners, she had affairs going on with Cole, Owen, Billy, James and even Sammy The Face – everyone except Jackie, whom she shunned for whatever reasons. These affairs occurred indiscriminately on *her* terms at *her* convenience, one-on-one or by way of the occasional threesome. I learned this the day I accidentally walked in on a snarl of naked, flabby, cottage-cheese limbs, unshaven female body hair and slick, hairless male privates fully erect, at various turns taut, thrusting and quivering. What I saw literally lasted no more than a second before I was able to flinch and slam the door in embarrassment. But again, it was too late. The damage had been done, the images burned into my brain forever. And though the lot of them generally kept things private and discreet, their sexual endeavors only led to an ongoing spur of bartering and accusations between the men over bragging rights to Darlene. (Somehow I think the true meaning of "multiple partners" was lost on them.)

But while Darlene and her men *acted* girlfriend and boyfriends in their own special comedy of errors, none of them shared a life-long commitment. Not so, Holly Gross and Hughie Lamb. Holly and Hughie weren't merely hump buddies, they had truly fallen in love.

Despite the ever-lingering perfume of eggs, Holly had no shortage of friends, which was testament to her natural charisma. Unlike Darlene, Holly shrewdly adopted the role of Most Demur, blessed by a talent for calculated timidity. Everyone loved little Holly Gross. It was unavoidable. Holly dispelled the stigma that all retarded people have crossed eyes and slack jaws. Instead, she had delicate dimpled features and soft brown hair that seemed to catch the sun, and when she spoke you almost had to hold a glass up to your ear just to hear her. In my mind I dubbed Holly the village cutie pie.

Hughie, meanwhile, reminded me of a Down syndrome Martin Luther King Jr. He was a plump, genteel, Southern black gentleman who liked to wear suits; a man rarely seen without a bible in his hand or heard without a scripture quote on his lips. Because of a plethora of medications, this also made Hughie walk, talk and react to everything very s-l-o-w-l-y; bobbing and weaving about the courtyard like a spaceman on the moon, sustained upright only by a winning, gummy smile.

As a couple, Holly and Hughie were able to reinforce each others' strengths and establish a bond, which gave them considerable satisfaction – if not distinction. What the two of them shared behind closed doors was refreshing in anyone's world.

Despite all the dubious sexual antics, however, accidental pregnancy was never a concern. This was because Holly and Darlene – like many female clients (with significant parental influence) – were each safeguarded by a tubal ligation, informally known as getting one's "tubes tied," a medical procedure to prevent fertilization, enabling all of the pleasures without any of the misgivings.

(Memo to self: Always knock *loud* before entering. *Yeeeesh!*)

By Saturday's end I was asking myself: *what kind of monkey house have I been welcomed into?* My first official week at ITF Village was evidence enough, filled with a spinning array of what's known in the field as "emotional outbursts." Arguments, accusations, blatant lies and tantrums – all requisites of on-the-job training. They'd taught us in orientation that *"people with cognitive disabilities are often victim to their emotions, reacting impulsively to feelings of the moment."* Factors such as immature moral reasoning, inborn temperament, and restricted social experience were also at play, all testimony to the ongoing struggle of "mental age" vs. "chronological age." But from what I could tell it was each person's individuality that ultimately dictated their actions.

CHALLENGED: A TRIBUTE

Petty power struggles were common. Owen would complain that Jackie kept throwing his personal belongings on the roof just to taunt him, and Jackie would complain that Owen's pet parakeet stunk. Cole complained that James took too long in the bathroom, and James complained (well, at least I *think* he complained) that Cole's music was too loud. Hughie spent his days patrolling the courtyard, preaching to the choir about the evils of fornication (when he wasn't busy snitching cookies from the rec room), while Darlene flirted with her men (or, as Dot was fond of saying, "cockteased"), and the men went slowly insane with wanton desire. Then, just as things would finally settle down, Billy Mattila would enter to stir the pot with a well-placed, well-timed insult towards someone's handicap, and everything would start all over again. Tempers would flair, threats would be flung, voices would crack and cry, only to be answered by medication and the need for consistent "counseling." It had all the sex, intrigue and backbiting of a D.D. *Dallas*.

But all of that paled in comparison to my first seizure.

Some people with epilepsy wear a seizure helmet to help protect themselves in case of a drop. Jackie Chuckam refused to be one of them. Jackie despised wearing his helmet and it was an ongoing struggle to get him to do so – especially in public. Seizure patients live a life of constant, underlying fear. Anything from crossing a busy street to sitting too close to a glass coffee table could be potentially fatal. And yet, most client seizures were so common and casual, they were often seen as little more than a checkmark tallied on a clipboard or frequency chart.

Luckily, Jackie's seizure activity was well-controlled enough with a minimal amount of Phenobarbital to allow him to venture alone into the community in relative safety. Because of his low frequency rate of episodes, personally I didn't bother to give it much thought, and in orientation they'd shown us a video of a simulated seizure so we'd know what one looked like and what to do (Waffle Stompers' consummate performance notwithstanding). But what they teach you in orientation is clinical and self-contained, never practical. Not till you see one in real life.

The bus ride to the grocery store had been uncomfortable enough, sitting in self-conscious silence between Jackie and Sammy, their folding metal, made-by-Monkey Wards laundry carts clanking next to us in the aisle. (As if these guys didn't need an excuse to look even *more* retarded.) Surrounded by the scornful eyes of the other passengers, their scowls treated us to the *tsk-tsk* and *tut-tut* of society at large, filling the overhead with one big, giant communal thought bubble that boldly chided: *Why don't people like that just stay the hell home?*

I hadn't ridden a city bus – or even thought of riding a city bus – since I was a small boy, with my hand linked to my mother's, taking the rare excursion down Wilshire Blvd. to the old Santa Monica Mall for a hot fudge sundae at the Woolworth's lunch counter. Back then, riding the bus was a young child's thrill, both daring and adventurous, perched high above the other cars, able to look down into them and giggle at the sum total of bald spots. Back then, believe it or not, city buses had *class* and people actually *dressed up* for the privilege to ride – whereas today mass transit has devolved into something foreign and disrespected by the California car culture, shuttling the poor, the elderly, the disabled, the ethnic and, of course, the retarded.

No sooner had we hit our stop than Sammy shot off the bus, dragging his cart behind him. I called for him to wait up but, no use, he was gone. Stepping down, I was grudgingly followed by Jackie and his cart – which promptly got stuck in the folding door. This erupted into a curbside performance of "*G-Goddamn it, let go!*" as he yanked on the cart over and over until I was able to rush back and help pull it free. My sheepish grin of an apology to the driver was answered by the bus door slamming in my face and a gust of exhaust.

Inside the grocery store I found Sammy struggling with the shopping carts.

"Sammy, I told you to wait up."

"I did."

I sighed. "Whatever. Okay, you each have your lists, get as much as you can on your own and I'll check it when you're done. Go." At that, I noticed Sammy's shirt was only half tucked in. Heading for the magazine rack, I tossed off nonchalantly, "And Sammy, tuck in your shirt." Two seconds later an old woman gasped as she stared past me. I turned back just in time to see that Sammy had innocently unzipped his pants, pulled them down, and opened the flaps to properly arrange his shirttails. Lunging back, I did my best Ballroom side-to-side shuffle to shield Sammy from general view. Once finished, Sammy pulled his pants back up and buttoned everything neatly. Admittedly, I was impressed by his fastidiousness – despite the laws against public indecency – and made a mental note we'd have to work on that sort of thing.

About ten minutes in, I shelved a copy of *Soap Opera Digest* and located Sammy who'd already filled his cart halfway with Zingers and Yoo-Hoo. After a brief "re-direction" for him to stick to the items on his list, I went to check on Jackie. Rounding the Entenmann's display, I noticed a small commotion over at the cart corral. There, I spied Jackie, climbing and yanking on the bars comically like he was revving a Harley. As people began to gather curiously, I was no different. Until it suddenly hit me – *shit!* – Jackie's having a *seizure!*

Pushing my way through the crowd, I frantically attempted to turn Jackie on his side per procedure, just as I'd been taught. Only this wasn't that kind of seizure. It wasn't your typical, well-known, body-convulsing-violently, grand mal seizure, it was a psychomotor – the goddamn Broadway show of seizures. A psychomotor doesn't spasm or jerk or lose consciousness. Instead, Jackie's eyes were wide and glazed, his attention focused simultaneously on something distant and nose-to-nose, his brain far, far away, caught in a beehive in the middle of a fireworks display.

Watching someone have a seizure is pure hell, but not knowing what to do is worse. Suddenly, Jackie dropped to the floor and began scooting along on his rump like a dog, smacking his lips and tittering ghoulishly. I was genuinely unnerved. Mixed up. Scared. But I knew I had to do something fast. Bracing my body against his, I squatted next to Jackie and blocked him into the corner of the cart corral, huddling us against the bars like two convicts forced to share a cell until the seizure made bail. In an eerie, ghostly voice he looked up at me and said, without stuttering, "Have you seen my father dead today?" I swear I peed a little.

Jackie's medical records indicated that ninety-nine percent of the time he came out his seizures after about thirty seconds with no problem, so I felt confident he just needed a little time to stabilize. What I didn't realize was just how long thirty seconds can last when people are watching you.

"Whaddaya suppose is wrong with him?" said one old geezer. "He on drugs?"

"Nah," said another old geezer. "He's from that *institution* place up the street." Then he rolled his eyes and added, "*You* know . . ."

"Any minute now I betcha he turns blue," spouted a third. "Not good when they turn blue."

Jesus Christ! Did the circus leave town or what? This isn't a fucking sideshow. I whipped around. "Look, do you people *mind*?" This only resulted in more befuddled stares.

Little by slowly by eventually, Jackie finally lifted his head and looked at me with clear eyes. His brain had returned from its visit with the pyrotechnic bees. "Jackie," I said, "do you know who I am?"

"Suh-Suh-Steve?"

"YES!" I was never so relieved. "How do you feel? You feel good enough to stand? You want to see a doctor?"

"What f-f-for?"

"Because you just had a seizure."

Jackie bristled. "No I d-d-didn't! No I did *NOT* have a seizure! I did *NOT!*" Now fully alert, Jackie scrambled to his feet and started for the door. "I don't need no damn d-doctor!"

As I moved to detain him, Jackie suddenly lashed out at me with a defensive sweep, moaning like a wounded animal. I stood there, petrified, our eyes locked. I was certain if I so much as flinched, the beast within him would take my head off.

Finally, I said, "Do you want to finish your shopping then?"

Jackie glared at me with that same Frankenstein grimace, then quickly looked away. With keen resolve he turned, retrieved his cart, and pushed off down the aisle in silence.

That night, when I replayed the event in my head, the whole thing left me feeling weak and incompetent. It dawned on me that not one of the gawking elite had thought to call 911 – including me. Why? Just what the hell was I thinking? Was it because I was still green and unsure how to respond correctly in that kind of situation? Or was it because I foolishly felt it was my responsibility – my *duty* – to take care of the situation on my own? And if so, just what was I trying to prove?

By the end of my second week I had aged a thousand years. Shift after shift, I found myself growing thankful just to get in and out without having to endure any more contact with those people than I had to. I was never exactly sure which direction the clients would take me next. How I'd be tested, what I would witness, or who would be the next one to prod me the way a child pokes a caged animal with a stick just to annoy it. Anything could happen. Anything at all. When it came to random acts of clientness, there was no such thing as traditional logic. I'm not ashamed to admit I was pretty overwhelmed by it all.

Joining my co-workers on break in the rec room, the TV entertained us with an old episode of *Lost In Space*, underscoring the room with snatches of dialogue and theme music. I sank deep into the couch and vowed to stay there for life.

"Rough night?" Anita asked.

"Rough *every* night," I replied.

"You'll get the hang of it."

"Maybe not," Dot chimed in. "No offense, but this job just isn't for some people." Dot propped her massive feet on the coffee table. "It's hard work."

"Danger, Will Robinson, danger!" said the robot.

"Hey, give him a break," Anita said.

"I'm just being realistic," Dot shrugged. "Look at him. He's only been here two weeks and his ass is already draggin'. He should get out now while he still has his sanity."

Anita smiled at me supportively. "Don't listen to her."

But Dot was on a roll. "Take my advice. Ask yourself, is this what you really want to do? If not, then quit now. The last thing these kids need is just another big brother hanging around out of *good intentions*."

Throughout the exchange Michelle had also been present, sitting curiously silent. I looked over to her, waiting to see if she had an opinion on all this. But Michelle merely stared back expressionless, as if it were some sort of test. How could I possibly admit the only reason I was here in the first place was to be near her? I thought I had played it smart. I thought I could score points by striking where Michelle lived, square in the social conscience. But instead, my reply to Dot came as a statement in the form of a question.

"Maybe this job isn't for me?"

Without a word, Michelle rose and exited. It was clearly an omen of defeat.

"Oh, the pain," Dr. Smith said.

Moments later, I tapped on Dawn's office door and peeked inside. The room was empty, bathed in deep yellow by the reflection of the setting sun. I wandered in and began to rehearse. First came the apologetic approach:

"I'm sorry to let you down, Dawn, but I don't think this is quite for me . . ."

Next I tried it efficient:

"Thank you, but I'm afraid I find myself forced to tender my resignation at this time . . ."

Just as I was just about to give the sincere approach a try, I heard a scuffle through the wall. It was coming from Jackie and Owen's apartment next door. What's Jackie thrown on the roof this time? Owen's razor? Owen's jacket? Did I give a shit? Not really. But the scuffle grew louder. Then louder still. All of a sudden, a loud *thump!* struck against the wall. Everything went quiet. Oh, my God, I thought. *Jackie killed Owen!*

Racing to investigate, I found them in their bedroom. Owen was throwing ineffective windmill punches at Jackie, who in turn lifted Owen off the floor and hurled him to the ground. This prompted me to shout an otherwise ineffectual "Hey!" It was as if I weren't even there.

Owen shot to his feet, furious. "That does it!" he shouted at Jackie. "I'm gonna call my brother and tell on you, you son-of-a-bitch!" Hearing this, Jackie made for Owen again, but Owen dodged through the door, jamming past me with a substantial body check, out into the courtyard and up the driveway.

Jackie bent down to retrieve his parents' picture from the floor. "Jackie, what happened?" I said. No answer. "Where's Owen going?"

Jackie looked up and grinned with delight. "He ran away again." And went back to arranging his picture.

Heading back out into the courtyard, Owen was nowhere to be seen. The entire complex was quiet with everyone in their apartments going about their daily routines, like they hadn't heard the scuffle, or had heard it so often they just didn't care anymore. I looked about apprehensively for some help or direction, but the staff, too, had gone missing in action. Great. And just as I was about to quit this damned place.

I took off up the driveway and followed it around to the street exit. Hitting the sidewalk, I anxiously looked both ways. There, in the distance, I spotted Owen rounding the block, flailing his arms in anger and making great strides. Stepping into a trot I made it to the corner, only to discover Owen now three times farther ahead of me than before. Damn, I thought, what does this guy have on? Rocket shoes? It wasn't long before Owen made it all the way down the road, which dead-ended at a chain-link fence atop a dirt incline. But that didn't stop Owen. He simply pushed his way through a hole in the fence and slid down the embankment, completely absorbed in his escape. Which wouldn't have been so bad if it weren't for the fact that this particular embankment led directly down to the 67 freeway.

"OWEN!"

I was now running. At the bottom of the incline Owen had made it to the edge of the freeway. By now the sun was almost down and headlights were spilling on. I made it to the top of the hill just in time to see Owen start to cross.

"OWEN, STOP!"

I couldn't believe what I was seeing. Oblivious to the traffic, Owen proceeded onward in blind fury, waving his arms and shaking his fists. Plowing through the hole in the fence, I slid down the hill into a thatch of weeds, spiders and broken beer bottles. The 67 was a two-lane, minor freeway, but at that moment it might as well have been the friggin' Autobahn. Horns blared. Tires skidded. Cars fish-tailed, swerving to miss him. I was frantic. Panic-stricken. Shouting. Praying. At once the cars began to slow down, creating a pocket in traffic. I saw my chance and took it. Stepping onto the freeway a few cars still rolled heavily past, refusing to stop. *Bastards!* Meanwhile, Owen had made it to the center divide and stopped, readying to cross the other side. I'm pretty sure by now I was screaming.

Sprinting blindly, I lunged for Owen and grabbed him by the waist just as he was about to take a fatal step. The two of us toppled backwards onto the center divide, hitting the ground hard. In a flash, Owen was back on his feet, yelling at me.

"Leave me alone! I'll tell my brother on you, too!"

Begging him to calm down, I put all my strength into overpowering the little hellion – who was a lot stronger than he looked. Finally, he eased up just enough for me to drag him back across the lanes of traffic to safety.

There, on the shoulder, standing in the lifeless patches of golden California grass, Owen began to cry. "He's always doing stuff to me and I don't like it!"

"Who, Jackie?" I said.

"I hate it there," he wailed. "And everybody hates *me.*"

"I don't hate you."

"Not yet." (Admittedly, I had to smile at that.) "Whenever I talk, they all say, 'Shut up, Owen,' and then *I* get in trouble. I wanna live with my brother. I wanna live with my brother . . ."

As Owen's sobs became more strained, I tried to remain positive. I reminded him he was learning to live on his own someday and wasn't that a good thing? Owen countered with, "They won't let me have a drinking fountain in my room." Not sure how to address that one, I deflected with how proud his brother would be to see him in his own place. When that didn't work I tried one last idea.

"How about your bird? You wouldn't want to leave him behind, would you?"

Owen sniffled and considered this. "No, Jackie might hurt him."

"Yeah. And you wouldn't want that, would you?" But Owen wouldn't answer me.

It was about this point I could sense the kindergarten teacher approach wasn't quite working like it usually did in the movies. But Owen had run away because he didn't think he was being treated fairly – and this struck a nerve in my core philosophy. So instead, I leveled with the man the best way I knew how. I told him that running away when things got tough was for quitters. And being a quitter sucked. I also told him there were always going to be people who try to bring you down. And those people were assholes. But, I told him, if he came back home, then maybe the two of us could beat 'em together.

At that, Owen slowly took my hand. It was a movie moment if ever I lived one.

At twenty-two years old, I confess feeling embarrassed by a man holding my hand. It had nothing to do with homophobia; hell, in the Drama department at

State greetings with hearty hugs, male or female, were commonplace. But holding hands, that was different. That symbolized trust. That required intimacy. Truth is, I couldn't even remember the last time I held my own father's hand – or the last time he'd offered it. Closeness like that had always made my father feel uneasy, like something only sissies would do – and so I should show little surprise those same feelings rubbed off on me. But as Owen and I climbed back up the embankment and prepared to walk home, I realized it was time I got over my – and my father's – personal embarrassments. I never thought the weird feeling of overcoming something so small could resonate so deep.

When we got back to ITF, everyone was finishing dinner and focusing on the things that mattered most in their lives at the moment. Doing the dishes, taking a bath, maybe doing a little laundry, watching TV, taking their meds, and going to bed so they could get up tomorrow and do it all over again. I helped Owen wash up, cleaned and dressed his scrapes, then did the same for myself. I helped him set his oven timer for a Swanson's Fried Chicken TV Dinner, and scooped myself a helping of noodles and gravy from the rec room kitchen warming bin, just in time to watch Mary Richards toss her hat into the air as a gesture of new-found confidence. It wasn't until I finally sat down to eat that I noticed the fork in my hand was shaking.

I never did tell anyone about Owen's little nature walk along the freeway. No reason to cause the man added grief, I thought. As for me, I decided not to talk to Dawn that evening after all. Instead, I decided to stick around a while longer.

For now.

CHAPTER 5

BLOOPERS, BLUNDERS, SCREW UPS AND OOPS

AS THE DAYS passed I continued my best efforts to win the affections of Michelle. Whenever I was scheduled to work a shift with her, I'd spend countless hours beforehand posing in front of the bathroom mirror – a truly magnificent specimen of lusty manhood – with half a dozen shirts trying to decide whether to dress "professional" or "sexy." (Ultimately, I would just choose to go with "clean" – which was a feat in itself.) In addition to Michelle, I also made efforts to win the respect of my clients. And while Michelle remained friendly but distant, Sammy, Owen and Jackie remained distant if not downright hostile. Oh, sure, somehow I managed to keep them groomed and well-fed, and skill programs were run with mixed success . . .

> "– *Very good. Now for the last step all you have to do is tuck in your sheets.* –"
> "– *No!* –"
> "– *C'mon, you want to get a 100% on your program, don't you?* –"
> "– *Fuck off!* –"

. . . but I couldn't shake the feeling that if I didn't show up tomorrow, no one would really give a damn. I was told time and again by the other counselors not to take it personally, but it was unavoidable. To the clients I was an outsider, just another set of pipes to boss them around.

This led me to try a different approach. One night, under the guise of fellowship, I brought an extra-large combo pizza to work, pulled my three clients together, and had a party for just the four of us. (Because nothing says brotherhood like spicy meats and gooey cheese.) No one else was invited. Flagrant pandering though it might've been, pizza was my password to a members-only clubhouse.

The bribe worked. Like a mailman who wins over a snarling dog by offering it a Milk-Bone, a simple pizza finally helped me break into their inner circle. In the eyes of my three clients, I was king. Ah, sweet pizza! Is there nothing you can't do?

As we gorged without shame and guzzled Coke by the two-liter, little by little they began to open up to me. We actually had a semblance of a conversation wherein I learned a few things. I learned that Owen longed to one day live in his brother's guest house in Palm Springs. (I guess we all have our dreams of retirement, I thought.) I learned that when Sammy had sex with Darlene, he preferred her to be on top so he could watch her enormous breasts bounce up and down. (Hm, okay, maybe just a *bit* too much information, Sammy, but I appreciate your willingness to confide in me.) And Jackie, even Jackie, made genial eye contact and asked me with enthusiasm, "Can we have p-pizza again maybe three, f-f-four weeks?"

"Of course!" I sang with gusto. "What do you guys say we have Pizza Night once *every* week?"

Everyone cheered.

The next night no one spoke to me. And I was out fourteen bucks.

The next month proceeded with an endless string of mistakes. I couldn't get through a single shift without at least one minor screw up, regardless of resolve. Everything from calling the clients by the wrong names, to the occasional grease fire, to over-loaded washing machines gushing with suds, to rubber bath mats melting in the dryer, to repeatedly walking in on clients in the middle of their "private time" – all playing like one gigantic montage set to the theme from *The Benny Hill Show*. And while most blunders weren't serious, each one seemed to only exacerbate the next. Working with Sammy, for one, felt like a mixed bag of enlightenment and disaster.

One night, while waiting for him to finish showering so we could pursue the vastly more significant task of sorting his underwear, I was stunned to discover that Sammy had been blessed with a beautiful singing voice.

"I-I-I don't have hopes and dreams . . . and I-I-I don't have plans and schemes . . . I-I-I don't have anything . . . since I don't have yo-o-o-ou . . ."

It was a voice both elegant and moving; a classically-rendered pitch worthy of any street corner doo-wop foursome, in perfect time to the rumble of cheap plumbing.

When Sammy stepped out of the shower with a towel cinched around his waist, I discovered the port-wine stain on his face continued across his left shoulder and down his back in splotches and puddles, amplifying the appearance of disabled vulnerability. I stopped. Poor guy, I thought. As if his lazy eye and disjointed face weren't bad enough. Whether it was this moment of pity or the charm of his singing prowess that caused me to feel charitable, I'm not sure. Regardless, I was suddenly seized with a sense of ardent altruism.

As Sammy began to dress, I noticed two hearing aids sitting atop his dresser. Now, Sammy wasn't completely deaf, just enough to be ranked as "legally" deaf. And he was certainly more than capable of inserting his hearing aids himself. But that didn't matter. I was determined to help him. Never mind the fact I had never seen a hearing aid up close, let alone knew how to work one. To me a hearing aid was simply a peculiar little lump of plastic dangling on the end of a wiggly tube. How hard could it be?

"Here, Sammy, let me *help* you." (Notice the emphasis on the word *help*.)

Ever so gingerly, I jammed the hearing aids into his ears to ensure they fit nice and snug. "Can you hear me?" I asked. "Testing, testing. What's this little dial for?"

"*AAAAAIIIIIEEEEE!!!*"

As I turned the dial I heard a muffled "*screeeee*" of feedback. Sammy threw back his head and cringed as if I'd pierced his eardrum with a prison shiv. He quickly slapped my hands away and cranked the dial back down, wincing in pain. Not knowing what to do, I immediately apologized and asked if he was okay. Sammy trained his good eye on me with a slow burn. "You want me to *die*? *Dumbass!*"

Then there were simple mishaps born from lack of experience.

One evening, Cole asked to speak to me in private, stating he needed a *man's* opinion on something. Thinking maybe he was seeking some advice on how to score points with Darlene, I was only too flattered to oblige. When we stepped into his bedroom and closed the door, Cole subsequently dropped his pants and cupped the goods in his hand for the sake of my scrutiny.

"*Yikes!* Cole, put that thing away, will ya?"

"But what should I do about this bump?"

"I don't know. See a doctor."

Needless to say, when a man flashes you his penis, regardless of circumstance, the moment tends to be a bit jarring. And yet, I was struck more by how nonchalant the whole thing was for Cole. In his world – that is, the D.D. world of a client – physical modesty didn't exist. Over the years, people like Cole have been subjected to countless exams by doctors, poked and prodded by nurses, bathed and dressed by houseparents, and fully exposed to their peers in pursuit of sexual spoils. In other words, they've been seen naked more times than all the *Girls Gone Wild* put together (including the 1993 collectable Mardi Gras series, volumes 1-12). So to Cole, dropping his pants for a counselor was as mundane as washing his hands.

In Cole's case he had a much greater legitimate worry – *What do I do about this thing on my weenie?*

Now, I figured my role in this was supposed to be one of advisor. And once I got over my initial shock (and had Cole pull his pants back up, thank you), my mind flashed to the appointment calendar hanging in the office. I remembered that the clients were scheduled to be seen the next day in clinic for a checkup. So to me the solution was obvious.

"You're seeing Dr. Neil tomorrow, right?"

"Yeah," said Cole.

"Well, why don't you wait and ask him about it?"

Cole looked at me a bit puzzled. "You mean show it to *him?*"

"Well . . . yeah. Why not? He's a doctor. He'll know what to do."

Cole shrugged and zipped up. "Okay, if you say so. Thanks, Steve."

"Anytime, bud. Glad to help."

It wasn't till the next evening I learned Dr. Neil was a *psychiatrist.* Apparently the only penises he was interested in were the ones associated with Freudian dreams of doughnuts dancing with cigars. So much for my role as advisor. No matter. Cole was seen by his regular physician two days later, a simple ointment was prescribed, and the staff had a good laugh at my expense – for *days.*

Otherwise, for the most part, everyone – clients and staff alike – ultimately remained patient in guiding me through my initial training. And I, for one, sincerely tried to get the hang of things. I wanted to *feel* what they felt and *know* what they knew. Little by little, I found myself investing in the well-being of the clients. I didn't want to just sleepwalk through my duties, I truly wanted to provide the best and brightest degree of care that I could.

Or so I hoped.

> *"Genius may have its limitations, but stupidity is not thus handicapped."*
> *– Elbert Hubbard, American writer and philosopher*

Shepherd Hills didn't own a platoon of short yellow busses, the kind commonly used by school districts to transport children with disabilities to Special Ed classes. Instead, each of the main campus units had its own van to transport clients to and from doctor appointments, outings, and for general errands. But ITF was different. ITF was more deserving. We were awarded a dark blue, curb-scraping, bone-rattling Ford LTD Country Squire station wagon with faux logs-on-the-side vinyl appliques, and a rusty wheelchair rack affixed to the rear bumper, as conspicuous as a shark's fin in a children's swimming pool. Our wagon was justly nicknamed the "Blue Beast." While the other units were driving comfy vans with air-conditioning and cruise control, we hauled our clients around in a creaking, sputtering, automotive afterthought with bad shocks and a transmission that sounded as if it were filled with iron marbles. A real working-class battlewagon.

By the end of my first month at ITF, Jackie had grown tolerant of me at best. More often than not the daggers were still flung, but at least now he would respond when I attempted to run programs with him. Why, once he even let me shave him. *Once.* Regardless, bearing in mind that Jackie was a very *large* man – with a few good inches on my height and a few good muscles on my flab – life was peaceful . . . until he would lose his temper. Jackie had some issues that would get the best of him now and then, causing him to go off like King Kong at a tea social. His favorite choice of expressing his anger was strangulation, and he was a throttling virtuoso. In short, you did *not* want to be near Jackie when he blew.

Hearkening back to orientation, we were told that our training in Management of Assaultive Behavior was good knowledge to have with this population "just in case." But the only good it served was to remind me of my fear of fighting – that is to say, my fear of getting punched. I hate fighting. Whether it be a fist fight or an argument, I live in constant fear of hostile confrontation. I've only had two fights in my life. The first I won, which is quite empowering to a child of six. (In actuality, it wasn't a fight so much as it was a series of awkward jabs, kicks and clunks that ultimately resulted in sitting on my opponent, thus ensuring sweet victory.) The second fight I lost, which is quite emasculating to an adolescent of twelve. And that turned me into a flincher. It showed me I was vulnerable and taught me that pain, duh, *hurts.* (Spankings by Daddy, of course, notwithstanding.)

It's also important to remember here that Jackie had epilepsy. And although his seizures were generally light, some of the longer ones could still require a visit to the E.R. just for reassurance. Add to the mix the fact that Jackie also had an overwhelming dislike for doctors, so much so that many an appointment was missed simply because he refused to attend. Seizures, outbursts, and a hatred of doctors. You can see the potential for quite a volatile situation.

By the end of June it was shaping up to be an especially hot summer, and that particular Wednesday night was the hottest night yet. It was a dark, moonless night. Jackie had walked up to visit the units on the main campus in search of a little charity by way of free cookies and punch, and thereby dodge yet another request to bathe. On the way back, he had a seizure outside the rear main gate and was found lying unconscious in the dark by James. Maybe it was the heat, maybe it was because he hadn't had a single seizure all week, but this one hit strong enough to take him down. This time I knew what to do. I wasn't about to go through another fiasco like the one at the supermarket. This time I sprang forward with knowledge and authority.

"I'll call 911!"

"NO!" the staff shouted in three-part harmony.

"Why not?"

"It's better if we just take him," Michelle directed.

"It'll be faster and that way someone can be with him," added Anita.

"'Sides, paramedics don't know shit about our guys," heeded Dot.

Though this line of logic didn't make sense to me, I thought, who am I to argue? "Okay. So who's gonna go?" Silence. A shiver ran down my spine as I felt the chill of six eyes focus on me. "Aw, shit," I muttered.

"You're up, Sparky," Dot grinned.

Fine, I thought. No problem. I can do this.

With no time to lose, I backed the Blue Beast up to where Jackie lay. As Dot, Anita and Michelle lifted him into the back seat, I ran inside the office, signed the car out, zipped back outside, jumped in behind the wheel and took off. Grossmont Emergency, here we come.

So I'm driving . . . and I'm driving . . . and meanwhile, in the back seat, Jackie began to wake up.

"W-W-Where are we going?" he asked groggily.

Oh, great, I thought. Here's a guy who hates doctors, and if he realizes we're on our way to E.R., he's gonna *kill* me. So I did what any experienced professional would do in this situation. I lied.

"Uh . . . we're just going for a drive, Jackie. Relax and have fun."

For the next 8 1/2 miles my head bobbed like one of those novelty plastic dogs on the rear dash of a '55 Chevy as my eyes darted non-stop between the road and rear view mirror, on the lookout for a Jackie attack. I desperately searched the back of my brain for what little MAB training I could remember from orientation, only to realize I hadn't remembered a thing. Meanwhile, Jackie's streaky white hair captured the reflection of every oncoming headlight, the same way flashes of lightening dance off Dracula's glistening fangs just before he sinks them into your neck.

We pulled up to the E.R. entrance and I dashed inside for assistance. "Hey! I'm from Shepherd Hills with a seizure patient. Can I get some help?"

No problem.

I headed back out to the car with a wheelchair, followed by an orderly who was supposed to help me lift Jackie out of the wagon. Unfortunately, the orderly took it upon himself to reassure Jackie. "Okay, sir, let's get you inside so you can see the doctor."

"DOCTOR!" Jackie sprang alive. "No! No! No way! I don't wanna see no d-d-damn doctor!"

Oh, great, I thought. Now we'll never get him out of the back seat. So I explained the situation to the orderly and he said no problem. Happens all the time. We can handle it.

I opened the back door to the wagon. The dome light was burned out. Jackie reeled into the darkness like a coiled wolf in a defensive daze. What little light there was emanating from the emergency room doors was seized by that white thatch of hair hovering above his head like a ghostly veil. I took hold of a shoulder and a leg, the orderly took hold of a shoulder and a leg, and we began to cautiously ease Jackie out. Suddenly, Jackie began to writhe and kick and snarl and spit and ultimately he pushed us off, refusing to come out of the car.

Oh, *great*, I thought. That's it! He realizes where he is and he won't budge. So I asked the orderly, "Can we get a doctor out here to sedate him maybe? 'Cause I tell ya, he ain't comin' out of the car."

"No, no," the orderly assured me. Happens all the time. We can handle it. So we tried it again.

I grabbed an arm and a calf, the orderly grabbed an arm and a calf and, again, we began to pull. Once more, Jackie spit and yelled and growled and twisted and locked his hands and feet against the car door frame and simply would not come out of the car. So I said to the orderly, "If the doctor gave him a shot maybe that would calm him down . . . No?"

About this time an ambulance pulled up and the driver got out, off duty. The orderly called to the driver. "Hey, we got a guy here who won't come out of the car. Can you help us?"

No problem.

The ambulance driver sauntered over – because I'm sure this happens all the time – opened the other back door and climbed in *behind* Jackie. "You guys pull and I'll push," he directed with casual poise. Okay, sounds like a plan.

Slowly, the whites of Jackie's eyes stole focus from his hair. I grabbed a wrist and an ankle. The orderly grabbed a wrist and an ankle. The ambulance driver braced himself against Jackie's lower back. "On three," he said. "One . . . two . . . *three!*" The ambulance driver put his full weight into Jackie . . . the orderly and I pulled and yanked as hard as we could . . . Jackie let out a terrific primal yell unto the heavens, as if some strange primitive beast deep within him were trying to tell us something, "NYAAAHHHG!!!" . . . and he *didn't budge an inch.*

"Wait a minute! Wait a minute!" the ambulance driver yelled. Then his tone grew softer . . .

"*Is his seatbelt on?*"

Silence.

You know how time stands still ever so briefly when you've just realized you're a complete moron? Welcome to my world.

I checked Jackie's waist and realized, yup, it was on. And that's when it dawned. Apparently, when Anita, Dot and Michelle put him in the back of the wagon, they must've buckled him in. Meanwhile, in my haste to play surrogate paramedic, I had been busy signing the car out, so I had no knowledge of this. By the time we made it to E.R., it was so dark and Jackie's clothes were so tousled, the orderly and I never even noticed the seatbelt. So, of course, the orderly did what any experienced professional would do in this situation. He turned to me and shrugged. "I won't tell if you won't tell," he said.

Grimacing at us the way Moe did countless times at Larry and Curly, the ambulance driver reached around to unbuckle Jackie. "No, don't!" I shouted. "If you unbuckle him, he'll kill us all!" But it was too late. *Click.*

On cue, Jackie *lunged* from the back seat – and landed, *whump!*, butt-first, square in the wheelchair. I froze. Slowly, Jackie lifted his head to lock eyes with mine. With a small whimper he simply said, ". . . Doctor?"

Inside the emergency ward, Jackie lay still in his bed. I sat quietly next to him on a metal folding chair. Feeling like a total idiot, I prayed no one would ever find out what I did; I was certain I'd be fired instantly. Suddenly, a rounds nurse threw back the curtain and stood framed in a halo of fluorescent light

"Jonathan Chuckam" she said, reading the name from his chart. It was the first time I'd ever heard Jackie called by his real name. Jackie opened his eyes and looked up weakly to see the nurse standing over him. "Okay, then, your blood labs are back, everything looks normal, your doctor says you're free to go. Any questions?"

Jackie eyed the nurse blankly, slowly reached down, pulled up his shirt, and pointed to his mid-section with a husky utterance. "Guh."

I glanced down. There, emblazoned across his waistline, was a red strap mark.

"Hmm, what was that?" the nurse said, still gazing at his chart.

She hadn't seen.

In my heart, I knew it was moments like this one that define character. This was a turning point. I had no choice but to be forthcoming. It was my duty to help safeguard Jackie from harm and stand up for the values of Shepherd Hills. Our very mission was at stake, as was my own self-worth.

Ever so gently, I pulled Jackie's shirt down and tucked it back in. "Nothing," I reassured her." He'll be fine."

The nurse looked up at me. "Great." Then she smiled. "You know, these guys are so lucky to have people like you to look after them."

To which I smiled back and replied, "Thank you. I try."

And so came to pass my first month on the job. A momentous month of blunders, botches, screw ups and oops – more than I care to admit or remember. That night, after I took Jackie home, made sure he got to bed okay, filled out an incident report, charted an ID note and finally clocked out, I drove home remembering what my Aunt Betty had said to me when she heard I was working for Shepherd Hills:

"Stephen, there's a place reserved for you in heaven."

Which, to me, is a shame. Because I'm sure as shit gonna burn in hell for what I did to Jackie Chuckam.

Two days later, Dawn called me into her office and handed me my 30-day evaluation, a standard feedback form rating the performance of new hires. I cringed. I was sure somehow word had gotten back to her about the E.R. run. Of course

Jackie had shown her that mark on his stomach and ratted me out, and only one thing went through my mind as I prepared for the worst: *Shee-it!*

My review read as follows:

30-DAY PERFORMANCE REVIEW

Employee: **Steve Grieger**

Dept: **Independent Training Facility**

Steve is an asset to the ITF team. He is dedicated, reliable, caring, and demonstrates a fine sense of responsibility to the requirements of the clients, his position, and the program. He has a thorough understanding of normalization, and is a faithful advocate for the protection of client rights.

Goals:

1) Steve will continue to utilize creative opportunities to provide general care and advocacy to the clients, and follow daily assigned work duty schedules.

Evaluated by: Dawn Barry

Date: 07/02/82

I signed my evaluation in relative silence and handed it back to Dawn. As I turned to leave, the words "keep up the good work" echoed behind me. Imagine that? I thought. I guess I have a job to do.

If the milestone with Jackie and the seatbelt established anything, it was my determination now more than ever to *get it right!* To serve, protect and advocate for my clients, regardless of causing a little occasional waistline discomfort. And in that – despite the things like Billy's insults, Owen's freeway shuffle, Jackie's contempt and even Cole's weenie – I felt obligated to become diligent, more dedicated, more deserving. For the rest of the summer I wanted to be there for my clients as they would continue to face the challenges of everyday living and the dreams of independence.

Besides, I still hadn't made it to first base yet with Michelle.

CHAPTER 6

5:30-ISH IN THE GARDEN OF GOOD AND EVIL

NOT ONLY DID I start to shape up, but I began to ease up. On myself. Instead of purposely trying to avoid screw ups, I accepted them. Instead of arriving to work each day with a head full of cloudy hesitations or designs on how to flirt with Michelle, I began to actually *listen* to the clients. So what, I thought, if Owen was obsessed with Lawrence Welk? To him it was important. So what if Hughie liked to preach the gospel unto deaf ears? To him it was meaningful. Just as Jackie's bicycle, James' bathroom time, and Darlene's job at Chuck E. Cheese were to them. In that first month I'd even grown accustomed to Sammy The Face's face until soon it didn't bother me at all. Granted, the passing of time had a little to do with it, but it was more than just a matter of growing familiar; it was finding the ability to look beyond his face and hear Sammy's voice. In fact, I discovered the man could be downright hilarious.

This became evident the time Sammy asked me how to set his kitchen timer for 70 minutes. When I asked him why he needed 70 minutes, he explained he was cooking TV dinners for himself and Darlene, and the directions required each to be heated for 35 minutes. Thus, applying clear logic, Sammy had added 35 and 35 on his calculator for a total of 70, henceforth, "How do I set the timer for 70 minutes when the dial only goes up to 60?" I had to admit it was a fair question.

After trying my best to explain the properties of time, Sammy now looked more confused than ever. Ultimately, I gave up and summarized the whole thing with a well-disposed chuckle only a houseparent can provide. "Oh, Sammy. What would I do without you?"

Without missing a beat, like some seasoned vaudevillian, Sammy replied, "I don't know. Get a lot more sleep?"

I whipped my head toward Sammy. This was obviously a punch line he'd picked up somewhere, perhaps from an old sitcom or a jovial family member. But what impressed me more was the fact that *he* knew what he said was funny – and he knew that *I* knew what he said was funny. Not just because I didn't see it coming, but because it was a genuinely witty comeback. Meanwhile, Sammy stood there eyeing me with a goofy, cock-eyed grin, awaiting my reaction. When I acknowledged his joke with a solid laugh, I could see triumph register in his eyes. He had been validated and we, for lack of a better word, had bonded. After that, I no longer thought of him as just Sammy The Face. I began to give Sammy a lot more credit. And a lot more respect.

It was moments like these that helped me begin to see something in the job I hadn't counted on. *Humor.* And from that humor I began to ease into a natural, good-natured sensibility set in motion during one particular laundry demonstration when I was able to coax James from the sanctum sanctorum of his bathroom to join us. James was a good guy, but I'd kind of dismissed him as an "also-ran," a man of few mumbles, the odd-client-out whom the staff had the least faith in to succeed. As I both lectured and measured the soft soap, I noticed James wasn't paying attention. This was nothing new.

"James," I called. "James, you getting this?"

No answer.

"James. Yoo-hoo. Anybody home?" I swept James' sheepdog bangs aside to look him in the eye. It was the first time I'd actually seen his eyes – two drooping, bloodshot pools like those of a Basset Hound. This, coupled with a round, chinless jaw, bore him a striking resemblance to the old children's board game Mr. Mouth. James stared at me vacantly.

"You with me, Jim?"

All at once, I saw a light go on in those bloodshot pools. James' head craned a few inches higher than usual, and a big smile crept across his face.

"What are you smiling at, Jim?"

His smile broadened and he bestowed a throaty giggle. "Muh-muh-muhm. You called me Jim," he said.

I took a step back. Typically, James spewed a gnarled tangle of syllables, but every now and then a comprehensible word or two, perhaps even a full-on phrase, would break free to see the light, like a game of verbal Peek-A-Boo. But this was more than just a moment of clarity. Somehow I'd made a connection. "Jim?" I said. "Is that it? You like it when I call you Jim?"

"Muh-muh-muhm," he nodded enthusiastically. "Jim, yeah. I'm Jim."

It was simple, really, but from that connection came the insight that no one had ever called James "Jim" before – nor ever thought to ask him if he had a preference. And so, from that moment on, while the rest of the world knew him as James Cornell Livingston, to me he became – and always would be – just Jim.

> *"I used to work at an assisted living home for adults with D.D. One time I took a couple of the male residents from the home to see the movie* **There's Something About Mary.** *If you saw it you probably remember that Cameron Diaz's character has a retarded brother in the movie. When this retarded guy came on screen and started talking, one of the guys laughed and turned to the other and said mockingly, 'That's you.'"*
> *– Anonymous Care Provider*

Not only did those little moments make me laugh, in time they encouraged me to consider things from *their* perspective. For instance, I learned that within their culture the worst insult one peer can hurl at another is to call him or her a "retard." Even the mere suggestion is stark and abhorrent; being called a retard is experienced as a direct assault on one's sense of personal worth. Instead, the client lexicon was, in its own way, keener. Steeped within their vernacular there existed a variety of shorthand terms that could be used to represent anything from a playful taunt to an all-purpose invective. Phrases like "you're not the boss of me," "old man," and "clown" were some of the most common ones bandied about, but the expression that amused me most was "your head."

Aw, your head!

"Your head" was a catchall catch phrase that encompassed "get lost," "up yours," "bite me" and "screw you." Who's to say if they even knew what the other was inferring – somehow, for them, it worked.

Another example of perspective was the time I found Hughie lying on his bed, groaning and clutching his stomach. When I asked him what was wrong, he said, "I just had a snack. Honest." I asked him what he ate and he said, "Just some pudding and ice cream, that's all. Honest. *Ohhhhh!*" Meanwhile, on the nightstand next to him I spotted a large empty jar and even larger plastic tub – both licked clean.

"Did you eat *all* of this?"

"Yeah, it musta spoiled. *Ohhhhhhh!* I think I gonna heave!"

As Hughie diligently aimed the contents of his belly into the trash can, I felt it my duty to help illuminate the error of his way. "Hughie," I said, "this isn't pudding and ice cream."

"It not?"

"No. It's mayonnaise and margarine!"

"Oh, sorry. My mistake. *Brr-aauugghhh!*"

The infamous "my mistake." Yet another phrase in the colorful repartee of clientisms. That and "sorry" were great weapons in the ongoing battle to fend off the normal world. To a client, "my mistake" was a shortcut to quickly concede defeat and sidestep responsibility. Clients can't be bothered with learning from their mistakes – it takes too much brainpower and leaves one susceptible to future accountability. And who the hell wants that? Saying "my mistake" says, "Okay, you win-I was wrong-you were right-now watch me forget about it in three . . . two . . . one."

"Sorry," on the other hand, was another way to tell people, "Get off my back!" The sentiment was rarely used to express remorse. Think of how the rest of the world uses "I'm sorry." When we say it, the recipient generally acknowledges the user's sincerity and all is forgiven. But for a client, "I'm sorry" was merely the speediest bridge to forgive-and-forgetness; just the means to an end. (Then again, I think in poor Hughie's case, this time the sentiment may've been genuine.)

And then there was the perspective of the *staff*. Some, like Michelle, were staunch advocates, while others, like Dot, believed in tough love – if not rough justice.

By July 4th I was still there and Billy Mattila was still an asshole. It hadn't taken as long as I thought for me to fall into a certain comfort zone within my duties, nurtured cheerfully by the fact that I genuinely liked most of the clients. True, progress was slow and each day had its share of unexpected challenges, but somehow that made the art of care-giving strangely seductive. Maybe it was those hidden high-school teacher instincts calling to me, but watching the clients make their way, day-to-day, carried a certain undeniable joy.

Except for Mattila the Hun.

From the moment our paths had crossed, his standing with me continued to lose footing. One day I had to transport him and Holly to a late afternoon medical clinic off the main campus. Being that we were the last appointment of the day, as we exited the clinic the doors locked behind us. All that was left now was to transfer Holly from her wheelchair into the Blue Beast, load it up and head for home.

Climbing into the car first, Billy asked if he could listen to the radio until we were ready to go. Still hopeful to earn brownie points with him, I happily obliged. Just as I turned my back to lift Holly out of her chair, the passenger door slammed behind me and I heard the sound of a distinct *"click."* Billy Mattila had locked us both out of the car. The clinic was now dark. Pleas, shouts and demands to open the car door were only met by jeers, sneers and Billy's spiky middle finger. These were the days before cell phones, so several blocks later – with an incontinent Holly in tow – I finally located a pay phone and persuaded our Maintenance Department to drive across town and unlock the door. Billy feigned innocence throughout.

Now, I knew even then, without anybody having to tell me, it was sacrilege to hate a client. But sometimes you just get a guy who pushes all the wrong buttons. More than just an instigator, Billy was a mean-spirited, unreasonable, unreachable punk. When he laughed, his face looked like it could pierce a brick. When he spoke, it sounded like he had a mouthful of sour piss. Morning, noon and night, Billy stalked the courtyard of ITF Village, telling the other clients to "shut da fucks up," and greeting the staff with such heartfelt sentiments as, "Go home, we don't want you here," or his favorite jingle, "I hope you *die!*" (This was often followed by spitting or blowing his nose in the targeted victim's general direction.) I would've liked to have chalked it all up to overcompensation for his psychological shortcomings, but Billy couldn't use his disability as an excuse. He was a bully who possessed an ugly spirit – an asshole who *enjoyed* being an asshole.

Yet it wasn't as if I could just wish him into the cornfield. Dawn countered that Billy never did anything *bad enough* to put anybody at significant risk or infringe on the residents' rights. So, like it or not, it was our job to work with him. How his roommate Hughie found the strength to put up with him remained a mystery – until that Fourth of July.

It was late afternoon and we were all gearing up for a traditional barbecue of burgers and dogs, potato salad and baked beans. I was in the rec room finishing a training session on budgeting skills with Sammy, Cole and Darlene, utilizing a pictorial budget sheet with pictures of food, a telephone, and the SDGE logo to symbolize groceries, Pac Bell, and the gas and electric bill. Several other clients lazily lounged outside on the patchy grass, sunning themselves next to an idle badminton net, as Michelle and Dot manned a lone Weber grill. The aroma of charred meat perfumed the courtyard. All that was missing were a few bottles of Bartles & Jaymes.

Meanwhile, Billy was pacing up and down the top of the driveway, when for no apparent reason he began to tease Holly.

"You stink, Holly Gross!" he shouted. "You crap in you chair and den you eat it!"

This went on for several minutes. Despite warnings from Michelle and Dot for Billy to stop "being inappropriate," he refused to let up. Instead, his ranting only grew louder before it finally disrupted my class and drew infantile snickers from Darlene and Cole. Unable to stand it any longer, Sammy said, "I'm gonna put a stop to this," and bolted from the rec room with clenched fists. Class dismissed.

As Sammy hit the driveway, I made it out in time to stop him from going after Billy. At the same time, Hughie, the wandering Southern Baptist, was making his own way to confront The Hun, no doubt to preach some Christian sense into him and defend his girlfriend's honor.

The two were just far enough away so we could hear them as Hughie raised his bible. "You stop that there yellin' at Miss Holly, Billy Mattila. Blessed da peacemakers."

Billy hissed and turned his back to Hughie. "Leave me alone, you fuckin' nigger."

It was the last time anyone at Shepherd Hills ever said, or dared think, something like that about Hughie Wendell Lamb.

WWWWWHAM! – In a blind, unforeseen rage, Hughie *flew* after Billy. Armed with fists of thunder he began pounding the life out of him; a blitzkrieg of blood, tears and unbridled hostility. The rest of us froze. *Was this really happening?*

"*EEE-EEEEE-EEEEEEEEEEEE!*"

Billy screamed like a schoolgirl on fire falling off a cliff.

"*EEEEEEEEEEEEEEEEEEEEEEEEEEEEEEEEEEEEEEE!!!*"

At last, he broke free and began to run. Dawn thrust her head out the office door. "Quick, Billy, this way!"

Billy sailed past me – and though I admit I was tempted to trip him, I didn't need to. Hughie was right on top of him. Dawn yanked Billy into the office and hastily tried to lock the door, but Hughie blew right through it. By this point I was running back to the office because I figured perhaps this was one of those "occasional aggressive behaviors" I was hired to help handle. I entered just in time to see Billy try to lock himself in the bathroom. But Hughie burst in there too, slammed him into the corner, and started beating him. And beating him. And beating him. Billy screamed and cried, his face tenderized like a hunk of cube steak.

Suddenly, Dot – of all people – emerged onto the scene, quick and to the point: "*Hughie, stop!*"

And just like that, he did.

Like turning off a light switch. Like nothing had even happened.

Hughie walked away, went to his apartment and closed the door behind him. Dawn drove Billy to E.R.

All through dinner not a single word was spoken about the incident. It was as if the clients were still in shock – not just because of the fight, but because it was *Hughie* who had participated. Beans and potato salad were passed around family-style in silence. Dot, Michelle and I took our cues from the group and steered clear from the subject.

That night, I retrieved Hughie's bible from the top of the driveway and wiped Billy's blood from the cover. I joined Dot and Michelle in the office where the three of us sat quietly, putting our final touches on the day's data sheets. No one suggested we go out to look at fireworks. Instead, the courtyard remained abandoned, as all the clients had chosen to go to bed early. That's when Dot leaned in toward us and whispered, "*Wasn't that fucking great?*"

Michelle looked up and scowled at Dot.

"Oh, come on," Dot said. "The little shit deserved it."

"Are you kidding? Hughie could've killed him!"

"But he *didn't*. And that's the beauty. You think Asshole will ever tease anyone again? Fat chance. Sometimes things just take care of themselves."

From there I sat back and marveled at the debate that evolved between Dot and Michelle. A debate about client ethics. I'd been warned time and again the biggest mistake you can make in this field is to take it personally. Then again, I thought, if we *don't* take it personally, what becomes of the human factor? Michelle, on the other hand, stated that while it's one thing to vent your frustrations, it's another to flounder in them – whatever the hell *that* meant. Personally, I wanted to jump in with my own two cents; I wanted to say that justifying Billy's mean-spiritedness just because he was retarded made about as much sense as justifying Rhoda Penmark in *The Bad Seed* just because she was ten years old. But it was times like these my jokiness could be too easily misunderstood, so I figured it was better to simply listen and learn.

Soon it became apparent this was a debate that neither side was willing to concede. And, in truth, both sides had merit. But the fact remained that the main reason Billy still lived at ITF was because Dawn kept him there. And while it's understandable, even admirable, that a manager may want to give a client every possible chance to succeed, it's only because they have staff to do the hands-on dirty work for them. Direct care staff live the day-to-day challenges with the clients, side-by-side, hip-deep in metaphoric muck. So, when faced with someone difficult like Billy, the most natural words out of your mouth become, "Why can't we just get *rid* of him?" And even though "get rid of" is an ugly thing to say, damn, it feels good to say it.

So then, what becomes a bully most?

The incident with Hughie Lamb and Billy Mattila happened so fast, no two accounts of it were the same. This ultimately made the entire episode symbolic if not surreal. Their mutual disabilities aside, Hughie and Billy acted out "normal" instincts – as "normal" as anything so violent can be understood. As for me, bullies were nothing new in my life. In fact, I saw the natural bully instinct quite early in my father, even before I was grown up enough to understand it.

I can't recall exactly how old I was, just that I was old enough to commit it to memory. On a night like any other, my mother had just finished preparing dinner. After taking good care to serve it to her family, it quickly became apparent she had accidentally done something wrong. Used the wrong seasoning, mixed up the sugar with the salt, I don't remember. What I *do* remember is that whatever it was instantly became fodder for my father's ridicule. Sharing his venomous glee with his children, Daddy roared at her alleged incompetence with a bray that sucked all the air from the room, and called for us to laugh along with him. And though the finer points of his riff remain fuzzy, I remember wanting to please him so much, out popped my innocent contribution:

"We have a *stupid* mommy, don't we, Daddy?"

Later that night, dressed in my pajamas on the way to bed, I peeked into my parents' room to see my mother sitting alone in the dark, brushing her hair. She was crying. I was shell-shocked. I'd never seen my mommy cry before. And in that very moment I found myself for the first time worrying about my mother's happiness more than my own.

Only years later as a young adult was I able to fully comprehend just what my father had suckered me into. For a mother to hear something like that coaxed from her own son must have been humiliating, as were all the other hurtful, spiteful tongue-lashings we would *all* endure for the sake of my old man's amusement. Sorting through those memories, hundreds of vicious criticisms snowballing into a single mass, I still remember some of the bits and pieces that pierced my head and heart:

> *"You're lucky to be livin' here! . . . All you're good for is costin' me money! . . . You're so ugly – why don't you pop your pimples? . . . When you gonna lose some weight? – you got the tits of a woman! . . . You'll never make it in the real world! . . . you can't-you aren't-you won't-you'll never! . . . Youse are all just DUMB!"*

At the very least I believed the clients deserved to feel their world was safe, let alone fair.

Billy returned home that night from the E.R. with a broken nose, two black eyes and a body marked by the blacks of survival-of-the-fittest, and the blues of what-goes-around-comes-around. To Dot, that afternoon the true nature of mankind unexpectedly burst forth, pounding its chest with indignation, righteous if not justified. And though I would never admit it to Michelle, I secretly agreed with Dot.

CHAPTER 7

PARTY DOWNS

MICHELLE HAD IT. So did Anita. Dawn, definitely. Hell, even Dot had it. What each of them had was the respect of their clients. Whether they always deserved it or not.

From what I could gather, most of the clients at Shepherd Hills had either grown up there, or had transferred in from some other institutional-type setting or group home when they were younger. Even those clients with strong family ties had spent a large part of their lives living outside their parents' homes. Therefore, it was understandable that many clients tended to develop their strongest bonds not with their families or even their peers, but with their direct care counselors. It gave them an enhanced sense of security. Prime example, Anita Rodriguez was the primary counselor for Holly, Hughie and Darlene. There wasn't anything they wouldn't do for her or vice versa. Anita helped give the Downs their voice and was rewarded with reverence and friendship – the same way only the best teachers are rewarded. And so, after three whole months, I too had now reached a point where I yearned for that same sort of mutual respect with the clients of ITF Village.

With an entire summer at The Hills about to end, my return to college was looming fast. During that time I'd grown fascinated by everyone's individual abilities, personalities, passions and quirks. However, the one thing I felt the clients still lacked was a little quality social time in the *real* world. Trips to the grocery store and the occasional mall walks just didn't seem to be cutting it. Whether or not by design, the clients populated a unique hidden fortress. Theirs was a culture held at bay by the rest of society. I wanted to change that. I wanted to fling open the door and expose their civilization for the benefit of all mankind – normal or otherwise. I wanted them to experience an awakening of life. And that meant only one thing: *A party!*

Marc Upcott had been a good college friend and fellow Drama student who worked part-time as a deejay for the university radio station. He was someone with whom I'd shared a handful of classes and a fistful of brews. As a member of the Alpha Delta Phi fraternity, he was also no stranger to parties – or ever in want of a reason to have one. And even though I didn't share his passion for the Greek order, when I called him to help set something up, he was more than happy to arrange a dance for the good people at Shepherd Hills, sponsored by his fraternity as a charity event. With Dawn's approval she allowed me to tap Michelle, Dot and Anita to help escort six of the clients – Owen, Darlene, Hughie, Holly, Jim and Jackie – to the festivity. Together the two of us envisioned it to be an openhanded meeting of sub-cultures. And in my mind, a great way to impress Michelle one last time.

The day before the event, just as I was about to cross the threshold into the rec room, I overheard Michelle chatting with Anita. "Yeah, Steve's a nice enough guy," she was saying, "but he just sort of takes up space. You know? I don't think he really gives a shit about anything. He just gets in the way."

I stopped dead. And so did my heart.

Gets in the way? What the hell did *that* mean? If I'd overheard anyone else say it, it probably wouldn't have bothered me as much. But this was Michelle talking. And it stung.

At any cost, it was the kind of conversation I had no desire to confront. Whatever it was they were talking about, I didn't want or need to hear any more. Luckily, neither of them had seen me, so I backed out quietly into the courtyard. I found myself an isolated lawn chair where I sat for the rest of my break, humbled and despondent, pathetically replaying Michelle's words over and over in my head like a lovesick fool.

I realized then it wasn't just the clients' respect I wanted, I wanted Michelle's more.

The night of the benefit began in grand style. To the over-amped reverb of late-'70s white-boy funk, the ten of us were joyously welcomed by a roomful of rowdy frat brothers and sorority sisters. It didn't take long for the gang to assimilate, each in their own way.

Owen immediately set the bar by dancing with a coed on each arm, singing his own words to the music, working that game-show-host appeal. Funny thing about Owen was that when he wasn't busy wallowing in his own intemperate frustration, there was a gruff spirit in his compactness that could be engaging, like that of a pint-sized Fred Mertz. He came that night prepared to usurp his share of the limelight, wearing a bright magenta corduroy sports coat adorned with a peculiar hybrid of brass buttons, gold zippers and lapels like the mainsails of a Spanish galleon. The coat had been a gift from his brother and Owen always pulled it out whenever it was time to paint the town. Never mind that he looked like a misplaced member of the Lollipop Guild, to Owen any excuse to dress up was almost as dear to him as his beloved tape recorder.

Meanwhile, Darlene propped herself up on the edge of the stage dressed in her cherished square-dancing dress so she could flirt with the band. It just might've worked too, if only she'd left her Chuck E. Cheese cap at home. Over by the snack table, Holly and Hughie were off on their own quest, obsessed with inhaling every last inch of a seven-foot hoagie. Jim, on the other hand, was temporarily missing in action, as he had personally commandeered the downstairs bathroom for his own private war room. This left Jackie, who chose to eschew the rest of us and tolerate the party on his own terms. Remaining true to his nature, Jackie leaned against the bar with his arms crossed, staring stonily at the wall. Seeing this I began to wonder why I brought him, or why I even bothered.

Oddly enough, however, it was my co-workers who turned out to be the most reluctant to participate in the night's events. While the clients intermingled with their slightly intoxicated yet erudite hosts, Dot, Anita and Michelle exiled themselves to a table tucked in the corner, masked behind a cloud of cigarette smoke.

As the night progressed I roamed the floor, shaking hands with everybody, acting the proud emissary. In a sense it felt good to be "home" again. In college I had found comfort. In college I learned to socialize. SDSU was where the insecure fat kid was finally able to stop sucking in his stomach and *bre-e-e-athe*. It was a safety zone to sample all the things you're supposed to in higher education: free speech, revolution, assorted vices, hangover cures and non-specific urethritis. A place to tilt at windmills until they would fall on you; a place where dreams were allowed to stay up all night long. But most of all, it was place where I no longer thought of myself solely as my father's son. And so, in wanting to give the clients that same feeling of liberation I'd savored, I brought them to the scene of the crime. Tonight, I was going to make a statement by bringing my two worlds together – or be damned trying.

I wandered over near the bar to see how Jackie was fairing and eavesdropped as the bartender offered him a beer.

"I c-c-can't," Jackie declined. "Not with muh-muh-my meds."

"Oh," said the bartender. "Then how about a Pepsi? No alcohol."

"Better not," Jackie waved him off, cautiously. "You never know. They put d-dope in candy."

That left the bartender one last idea. "Well then, how'd you like to help me out?"

"M-M-Me? H-H-H-How?"

"Whenever someone orders a beer just pull on this tap and fill the glass. Like this, see?" I watched from a distance as the bartender demonstrated how to work the tap. "Wanna try?" The tap system was the house pride and joy – a gleaming, stainless-steel assemblage treated with near reverence by most of the brothers. To have been asked to assist with such an important duty as this was colossal. But what really impressed me was how the bartender *spoke* to Jackie. Clean and straightforward. Why couldn't more people "out there" do that?

Jackie beamed. Stepping into the inner U of the bar, he was anointed with an apron. With gentle, hand-over-hand assistance – not unlike the assistance many a houseparent practiced during skill-trainings – the bartender schooled Jackie in how to manipulate the colorful plastic toggle to produce the perfect measure of beer and foam. The next thing I knew, Jackie was pouring and doling out orders like a pro. And I thought, way to go, Jackie. I could tell it meant the world to him.

Soon the party kicked into full swing and I joined my colleagues at their fortress of nicotine retreat. Not surprisingly, I found Dot in full sourpuss mode, doing her best to bring the others down with her. Everything to her was a waste of time; she didn't like the music, didn't like the food, didn't like the hosts, and was embarrassed for – and *by* – the clients. But despite Dot's sourness, Anita and – more importantly – Michelle saw the positive effects the celebration was having on the clients and threw me their nods of support.

All at once, the music shifted. Owen took the floor as the crowd encircled him, stomping and clapping. Accompanied by a series of drum rolls, Owen whipped off his coat and began swinging it over his head, a tireless matador flourishing his corduroy cape. The entire room laughed and cheered him on – all except for Dot. Instead, she turned to me and sneered, "Aren't you gonna stop this? They're treating him like he's a trained monkey."

In an effort to lighten the mood and loosen the size-nine board from Dot's ass, I jokingly replied, "Well then, throw him a peanut! He'll never know the difference." I handed her a bowl of nuts. Dot stared at me, unsure. To punctuate my wisecrack, I scratched my armpits like an ape and swayed to and fro with an "ooo-ooo-ooo." Dot's lips curled. Finally, she began to laugh. *Success!* I thought. I finally won her over. Then I looked at Michelle.

Michelle wasn't laughing.

Shit. Instantly, I realized that I'd said the wrong thing. But the damage had been done and in her eyes – regardless how harmless my remark had been intended – I looked like a complete jerk. Michelle got up from the table and walked out the door. I got up and went after her.

The front lawn of the frat house was jammed with parked cars blocking my way. By the time I caught up to Michelle she was filled with blind anger. I tried to apologize – it was just an innocent comment, after all – but she wouldn't have any part of it. She tore into me about being insensitive, being a phony, not taking the job or Shepherd Hills seriously. I had no defense. Then she hit me with the killer:

"Why are you there, anyway? Just to get one more *'experience'* to put down on your fucking resume?"

With that, Michelle stormed back inside without even giving me a chance to reply. (Not that "I'm there to get in your pants" would have helped much.) In that instant, all the bubbles of false hope I'd amassed over the summer burst. Who was I kidding? What naïve notion made me think for one second Michelle Montgomery could possibly be interested in someone like me? My head looked like a sticker burr with glasses. My body looked like a pear with a bite missing where the butt should be. The best I could ever hope for was to land the role of dancing bear to her barefoot contessa. And now, even that dream was shot to pieces.

I drifted back into the house and stood in the doorway, figuring I'd better let Michelle cool off before trying to approach her again. The frat house president was up on stage, busy blathering about how this was a "very, very meaningful night" for a "very, very special group of people," and those of us who worked with them had a "very, very special calling in life." I remember thinking, What a very, very dick.

Following his very, very speech, the president proclaimed they were now going to announce the winner of the night's raffle. He was joined on stage by Darlene carrying a fishbowl-sized Margarita glass full of ticket stubs. The glass was as round as she was. Swinging her square-dancing petticoats for effect, she was greeted by a few harmless wolf whistles.

"Hi, I'm Darlene. I work at Chuck E. Cheese. Fun for the whole family."

A few more whistles and some good-natured chuckles.

"O-yez, o-yez!" the president playfully stalled. "Who, oh who, is destined to walk away with this lovely little portable TV, donated for tonight's event by Sound Design Stereos located at 54th and Main? Sound Design Stereos, the place dedicated to meet all your stereophonic needs for life. Hurry, their 'going-out-of-business sale' is on for only three more days!"

Darlene rooted her hand into the bowl, pulled out the winning stub, and drew it to her nose. "Number two . . . five . . . what's this other number?"

"Two," the president whispered.

"Two! Number two-five-two. Who has number two-five-two?"

Checking his ticket, a shy grin slowly crept over Jackie's face. "That's m-m-my ticket."

Across the room Holly shouted, "Jackie Chuckam! It's Jackie Chuckam's! He won, he won!"

The other clients started cheering and everyone began to applaud. Even Jim poked his head out of the bathroom long enough to see what all the hoopla was about. Half the frat guys started chanting, "*Bar*tender, *Bar*tender, *Bar*tender!" Hands appeared from everywhere, patting Jackie on the back and guiding him to the stage. In a joyful daze, Jackie stepped up to the mike.

"Tha-tha-tha-tha-tha-tha-tha-tha –"

Slowly, the applause fell away.

"Tha-tha-tha-tha-thank –"

Whispers turned into an embarrassed rumble as the room faded to silence. All eyes were on him – and he knew it.

"Y-y-y-y-y-ou-ou –"

My heart sank. All I could think was, at that moment, the only thing anybody saw up there on stage was a stuttering, stereotypical retarded person.

I didn't know what to do. Why isn't anybody helping him? Should I go up there and be with him? Should I let him stand there and work it out for himself? Should I ask the band to start playing? What?

Suddenly, one of the frat boys who was drunk off his ass began to laugh. He shouted to Jackie, "English, dude, speak English! If you *can*!"

That made me move. I bounded up on stage and stood next to Jackie. I told the crowd, "Thank you" on Jackie's behalf. But apparently that wasn't good enough.

Owen charged the drunken frat ass. "Hey! You can't talk to my roommate that way!"

Frat Ass looked down at Owen and scoffed. "Get outta my face, retard."

"*RETARD?!*" Owen bellowed.

(*Uh-oh.*)

Jumping off the stage, I pressed myself between the two of them. But it was too late, the fuse had been lit. With all his might, Owen swung his sports coat at Frat Ass, only it caught me instead – *swack!* – zipper-first across the face. Down I went.

STEVE GRIEGER'S OFFICIAL
LIFETIME FIGHTING RECORD
Won: 1
Lost: 1
TKO by Zipper: 1

The place exploded.

Instantly, everyone was out of their seats. The clients swarmed the scene in defense of one of their own, screaming, cursing, vicious – no longer the sweet holy innocents everyone thought them to be. Michelle, Dot and Anita shouted orders to no avail, frantically trying to maintain control amongst a sea of confused collegiate faces.

"– I'll kill you, you bastard! –"

"– Owen, calm down! –"

"– Kick him! Kick him! –"

"– Get him! –"

"– Darlene, Holly! Stop! –"

"– Bob-bobby-brown-grrr! –"

"– James, stop biting! –"

CHALLENGED: A TRIBUTE | 79

Jackie looked on, his face warped with humiliation. Unable to stand it any longer, he ran out the door and disappeared into the night.

What was meant to be a benevolent meeting of cultures instead became a culture clash. Eventually, Marc and two of his frat brothers tackled Frat Ass and carried him upstairs. With my eye already swelling, I scurried to my feet, grabbed the portable TV, and followed after Jackie. I never once dared look at Michelle.

Outside, I found Jackie standing with his head down, seething with frustrated fury. His entire body was quivering, and even under the dim streetlight his ears looked bright red, as if they'd been boiled. I stopped about ten feet away.

"Jackie? I've got your prize."

"I don' wan' it!"

"But you won it."

He shook his head sharply. "No! No! They just gave it a-me 'cause I'm re-...re-...re-...re-*eeeee*-..." Infuriated that he couldn't get the word out – that dreaded, vile word, the one word he hated most – Jackie pounded his fist on one of the cars, as if trying to punch it free. "*GODDAMN IT!*" he screamed. "*I CAN'T HELP IT! I CAN'T...CAN'T...CAN'T...CAH-CAH-CAH-...cah-cah-cah-... cah-...cah-...*" His voice faded to raw silence.

My first instinct was to take a step back, afraid that he might suddenly lunge at me. Instead, I inched forward, worried he might begin to seizure.

With a weak, defeated moan, the words "Lea' me alone" dribbled from Jackie's lips. He ran to the Blue Beast, dove into the back and slammed the door. I slowly followed after him and eased the door open. I placed the TV on the seat next to him. Then I closed the door, walked around to the driver's seat, and got in without saying a word. In the background I could hear music coming from the band, a million miles away. But at that exact moment, the only world that existed was in the car – and no one else was permitted. As Jackie gradually gave himself up to tears, I sat with him in the shadows of Alpha Delta Phi, looked straight ahead, and fought the lump rising in my throat.

Later that night, after we took everyone home and they went to bed, Michelle asked me, "How's your eye?"

"Hurts," I said. "Yours?" This time she smiled. There was an awkward pause. "It was my fault, really. I guess I just sort of . . ." I took a half beat ". . . '*got in the way*.'" Whether or not Michelle caught the reference, it didn't register on her face. I shrugged. "So . . . Guess I'll see you tomorrow."

As I started to walk away, Michelle called after me. "You want to go for a drive?"

We drove out to the beach with hardly two words spoken. It wasn't until our feet hit the sand that we got to talking. I asked Michelle how she handled going to school *and* working full-time at The Hills. I remember I said, "Don't you ever feel like you're not getting anything back?"

"All the time. It's called 'The Martyr Syndrome.'" She smiled. "Personally, I thrive on it."

"No, but . . . how do keep it from making you cry?"

Michelle softened. "Look, Steve . . . I can't tell you, 'hang in there, it gets better,' because it might not. But it doesn't get any worse, either. This job is what you make it. So make it matter."

It was then that Michelle asked me if I'd ever read the background files on Jackie's family history. I was reluctant to admit in the three months I'd worked there that I hadn't. She told me the reason Jackie was so cold to people was because he'd been burned a lot in the past. Counselors. Friends. And especially his family. His own parents lived just a half hour away, but they never came to visit. They were too ashamed.

"Why?" I asked.

"Because Jackie wasn't born retarded. His father dropped him when he was a baby and screwed him up for life. He doesn't want to have anything to do with him." Michelle cleared the emotion from her throat; her eyes were large and liquid. "And what's more . . . Jackie *knows* this. He *knows* that he was once normal and never will be again."

I stopped walking. This was something about Jackie I'd never expected to learn. Something I'd wished I hadn't learned. Not now.

With the waves gently lapping the shore, I recalled all the things that had initially attracted me to Michelle as far back as Ballroom Dance. She was as naturally graceful as she was beautiful. Whenever we paired up, all I had to do was place my hand in the small of her back and she would guide me as I pretended to lead.

Drizzle began to fall in veils and the moment eased into something dreamlike. An uncomfortable juxtaposition of heartache and "just-friends"-ship and pity and empathy and Michelle, always Michelle.

Michelle . . .

Michelle took my hand and lightly squeezed it. Neither one of us started it nor stopped it, but together we eased into an embrace; the gentle touch of her hand on my neck, the scent of rain in her hair.

That's when Michelle Montgomery kissed me. For the first and last time.

PART II

RIDING THE SHORT
ROLLER COASTER

CHAPTER 8

HOLIDAY SPIRITS

THE NEW FALL semester at SDSU was scheduled to begin the final week of August 1982. It meant that all returning students had long since registered and would soon reunite with their studies, their homework, and their parties full-time. For Michelle, this meant a return to the full-time pursuit of her degree in Sociology, while for me, it meant continuing the pursuit of my own education as a teacher. For Michelle, it meant she would be leaving Shepherd Hills. For me, it meant I would be staying.

With Michelle leaving, this left an opening for a full-time houseparent – a position I wanted to explore just a little longer. Dawn promoted me without hesitation. Not only had I grown comfortable in the job, but remaining at ITF full-time afforded me the chance to save a little extra money before returning to school. In the meantime, I could work on my writing and stockpile a wealth of character research. The opportunity was win-win – and I was all too keen not to take advantage of throwing the fact in my old man's face that I had a job I enjoyed.

Soon Halloween arrived, with most of the clients donning some form of homemade costume. Each of the different day programs had planned their own party, so dressing up was a given – whether or not everyone actually understood the reason they were dressing up. To some all Halloween meant was an excuse to mac out on sugar, so sure, go ahead, put a goofy-looking hat on my head. Whatever. Just gimme da *candy*.

83

Most of the costumes at ITF were nothing to write home about; a cluster of hobos and square dancers, costumes that required little effort and were readily at hand. There were also those like Billy who regarded himself too cool for such silliness and refused to dress up, and Jackie who could get by on his own natural gray-and-white fright wig, which had grown capable of scaring small children. Owen went to work dressed as a pirate, complete with eye patch, earring and scarf, although the staff insisted he leave his parakeet at home. Cole dressed as (who else?) John Lennon, and for a few hours actually became John Lennon incarnate. But the one who impressed me most was Jim.

The day before ghosts and goblins were poised to descend, it was my turn to pass meds. As I handed Jim his Thyroid pill I casually asked, "So, Jimbo, what're you going as for Halloween?"

Instantly, Jim lit up, elated someone had shown an interest.

"Muh-muh a wit!" he answered.

"A . . . a what?"

Jim crooked his finger and beckoned me to follow. Creeping across the courtyard like Peter Lorre in *M*, Jim led me into the sanctuary of his *Star Wars* bedroom lair. (For a minute I was afraid he might show me his Wookie.) Pushing aside a stack of neatly folded, stained-but-clean T-shirts, Jim dug deep into his closet and withdrew a frail, plastic witch mask, complete with hooked nose, warts and evil scowl. It was the kind of mask you see on sale each year at the grocery store; a bargain bin holiday staple. The mask was a good ten years old if it was a day. With great reverence, Jim slowly pulled it over his face, taking extra care not to snap the original elastic strand stapled to the sides. Jim's eyes peeped through the eye holes, eagerly awaiting my response.

"Oh," I said, nodding. "A *witch*. Great costume, Jim."

Ah, but Jim raised his finger to signal there was more. Rooting through the closet further, he proceeded to excavate a black nylon witch's hat and black horsehair wig. He donned both with the same level of care he'd shown the mask and smoothed his tangled 'do. Lastly, Jim gathered a black Member's Only jacket from its hanger and put it on – backwards. He turned and mumbled some sort of instructions to me, thumbing the zipper behind him.

"You want me to zip you up?" I said.

Affirmative mumbles.

As I zipped the jacket up, Jim's costume was now complete. He turned back to face me, crouched into a stance with clawed hands a la The Wicked Witch of the West, and let go a fierce cackle.

"Eeeee-hee-hee-hee-hee!"

It was the most articulate thing he said all day.

At that moment it became delightfully clear Jim loved Halloween. More than Christmas, Thanksgiving and his birthday combined. This was Jim's favorite time of year. It not only defined him, but showed me a wholeheartedness I'd never seen

CHALLENGED: A TRIBUTE | 85

in him before. Each year, Jim would come alive under the guise of his self-made, self-realized, signature get up. He was a closet character actor; a one-night-only indomitable spirit. I smiled. Jim would never be too cool for Halloween.

Thanksgiving came and went at my parents' house the same as it always had – a day that was never anything more than an excuse for my old man to devour a bargain-value ham. Still, as the holiday season hastened, I'm not sure what I expected differently from ITF. I had no reason to anticipate the trappings of a traditional Christmas with stockings hung by the med cabinet with care, or twinkling lights strewn over the ice plant. In fact, most of the clients were planning to spend the holiday visiting their families – some up to a full week. Yet there would always be those, like Jackie and Jim, left behind with no place to go. And so I felt a certain sense of duty that I should be there. Moreover, I *wanted* to be there. To help support them any way I could.

For me, working on Christmas day did not pose a problem. Christmas didn't exist at our house – at least not in the traditional sense. Christmas with my father was manifested by a small artificial tree he'd allow us to pull out of storage, and the hollow ritual of passing out presents that didn't mean anything to any of us. My dad was a classic Scrooge – and for him, Christmas was sport. Depending on his mood swings from Yuletide to Yuletide, he'd either ignore the holiday completely, or worse, attempt to ruin it for the rest of us on purpose. The memory of Christmas when I was nine still carries me relentlessly, against my will, back to that awful day.

Clinging to a tinsel-thin strand of hope that maybe we'd have a *nice* Christmas that year, I was awakened when out in the yard there arose such a clatter, I sprang from the bed to see what was the matter. I peered into the early morning light of another dry California day – only to see my father filling buckets with water and sloshing them with soapy, grungy sponges. There, spread out across the brown and yellow lawn, was every window screen from the house, including the back patio screen door.

"Get up!" Daddy bellowed as he caught me peeking from behind the curtain. "Time to wash all the screens and windows!"

Was he *crazy?*

"Are you *crazy?*" my mom said, now appearing on the front lawn in her flannel housecoat. "It's seven o'clock in the morning!"

"Gotta get an early start before it gets too hot," my father countered. "Make breakfast, let's go!"

"But it's *Christmas!*" My mother was flabbergasted.

"So? It's a day off, gotta make the best of it."

"Why can't you do this on the weekend?"

There was nothing my dad loved better than coercing an argument to entertain the neighbors, and I could see him trying to sucker my mother into his daily required heated confrontation. With no possible logical answer to her question, Dad reverted to his favorite stand-by response: "Awww, youse are stupid. Youse don't appreciate *nothin'*!" (Though he grew up in Pittsburgh, I never quite understood why my old man would suddenly lapse into a Brooklyn accent whenever he became angry.)

Luckily, this day my mother was not about to be sacrificed for public spectacle. She simply turned and walked back into the house.

Fifteen minutes later I found my mother at the kitchen sink, repeatedly washing her hands, as was her ritual of self-pacification, muttering her dismay at my father's actions. Just the same, on the stove, eggs and bacon sizzled, dutiful wife that she was.

"When can we open presents?" I asked.

"Hi, honey," my mother said, turning all too quickly with a terse smile. "Later. Go help your father."

For the rest of that morning my old man played "walkin' boss" to my one-man reenactment of *Cool Hand Luke*, overseeing as I slathered all the screens and windows in soapy suds, then hosed them off onto the dead weeds. Because the majority of his abuse occurred behind closed doors, it had become second nature and almost acceptable. I knew nothing else. The true impact really only occurred when he took the humiliation public and I suddenly found myself on display.

Slogging ankle-deep in mucky, sudsy water, I looked up to see a pack of elfin-eyed school chums on the prowl, eager to show off their brand-new Schwinn Stingrays – complete with tiger-striped banana seats and chopper-regulation sissy bars – gathering across the street to watch the show. Nevertheless, I endured as my father grabbed me by the scruff of the neck – *"Youse missed a spot, numb nuts!"* – and tossed me about like Raggedy Andy. This in itself wouldn't have been so bad had it not been for the fact that suddenly, without explanation, Pop began to rifle off a series of my shortcomings while my peers sniggered in the distance. Of course, there were the usual jabs: I was dumb, I was useless, I was selfish, I was fat. I wasn't sure what hurt worse – the bruise left by his meaty paw on the back of my neck or the distress of it all in front of my friends. As it turned out, neither could compare when he crossed the line and uttered the worst thing he'd ever said to me.

"I swear to Christ, Steve, when youse die, the world won't miss you."

They say you can't unring a bell. But what do you do when that bell rings louder than a nuclear blast?

Merry Christmas, Charlie Brown. *KA-BOOM!*

So you see, working at Shepherd Hills on Christmas didn't bother me one bit. In fact, I happily volunteered to do a double shift.

> *"Never underestimate the power of the handicapped."*
> *– Damon Wayans as superhero Handi-Man from* **In Living Color**

On December 24th, Sammy asked if I'd take him Christmas shopping.

"What?" I said. "*Today*? Why didn't you say anything before?"

"Because I didn't think about it till just now."

Sammy was slated as one of the clients planning to spend the holiday with his family, and so it never occurred to me he would need to buy gifts. Cole and Darlene had already flown home to visit their families and *they* didn't need to buy gifts. Owen was packing to visit his brother and *he* didn't need to buy gifts. So in Sammy's case I'd just assumed his family would supply all of that for him as well.

But gifts Sammy needed – and so it was Christmas shopping-*ho!*

Anita and her clients were already on an outing for the afternoon, which left us without a car. (Employees weren't allowed to drive their own cars during working hours due to insurance liabilities.) For all its faults, I never really minded driving the Blue Beast. I didn't mind having it associated with ITF Village, nor the symbolic status it perpetuated on us as Shepherd Hills' bastard stepchild. I didn't mind driving the Blue Beast because the alternative was worse. *Much* worse. Whenever a unit required a back-up vehicle, we utilized a reserve van pool. The reserve van pool consisted of exactly one van, duly christened the Shepherd Hills "Sunshine Van."

Back in the late '70s the customized van craze hit Southern California with a vengeance. Vans were outfitted with kick-ass sound systems, shag carpeting, bubble port windows, captain's chairs, mag wheels, and murals depicting everything from majestic seascapes to busty she-warriors doing battle with fire-breathing dragons. The Shepherd Hills Sunshine Van was a full-sized, eight-passenger, 1977 Dodge Tradesman 200 that had been donated by a group of well-meaning drug addicts as part of some rehab indemnification. The interior was functional enough, complete with an optional ramp and wheelchair tie-downs. But the exterior was a different matter. The exterior was not optional. We didn't have seascapes or dragons to contend with. Instead, what we had been given was an airbrushed cartoon sun smiling euphorically over cartoonier clouds. Below this, running the entire length of the van, in bold, vivid-rainbow letters were the words: "SHEPHERD HILLS BOARD AND CARE." And beneath that – just so there'd be no doubt – "*A Facility for the Mentally Retarded.*"

Getting stuck with the Sunshine Van was humiliating; a true test of commitment for *any* houseparent. Carting a van full of clients out into the community was stigmatizing enough – playing chauffeur to drooping, drooling faces pressed against the windows, peering out onto a foreign landscape. But to see those same hapless souls peering out above a damnation like "*A Facility for the Mentally Retarded*" was borderline abusive. Even driving the damn thing *without* passengers was mortifying. There wasn't a single solitary houseparent on the entire Shepherd Hills campus who didn't dread one day getting caught behind the wheel of the Sunshine Van.

But Sammy needed a ride, so . . .

Surprise-surprise!, traffic was horrendous. (Apparently, when it came to Christmas shopping, Sammy wasn't the only one who "didn't think about it till just now.") As we inched our way toward the Parkway Plaza Mall, the Sunshine

Van took its place in line at the stoplight, treating us to an ever-thickening haze of holiday transit exhaust. When it finally came our turn to venture through the intersection into the parking lot, we proceeded forward – only to be seized by gridlock. There we sat, blocking the thoroughfare and vulnerable to the last-minute shopping angst of countless motorists.

Eventually the cross-traffic light turned green. However, instead of waiting for us to clear the intersection, a black, 4x4 Chevy Small Dick with tinted windows bore down to greet the passenger side of our little ray of sunshine. Seeing full well we couldn't move, the driver did the only logical thing. He blasted his horn.

"Why is that dipshit honking?" Sammy asked.

"Probably because he wants us to get out of the way," I said, concentrating on the traffic.

"Well that's just *rude*," Sammy responded astutely. "Can't he see we're stuck?"

At last, the traffic surged and we crept forward into the lot. It was then Sammy turned to me and proudly proclaimed, "It's okay, Steve. I gave him the finger for you."

"You *what*?"

Sammy was streetwise and confident. I knew that. He acted from his gut, not his head. But I was also sensitive to the fact that road rage – and subsequent gunplay – were currently at their peak in the news. Driving in Southern California is all about one-upmanship – a lesson I'd learned all too well from my father. When someone would cut him off, my old man would rebut by tailgating them with his high-beams ablaze, howling like the devil with a feather up his ass as my mother yelled at him from the passenger seat, and my sister and I cowered helplessly in the rear well. So all I could think was, *Shit!* God, *please* don't let the driver double back and start anything.

I immediately snagged the first space I could find and bolted from the van, all the while glancing over my shoulder. There's a scene in *Jaws* when Robert Shaw describes anxiously waiting his turn to be rescued from the water after the U.S.S. Indianapolis was torpedoed, and the sharks methodically pick off man after man after man. That's how I felt, adrift in the open parking lot until we could find shelter inside the mall.

ROOOAAAAARRRRR!

All of a sudden, the same black truck came screeching up from behind, blocking me in. I guess it wasn't hard to spot an elephant-sized, rainbow endorsement for mental illness amongst a parking lot of white and silver sedans.

The driver jumped out, just itching for a fight. He wore grease-stained Levis, grease-stained boots, and a grease-stained T-shirt advertising Thrush Glasspacks with that damn Woody Woodpecker clone chomping a cigar. His chest was as puffed as his mullet.

"Did you flip me off? *Huh?!* Did you fuckin' flip me off?"

All I could think was, this guy is going to tear me apart, and there's no way I can defend myself. I've got a client with me whose safety I'm responsible for – and there's no telling what he might do to Sammy. Like it or not, I was going to have to plead forgiveness for Sammy's sake, never mind my own.

But then sometimes the gods of testosterone smile on you.

As I began to stammer my way into an apology, Sammy burst from the Sunshine Van and jumped in front of me. His face looked like it'd been slammed in a door. And he puffed *his* chest out and said, "You got a problem, asshole? *Huh?!* What was all that horn-honkin' shit? You got a fuckin' *problem?*"

Mullet Head froze. He stared at Sammy's face and just froze. It was obvious he'd never seen anyone as startling as Sammy – let alone that Sammy was half his size and rarin' to kick his ass. Normally, Sammy's tone and mannerisms suggested those of a 7th-grade math nerd. But not today. Today we were visited by Sammy the Scrapper. "C'mon, asshole. You wanna start something? I'll give you the first punch. Let's go!"

Mullet Head was terrified. *I* was terrified. I had never seen this side of Sammy. And at that precise moment I'm not ashamed to admit I was pretty darn glad to see it. Cast before the rays of a cartoon sun over cartoonier clouds, Sammy White became the big brother I never had.

Raising his tattooed arms defensively, Mullet Head – looking every bit the caricature of small-town, small-minded mentality – gurgled what sounded like "fuck it," climbed back into his truck and roared off.

"Yeah, *your head*, motherfucker!" Sammy yelled after him. It was then Sammy turned to me, grinned . . . and winked. It was a wink that told me Sammy knew damn well he'd bailed me out, and that he took genuine pride in the accomplishment.

I will never forget that as long as I live. I was supposed to be the protector of this mildly retarded man and yet *he* was the one who ensured *my* safety that day. Granted, he did start it all by flipping the guy off, but that's beside the point. While Sammy may have lacked a sense of social boundaries, he more than made up for it with a strong sense of loyalty.

What could be more normal than that?

> *LINUS VAN PELT: Charlie Brown, you're the only person I know who can take a wonderful season like Christmas and turn it into a problem. Maybe Lucy's right. Of all the Charlie Browns in the world, you're the Charlie Browniest.*
> *– scene from* **A Charlie Brown Christmas**

Christmas morning I clocked in bright and chilly at 6 a.m. Working a double meant I'd be there until 10 p.m. Technically "closed" for the holiday, Shepherd Hills had become a virtual Marley's-Ghost town. Out of 150-plus residents, most had either already gone home with their families or would soon be picked up for day visits. Being a stranger to early morning frost, I jammed my hands into the pockets of my hooded sweatshirt and skated across the main campus dew to the warmth of the ITF rec room, where I promptly poured myself a cup of coffee and plopped down to set up morning meds. It was going to be a delightfully quiet, delightfully uneventful Christmas.

By 9 a.m., the majority of ITF was over the river and through the woods. For the rest of the day it was now just me, Jackie, Jim, Hughie and Mattila the Hun. With the place festooned in plastic wreaths and electric candles, we spent the afternoon watching Christmas movies on TV, taking time now and then to baste a donated Butterball in the oven. That night I planned to take the guys out for a drive to see Christmas lights on Candy Cane Lane. Candy Cane Lane was a residential street in Chula Vista just north of the Tijuana border where one entire block decorated their homes for Christmas. Today there are entire neighborhoods that do this and it's become quite common. But in 1982 it was unique, and Candy Cane Lane was the place to go.

About half-past four an unfamiliar face with long gray hair tied into a ponytail wandered into the courtyard. He was dressed in well-worn sandals, an army jacket with a peace symbol stitched to the pocket, and carried a camouflage knapsack over his shoulder. Could this be Billy's father? Or Jim's? Certainly not Jackie's. I went out to see what he wanted.

"Is this Shepherd Hills, ITF Village?" he said. When I confirmed it was, he introduced himself. "Rick Bauer. Sorry I'm late. I'm a temp, assigned to help out today."

"What, *here*?" I said.

"Where do I sign in?"

Being that this was the first I'd heard about it, I had Rick follow me into the office so I could check the schedule. Sure enough, Rick's name had been penciled in by Dawn at the last minute. Apparently, rather than allow me to work the shift alone, Dawn thought I required assistance, so she requested a temp from an outside agency. Though this wasn't unusual, I was miffed that she'd done so, especially without telling me. I'd selfishly expected to have the shift – and the clients – all to myself. Today was supposed to have been a day to kick back and skate through some easy overtime. Instead, now I was actually going to have to *work*. Meanwhile, about ten miles away, I could hear my father laughing.

Once dinner was finished, I wrapped up the leftovers while Rick did the dishes. Kitchen duty complete, it was time to hit the road.

Candy Cane Lane, here we come!

Rick and I piled the clients into the Blue Beast. I asked Rick if he wanted to drive. "No, I think you'd better," he said – and he didn't say anything more.

With Candy Cane Lane a good forty-five minutes away, I nestled in behind the wheel for a peaceful evening jaunt. As we eventually closed in on our destination, I merged neatly with a string of cars onto the designated off ramp, and grudgingly funneled into place with everyone else like cows herded into a chute. From here we would have to wait in line until we hit the edge of Candy Cane Lane. Great, I thought, more holiday gridlock. Just what I need. But at least this time we aren't stuck with the Sunshine Van, so things won't be so bad.

Rick reached into his knapsack and pulled out a Tupperware bowl. Popping the lid, I saw that it was filled with something dark and sweet. "Want a brownie," Rick offered. "Made 'em myself."

Now, so far this guy hadn't done much to impress me, and I was still sulking about him being with us at all. But a brownie right about now *did* sound kind of good; in truth, waving a brownie in front of a chocoholic like me is the same as waving a sirloin in front of a Pit Bull. Why, the son-of-a-bitch had even gone the extra mile and frosted them. How could I resist?

Rick handed me a single brownie. Quickly looking over his shoulder, he then proceeded to voraciously down the rest of the bowl. Well, that's rather selfish, I thought. What if the clients wanted one? Then I bit into mine.

Sleeping Jesus!

What was this, a bad joke? Did this guy not have taste buds or was I missing something? I took another bite. "Did you put any sugar in these?" I asked.

"Arrg-huhnf," he replied, mid-gulp.

"Hm," I said, popping the final bite. "What is that, alfalfa? Are these health brownies?" That would certainly explain the lack of sugar.

But Rick didn't answer. He was too busy choking back a laugh. That's when it hit me.

FUCK!

Damn you, Chocolate Jones, damn you!

I looked at Rick, dumbfounded. "Were those . . ."

"*Special* brownies," he grinned, his teeth smeared with gritty fudge.

"What are you, an *idiot*?" I wasn't sure if I was talking to Rick or myself. For a teenager raised in the '70s, I was probably the only person on the planet who couldn't readily identify the not-so-subtle taste of "special" brownies.

Licking his fingers and catching his breath, Rick detailed exactly how he went about making them; how he'd first sautéed the secret ingredient in butter and then stirred it into the batter. He went on to say that he'd never made them by himself before, so he wasn't sure whether or not they would work. All we could do now was sit back and wait.

Twenty minutes later I felt no effect. Neither did Rick.

"Hmph!" he grunted, disappointed. "Must not've worked."

Great! I thought relieved. Must not've worked. Just ahead, Candy . . .

. . . Cane . . .

. . . *Laaaaaaaaaaaaaaaaaaaaaaaaaaaaaaaaaaaaaaaaane.*

All of a sudden, the entire procession of creeping chrome and metal transmogrified into a one-way conga line from San Diego to Amsterdam. Peripheral vision, gone. Distance, imperceptible. Everything around me yonder, farther, further, remote.

Shit!

Is this what it's like to be *stoned*? On *brownies*?

Shit!

Why did it have to kick in *now*?

So again, I asked Rick, "You *sure* you don't want to drive?"

"No, you're doing great."

No wonder. After all he ate, he had to be stoned fifty times worse than I was. Stuck in the middle of traffic with no way out, I realized I had no choice. I would just have to suck it up and continue onward – employing every last working brain cell I had left *not* to ram the car in front of me.

What I'd thought would be a simple hop, skip and a Blue Beast through Candy Cane Lane turned out to be the longest journey of my life. Though the shortest distance from Point A to Point B may be a straight line, the scenic route is along Hallucinogen Highway. The one thing I *do* remember clearly about Candy Cane Lane itself was . . .

. . . was . . .

. . . a-a mUltiTudE-MultItude of-oF briGHt-Bright LIghtS-lighTs and-AnD a-a bIg-BIg sTuFFED-stuffed BUNNY-bunNy RabbiT-rabBit SittINg-sitting iN-iN a-a MoDel-moDEL T-T jalopy-jALoPy on-On sOMEboDY's-somBOody's FRont-froNt LAWn-lawn.

What the hell it had to do with Christmas I still haven't a clue.

The clients never made a sound. Did they even happening what was know? Care did I even?

Somehow (don't ask me how), we made it out of Candy Cane Lane. Finally. I grabbed the first onramp I saw and soon we were back on the freeway, heading home. The last rational thought I remember having was, *Must get these guys back safe, Must get these guys back safe, Must get these guys back safe.* Meanwhile, faintly in the distance, I could hear the clients screaming something at me, but I couldn't tell what they were saying . . .

"*Steve! Steve! Oh Lawd!*"

"*S-Slow d-down!*"

"*Da police, da police!*"

"*Bob-bobby-brown! Bob-bobby-brown!*"

It was Jim's warning above the rest that successfully snagged my attention. I looked down at the speedometer, which either read "88" or "You're fucked," and suddenly an Aurora Borealis of cherries and blueberries exploded in my rear view mirror. Instinctively, I hit the brakes. *VRRROOOOOM!* A police cruiser rocketed past me. I watched in chemically-dependent awe as the light show faded . . . faded . . . faded into the vanishing point on the horizon with a green

CHALLENGED: A TRIBUTE

flash. Humph. Why didn't he pull me over? No matter. I was running on pure luck, cruising on instinct, paying little attention to the signs. Except for one:

LAST AMERICAN EXIT

You guessed it, friends. When I got on the freeway I'd headed *south* instead of *north*. As I passed the sign, even Rick perked up.

"Where the heck are you going?"

If I'd had half a lick of sense I would've simply pulled over and waited for the effects to wear off. But I was young and stupid. And high and stupid. And stupid and stupid. The next thing I knew we were crossing the border into Mexico – with a station wagon full of four retarded people and two direct care workers baked off their asses as if it were the most natural thing in the world.

Falling in with a line of gear-grinding taxis, I gazed in Wonderama at an entirely different sort of Candy Cane Lane. There were street-corner puppeteers, discount fireworks stands, drunken American sailors in search of easy holiday cheer, and children trafficking cases of Chiclets 'neath the flickering lights of a shantytown *fiesta* – reds!, yellows!, greens! – as each individual bulb grew its own comet tail. *Wait, where are we again? Mexico? Am I supposed to drive on the right side of the street or the left side? . . .*

Somewhere I heard music: *". . . Feliz Navidad . . . Feliz Navidad . . ."*

"I hate fuckin' bean-ders," I heard Billy mutter from the back of the wagon.

"I love you all," I said to no one.

Rick was chortling like a merry Howitzer. "There may've been a little more than just weed in those brownies," he confessed.

But this was no *Alice's Restaurant*, and I was no whoever-the-fuck was in that movie. Instead of giggling inanely the way counterculture Hollywood typically depicted a good brownie buzz, I began to grow paranoid. Before long, the border festivities gave way to body shops and cardboard shacks. Trapped in my own rendition of *Fear and Loathing in Tijuana*, I started to abandon all hope of ever finding our way back. Each street grew darker than the last, cast in the shadows of ancient, factory-like structures of filthy red brick. And suddenly, I felt it. The fingers of doom tightening around my neck. *Was* there a way back? Or were we destined to drive off the edge of the world? Visions of *Reefer Madness* overtook me. I drove faster . . . *faster.* My mind was out of control. My entire sense of Being was out of control – lost on a savage journey to the heart of Nothingness – and there was no stopping me – no stopping, I tells ya! This is it! Top o' the world, Ma! *Top o' the world!*

AH-*HAHAHAHAHAHAHAHAHA-A-A-A-A-A-A-A!!!*

"Dude, look out!" Rick yelled.

I slammed on the brakes.

Slowly, our eyes focused.

There, before us, materialized the Virgin Mary herself, cradling the baby Jesus wrapped in a bundle of swaddling clothes.

All at once, I was calm again. Surely Mother Mary would show me the way home. Even Rick stopped giggling and stared at her with reverence. Mary and I exchanged serene smiles. Somewhere a choir of angels was singing. I never felt more at peace.

Right up until she whipped out a spray bottle of soapy water and bestowed the baby Jesus upon us to clean our windshield.

"... *Feliz Navidad* ... *Feliz Navidad* ..."

On cue, an ersatz band of apostles swarmed the car, banging the windows and begging for hand-outs. Within seconds we were surrounded. The car began to rock. Rick howled. Jim shouted. Hughie prayed. Billy screamed. Jackie cursed. I ... checked the map from AAA. (Which, in retrospect, really didn't help much, being we were in a foreign country and all.)

That's when a second epiphany told me it was time to get the hell outta there.

In an all-out, balls-out, wigged-out quest to flee the temple, I cranked the wheel into a hard U-turn and floored it, hastily bidding the international Christmas trade *adios*.

Slowly but surely, I felt myself growing calm again. Floating. Mellowed. Coming down.

Eventually we crossed the border back into the U.S. without incident – still with a wagon full of four retarded people and two direct care workers baked off their asses. Do you have anything to declare, sir? Yeah, I could *kill* for some snickerdoodles. Ba-da-*bing!*

Somehow (don't ask me how), we finally made it back home without so much as a scratch. How we all didn't land in a Mexican jail sentenced to forty years hard labor painting zebra stripes on a donkey's ass, I'll never know. I piloted the Blue Beast up the driveway and parked. Rick looked at me. "I guess they worked after all," he said. He then shook my hand, walked into the rec room, and promptly crashed face down on the couch for the rest of the shift. I felt a giant hand gently come to rest on my shoulder.

"Y-Y-You aw right?"

It was the first time I ever heard genuine concern in Jackie's voice for someone other than himself.

Gradually, my mind came back to itself. Jesus, what a night.

Someone once said that life is always funny so long as nobody gets hurt. But when all was said and done, I couldn't help but feel guilty for having put my guys in danger. I was supposed to be a role model, a protector, but instead I did something too reckless to forgive anytime soon. Then and there, like some funky Rastafarian version of Scrooge, I resolved to be a better man. Or at least a more careful man.

And so the lesson I learned that night was not "God bless us, everyone," but rather "*never fucking do fucking anything like that again!*" The clients deserved better.

Dawn never found out what happened. Jim and Hughie weren't ones to tattle, and Billy Mattila couldn't care less. But in Jackie's case, whether or not he really understood exactly what we'd done, he could tell that something was "off" about our spirited excursion, and not telling Dawn, I believe, was his way of protecting me. In time, the whole thing became glazed over by a blur of tunnel-vision weirdness, criminal repose, a little CHriStmAs-ChrisTmAS MaGic-mAgiC, and a whole shitload of luck.

And damned if it *still* wasn't a better Christmas than any I'd ever spent with my old man.

CHAPTER 9

TO MICKEY MOUSE AND CARMEN MIRANDA, WITH MUCH GRATITUDE

WITH THE ONSET of 1983, I heartily embraced the optimism we all know the New Year can bring. For the next few months my job sustained a pacifying sense of routine, and when April arrived I enjoyed a rediscovery of The Happiest Place On Earth by way of alternative intellectual giftedness. Each spring Disneyland hosts "Happy Hearts Days," wherein for two weeks admission tickets are available for people with developmental disabilities and their helpers at remarkably low prices.

Cha-*ching!*

Though Dot, and to a lesser extent Anita, painted the whole thing as one big pain in the ass, I was bursting at the seams of my mouse ears. I *love* Disneyland. Ever since those early childhood years when my father would cart us there from the bowels of L.A. for our annual excursion, Disneyland became that time-honored family getaway – even though my dad would remain in the car. I'll repeat that. He *stayed in the car* as my mother, sister and I frolicked amid the lands of enchantment on our own. Mom didn't drive and Pop had no use for Disneyland, so in a rare compromise he chose instead to while away the day in 80-degree heat with a cooler of Coors, a sack of ham sandwiches, a pipe full of Kentucky Club, and a portable radio to catch the game between naps. My dad was probably the only man

CHALLENGED: A TRIBUTE | 97

in history to ever "tailgate" the Magic Kingdom. But, to his credit, he did take us there, and his lack of kid-again spirit never diminished my passion for the place.

After discussing the logistics with Dot and Anita, we decided to divvy up the clients into separate trips. Because of the lifting required for Holly, I agreed to accompany Holly, Hughie, Owen and Jim for a day at the park.

The morning of our trip I was up and ready at the first sign of daylight. C'mon, c'mon, get in the car, let's *go*! Less than thirty seconds later we were careening the back roads of East County and onto the freeway. Punching the accelerator, the Blue Beast's carburetor made an audible *"sluuuurrrrp!"* as I lead-footed the old girl as fast as she could go, out of my head with excitement. It was Disneyland, man! *Oh, boy, oh boy, goody-goody-goody!* I must have been doing ninety, easy.

Not a smart move.

Out came the flashing red lights, and suddenly my Disneyland-sized hard-on shriveled down to a parking-lot-carnival embarrassment.

Damn.

As the cop pulled me over my heart plummeted. I had no money to pay for this ticket, so that killed me right there. Plus, I felt like a complete boob in front of the clients. So much for improved role-modeling. And, with Owen in the car, there was no way I was going to stifle this from making its way into The Hills' gossip mill. Strike three.

Glued to the rear view, I watched the cop dismount his motorcycle and whip out his ticket book. Double damn. The cop strut-sauntered up to my window the way all cops strut-saunter. He crouched to peer inside and scanned the vacant stares of developmentally disabled faces – all five of us. Admittedly, I briefly hoped this might win me some points – perhaps the cop would let me off with a warning, seeing as how I was such an obvious humanitarian transporting the obviously less fortunate. No such luck.

"Do you know how fast you were going?" he asked.

"Uh . . . No, sir. I sure don't." (The classic, spineless response.) Then, just for the hell of it, I tried, "We're from Shepherd Hills, on our way to Disneyland. I guess I just got a little overexcited."

No help. As he clicked his Bic and put it to the pad, I sighed and closed my eyes, resigned to the burden of a hefty fine and future eight hours of traffic school.

Then, from behind me, came Owen's signature rasp.

"Your barn door's open."

I opened my eyes and instinctively checked my crotch. All was zipped and proper. What was he talking about? Besides, he's sitting behind me, how would he know? Then I looked at the cop's crotch. The whole wagon looked at the cop's crotch. The entire *freeway* looked at the cop's crotch. There, as the officer shifted his hips slightly, flashed every boy's nightmare – that humiliating beacon of white cotton jockeys peeking through a breach of black polyester. A clear cut case of the cop caught with his fly down.

To Owen, his comment was as innocent and natural as could be, to the point where there was no graceful way to parry. The officer assigned to serve and protect simply stopped writing and slowly closed his book. "Drive carefully," he uttered, and walked back to his motorcycle, sans strut-saunter.

I turned the key and never looked back.

For millions of children and children at heart, Disneyland symbolizes a place of wonder, awe and underlying safety. It's the last place you'd ever think to see something that might challenge your social sensibilities. Dopey was just dopey, not incapacitated. Mickey didn't dodder around on crutches. Snow White didn't have a port-wine birthmark on her face. Goofy didn't have seizures.

Enter 5,000 disabled people.

Disneyland was open for business as usual that day to the general public. However, thanks to Happy Hearts, the floodgates had dispelled a State-wide *whooosh!* of California's finest handicapped, and the usual crowd of self-assured tourists was besieged by a tidal wave of metal braces, runny noses, impatient moans, Knucklehead Smiff haircuts, and fashion statements circa Mork from Ork. Oh, to have had the wheelchair concession *that* day. I'd be one rich houseparent.

The day's activities played out with typical amusement park fervor. We channeled up Main Street and into the various lands, spilling past jungles, rivers, mountains and castles. I spent the afternoon barreling through it all, pushing Holly's wheelchair, chasing after Jim who insisted on running ahead of us, answering Owen's endless array of questions, and calling behind me for Hughie to keep up. It was a day of blotting chocolate stains from shirts and brushing buttered crumbs from faces. A day spent trying to divide three expensive boxes of popcorn evenly between five hungry people. A day spent lifting Holly from her wheelchair into, onto, off and out of an entire squadron of pastel-colored cars, boats, trains, tea cups, people-movers, rocket jets, flying elephants and merry-go-round equine. It turned out, in fact, to be one of the best days of my life – despite the fact there was always some phobia that kept us from enjoying what I thought were the simplest, most harmless of rides:

"– Hey, you guys wanna go on Space Mountain? –"
"– *No, Steve, too fast!* –"
"– You wanna go on the Haunted Mansion? –"
"– *No, too scary!* –"
"– You wanna go on Bear Country Jamboree? –"
"– *BEARS?!* –"

This basically left us such innocuous attractions as It's a Small World, King Arthur's Carousel, the Mark Twain Steamboat and the Disneyland Railroad, all underscored by the Dapper Dans and their non-threatening barber-shop borefest.

As a thrill-seeking teen, these were rides I'd typically passed over and pooh-poohed. But now their significance suddenly became clear. For some people these attractions were all they had. It made me regard Disneyland – and the clients – in a whole different light.

But the greatest insight that day came from a simple observation. While cruising past the Mad Hatter Hat Shop, we spotted none other than Mr. Mouse surrounded by a throng of children. Costumed character sightings were nothing new at Disneyland, especially if you staked a claim in Fantasyland where you were guaranteed a face-to-faces with the Seven Dwarfs, or at least a couple of minor contract players such as Captain Hook and Mister Smee. But here, this time, our sighting hit pay dirt. Mickey Mouse. The biggie. The ambassador to worldwide commerce by way of animated antics. Mickey the Mouse, himself, in the flesh (deftly covered by fur, felt and plastic). Say what you will about shaking paws with Pluto, nuzzling with Minnie or trying to discern the difference between Chip and Dale, a *Mickey* sighting was gold.

As we approached for our chance at a close encounter, a jostling knot of sticky-faced children and their photo-hungry parents seemed to swell in front of us with every step and wheel rotation we took. They were rude, they were loud, and they all smelled like wet diapers. By the time we reached Mr. M, the crowd had merged into one big bottleneck of bumping and milling unpleasantry. There was just no way we were going to get some one-on-one time with the Mickster before his unionized break.

Then, in the midst of children shoving each other and parents directing them to hold still for their own individual Kodak moments, Jim called to Mickey.

"Muh-muh-mo-muh-muh! Mickey Mowp, Mickey Mowp!"

Immediately, instantly, and without apology, Mickey stopped, turned, and walked directly over to Jim. It was as if those other children had suddenly ceased to exist. Mickey snubbed them, one and all. All for the sake of "Happy Hearts Days."

It quickly became obvious that Mickey – and indeed *all* the characters – had been coached to give priority attention to anyone with developmental disabilities. For the next several minutes Mickey held court with us and us alone, repeatedly shaking Jim's hand, trading hugs with Hughie and Owen, and patting Holly on the head – while at the same time boldly dodging the huffy, jealous daggers of the remaining little darlings and their pissed-off parents. Holly closed her eyes and threw her head back with a wide-mouthed gale of laughter at Mickey's touch. Hughie hugged and buried his face into Mickey's downy-soft cushy body. Jim carried on his own conversation, "Muh-mo-muh-muh-mo-bobby brown," as Mickey politely nodded in response. It was like having a private afternoon with the world's most famous rodent; a command performance just for us. I never saw the clients look happier.

Sensing he was finished, I stepped forward and thanked Mr. Mouse with a hearty handshake of my own. "Nice gloves," I commented.

Mickey gave me a thumbs up and, with a few perfunctory handshakes and plenty of waves bye-bye-for-now, he shuffled, then trotted, then *bolted* down a hidden walkway through a private gate marked "Cast Members Only." Undoubtedly, it was well past his break time.

As the day drew to a close and evening fell over Main Street, nostalgic facades came alive amidst flickering gaslamps and electrified gingerbread trim. With the five of us lounging street-side at the Carnation Café, slurping Gibson Girls and Matterhorn Sundaes, I contemplated our afternoon turn with Mickey Mouse. It instilled in me the nature of altruism that occasionally tips the scales in our clients' favor. But even more it showed me how just a little bit of kindness can go a long way – a simple realization that hadn't really occurred to me till now. Was I simply caught up in the illusion of philanthropy cast under the auspices of All Things Disney? Maybe. Or maybe it was something more. Either way, it felt pretty darn good – and I didn't want that feeling to end with just our day at Disneyland.

The spring of 1983 soon passed, as did the spring semester at SDSU, then came the summer, followed by the beginning of the new fall semester. And still I hadn't returned to school. Then again, I told myself, why should I? Each day I wake already brings a unique outlook on life:

> OWEN: Steve? Will you take me to see that new movie?
> STEVE: Sure, Owen. Which one?
> OWEN: *The Return of the Deer Men.*
> STEVE: *Return of the Deer Men?* (*long, puzzled pause*) Ohhh! You mean *Terms of Endearment.*
> OWEN: That's what I said.

Besides, I knew college would still be there when I was ready. I knew college would regain a place in my life soon enough.

Meanwhile, Billy Mattila was still an asshole. Unfortunately, unlike Dot had predicted, the beating by Hughie did not quell Billy from teasing people as we'd hoped. If anything, his supreme snarkiness had grown worse.

One afternoon, during a more-tedious-than-usual cooking session, Mattila the Hun finally pushed my "nigger" button. Right in the middle of my demonstration, he deliberately stood up and threw me the Elvis lip – a willful sneer of disrespect if ever there was one. "I don't have to listen to you," he said. "Michelle not here anymore. She a *cunt* and you a *fat fuck.*"

That did it.

Don't take it personally, Steve, don't take it personally, don't take it –

I grabbed Billy by the throat and slammed him up against the wall. It was a good solid slam, a slam that both sounded good and felt good. I seethed. "Don't you *ever* talk to me that way again, you understand?"

CHALLENGED: A TRIBUTE

Billy couldn't speak. I was choking him. All he could reply was . . . *gurgle* . . . *gurgle* . . .

"Michelle and I are *staff,* you got it?"

gurgle . . . gurgle . . .

"You do it again and I'll fucking *kill* you."

"Stop," he finally managed. . . . *gurgle* . . . "I . . . sssssorry" . . . *gurgle* . . .

Holy shit, Steve, what are you doing? Let him go! You're killing him!

Thankfully, I didn't have to let go. In fact, I hadn't laid a finger on him. As my mind jolted clear from its subconscious, I discovered myself simply staring back dumbly at Billy's remark. Twisted fantasies about physically taking a client's throat in hand were unforgivable if not potentially dangerous. But still, at that moment of weakness, oh how I *wanted* to strangle him. Oh how I *wanted* to see his eyes widen with terror as life left his body.

Just before he hit the door Billy turned back, spat on the floor, and delivered a final blow. "Fuck you, fat, fat, fat!" And then he bolted.

Don't take it personally, Steve, don't take it personally . . .

The words echoed in my head – trained not to soothe as much as to taunt me. What was I carrying around inside me to hate Billy so much? What was to keep the beast within me – my *father's* beast – from one day rearing its ugly head for real? For the first time in my life I could actually sympathize with Nurse Ratched. Am I a bad person? No, I told myself. I'm not. I *know* I'm not. I would *never* do something like that to Owen or Jackie or Sammy or Jim or *any* of the others. It was *Billy* who got the best of me. It was *Billy* who deserved another dose of rough justice. I was *Billy* who just didn't fucking belong here. Fuck that he's retarded! He just doesn't *belong* here!

The next few weeks flew by in a matter of seconds. By month's end I was reviewing my data sheets with Dawn and tallying up the percentages of each client's progress in class. Percentages were variable as usual, but I was always pleased to report the occasional 100% compliance, or at least "progress maintained" by Cole, Owen, Sammy, Jim, even Jackie. When we reached cooking class with Billy the Hun, it was another story.

"Zero percent again," I reported. "Non-compliance. All refusals."

"Budgeting?" Dawn asked.

"Zero percent. Non-compliance. All refusals."

"Laundry?"

"Zero percent. Non-compliance. All refusals."

"Hmph," she uttered. "He's not doing . . . *any*thing."

"Not just that," I said. "Look at this." I pointed out a pattern to Dawn that I'd begun to notice over the last two quarters. It seemed anytime Billy was moved from one skill class to another – regardless of who was teaching it – the percentages of success for all the other clients in that class went down. In turn, when he was transferred out of a class, their percentages would begin to go back up.

"Don't you see," I said. "He's not only refusing to participate in his own programs, he's affecting the others in *theirs*."

"We don't know that for sure," Dawn countered.

"With all due respect, Dawn," I said in measured tones, "you don't work with them. We do. We see it. Not only is Billy hurting the others, he doesn't take this place seriously. Ask any of the other counselors."

Please, please ask the other counselors. I know *they'll back me up . . .*

Still, Dawn wasn't convinced. But the seed had been planted. "You know," I said, "There's got to be a way of tweaking this system to make it more effective. If we're an Independent Training Facility, how come no one ever graduates? This just feels like a big day care center. The whole thing's just grown . . . *stagnant*."

Are you crazy? Talking to your boss this way? . . .

I could tell by the sober look on Dawn's face I had better stop. The good thing about working for Dawn was that over time I had come to learn my limits. I stopped long before going too far and insulting her leadership, yet felt that I'd successfully made my point. Dawn and I had grown to forge a decent rapport, and I was always impressed by her open door policy. She was the kind of boss who'd allow you to come into her office and vent minor frustrations, brainstorm new ideas for the client's benefit, or simply chat about current movies. Little by little I found myself wanting to live up to that original performance review she'd given me, in spite of myself.

But at that moment there was only one thing I was trying to lay the ground work for, only one thing I was hoping to accomplish:

Get rid of fucking Mattila the Hun!

There was no denying it. Billy Mattila shared the same ugly soul as my old man. No more could I allow another bully to invade my life – or the lives of my guys. I was finally taking stock in doing what was best for everyone. And that meant the eradication of *all* bullies.

As I got up to leave Dawn's office, I lit a small backfire just to be safe. "I'm sorry if I overstepped my bounds," I offered sincerely. "I just want what's best for the clients as a whole." (Meaning everyone *except* Billy Mattila.) "I just don't want this to become a . . ." (*Okay, now, go in for the kill*) ". . . a *rights* violation."

Dawn stiffened. "No, no," she assured me. "I understand how you feel. You've given me a lot to think about."

It was then I drove the final nail in the coffin – and didn't even realize it. "Tell you what," I said lightheartedly. "If Billy Mattila ever leaves here, I'll come to work dressed as Carmen Miranda."

Dawn laughed. "It's a bet!"

Always leave 'em laughing, I thought. Good job. But even I knew deep down we'd always be stuck with Mattila the Hun.

Exactly two weeks later a special staffing was called. "Staffings" (also sometimes referred to as "watch your ass" meetings) are meetings of the highest regard and utmost importance. In attendance were Billy and members of his Interdisciplinary Team (a.k.a. "support team") including his social worker from the San Diego Regional Center, a nurse consultant from Shepherd Hills, Dawn, Dot, Anita and me. The proof had been well-documented. The discussion was short. Billy Mattila would be discharged from Shepherd Hills and transferred to a group home for aggressive behaviors before the end of October.

Hallelujah! I thought.

And . . . *shit!*

Where the hell am I gonna find a tutti-frutti hat?

As luck would have it, Halloween was once again on the horizon. And as it beckoned, so did my urge to rekindle a fire that had been extinguished since childhood. Inspired in part by Jim's enthusiasm for his annual ritual, and bound by my promise to Dawn, I would pay up and *dress* up.

At the ITF Village Halloween party, Dot pounded on the office bathroom door. "C'mon, why's the door locked? Open up!"

"Okay. You asked for it."

To the tune of "Chica Chica Boom Chic," the door burst open and out stepped seven feet, eight inches of tutti-frutti splendor. Having hit every costume shop in a 30-mile radius, I was able to piece together a fairly decent facsimile of the Brazilian Bombshell herself. Multi-colored skirt, open-toed sandals, extra-large, frilly blouse (after all, I was a *big* girl), and lotsa cheap, dangly bracelets. At one costume rental downtown I even found an 18-inch plastic pineapple and banana hat.

"I'll take it!"

Next, I scoured the used record stores and found a copy of *The Compleat Carmen– Miranda, That Is!* It was the only copy in all of San Diego County. And it was 99 cents.

"I'll take it!"

I transferred the record onto a cassette and tucked a mini tape recorder into my belt. When I finally burst from the office bathroom, the clients went wild.

". . . *Ai-yi-yi-yi-yi, I like you verrry muuuuuch!* . . ."

Hoots, hollers and giggly shouts of "*Steeeeeve, oh, Gaaaaawd!*" greeted me as I danced and swayed and bumped and stumbled to keep my pineapple perfectly poised. No one at work had ever seen me act the clown before, especially with such goofy abandon as this, and eventually the sheer spectacle of it all drove everyone to join in as the whole lot of us danced foolishly about the courtyard, like a bunch of spirited, nonsensical school kids let loose at recess on Halloween.

Later, after all the apples had been bobbed and the Jack-O-Lanterns began to grow dim, everyone gathered in the rec room with bloody punch and cemetery cake to watch the camp classic *Who Slew Auntie Roo* on TV hosted by Elvira. Bathed in sweat, I removed my hat, set it on the counter to air out, and joined the others on the sofa. From across the room I caught sight of Dawn looking at me, still grinning and nodding her head approvingly at my antics. It felt good to make the boss smile. Then I looked the other way – and saw Jim struggling to peel a banana he'd plucked from my hat.

"Jim, don't!" I shouted. "It's plastic."

"Pastic?" he grunted. "Oh, sorry. Muh-muh mistake."

Little did my fellow Halloweeners know the dignity I'd sacrificed that night in the name of giving Billy Mattila the boot. And little could I share that my dance of joy dressed as a giant fruit salad was not so much guise-inspired as it was a celebration of Billy's departure. But it was worth it. Hiding behind the mask of Halloween vogue, I was secretly throwing myself a one-man vengeance party. *Hot damn! Mattila the Hun is finally gone!* Was I ashamed? In truth, a little. If it had been any other client I would've felt obligated and duty-bound to help them succeed. But I was only human, my co-workers were only human, and the clients were only human. And I could see that they – *we* – just couldn't take anymore of Billy; despite his disability, despite our mission statement. Nor should we be forced to – I was convinced of that. Let someone else take a crack at him, I thought. I, myself, had failed – and can't say I really gave a damn.

Some weeks later a small, frail man wandered down the ITF Village driveway dressed in tattered jeans and a white cotton shirt that looked as if it'd been battered clean on river rocks. He wore wire-rimmed glasses that looked as fragile as he did, and sported a thick moonshiner beard, the kind that crept from the top of his cheekbones to the base of his throat. His voice was weary and as worn as his boots. "Excuse me," he said, "but does Billy Mattila live here? I'm his father."

Dot and I exchanged looks of incredulity. To our knowledge Billy had never had any family contact, at least within recent years. Initially, I didn't see any resemblance to Billy in the man's face; brown, wind-burned and creased like a worn leather sofa. But the more he spoke the resemblance became clear. The man had Billy's voice; his mouth filled with what was surely the same unpleasant fluid.

The man went on to explain that he had gotten the information on where to contact Billy from a former social worker. We informed him that, unfortunately, Billy no longer lived here. Oddly, the man seemed slightly relieved to hear this. When I asked him if he'd like the name and contact information for Billy's current social worker, at first the man didn't answer, didn't even seem to acknowledge this as an option, then suddenly snapped awake and said, "Yes. Yes, of course. Thank you." Then the man made a rather strange request. "May I see where he used to live?"

As Dot and I showed the man Billy's old apartment, his face registered approval. It was then he told us that he and Billy's mother and sister were "between homes." The three were currently passing through San Diego and living out of their car, although he wasn't sure how long that would last. "I just wanted to come by and say hello before we moved on," the man said. "His mother and sister are in the car."

CHALLENGED: A TRIBUTE | 105

At that, Dot arched an eyebrow and excused herself with a sudden false urgency to pass meds, leaving me alone with the man.

When I asked if they'd like to stay for dinner, the man said no. Instead, he handed me a five dollar bill and asked if I'd give it to Billy so he could buy something he likes. "Maybe some sodas. Or candy. I know he used to like Butterfingers." I awkwardly reminded the man again that Billy didn't live here anymore, so my taking his money wouldn't be appropriate. The man looked as if he didn't understand this. As he turned to leave I asked him once more if there was anything I could do for him.

"I just wanted to see where he was living," the man said softly. "This looks like a very nice place." He then added, "I know Billy can be pretty hard to handle. He used to attack me when he was a boy. When we couldn't give him what he wanted, he'd attack all of us. It got so bad sometimes I wished he'd . . ." The man paused and his gaze grew distant. "Well . . . It just got real bad, is all." The man quivered a little and nodded. I could tell by the way he shifted uneasily he wanted to get something off his chest. "I heard out in California that people like Billy are guaranteed placement. So, 'bout ten years back we drove out here and left him off at the Regional Center. See, we're originally from Georgia. Thanks to this worker, she found him a new place to live. Otherwise, I don't know what we'd've done." With great, quiet sincerity, the man looked deep in my eyes and shook my hand. "Thank you for taking care of my son."

Strangely, I suddenly felt ten years old again, standing in the garage watching my father tinker with an HO-model train set he'd built for himself. As he yanked the garage door shut, I was accidentally standing in the wrong spot. The door came crashing down on my head and I began to cry. Not the kind of cry caused by pain – although make no mistake, it did hurt – but the kind of cry a child makes out of distress, trying his best to stifle it for fear of further punishment. Instead, my father surprised me. Instantly, Dad folded me into a hug with his powerful, grizzly bear arms and rubbed my head. "Are you all right?" he said. "I'm sorry, I'm sorry . . ." Thinking back, it was the only time I clearly remember him showing me a moment of tenderness; a hint of honest, paternal love. From that I grew to think of my dad as a man who maybe wanted to love his son but, like Mr. Mattila, for reasons all his own, was simply unsure how to do so.

I watched Billy's father shuffle back up the driveway to his car – an old blue station wagon not unlike the ITF wagon, with faux wood paneling seared off in patches clear down to naked metal. Joining the other two figures inside, the car gradually pulled away in a wheeze of sputters. Not sure what to think, I looked down – and saw the five dollar bill still in my hand.

Little did Billy's father know just exactly what sort of "care" I had actually given his son. Little did Billy's father know that I was the one who'd headed the revolution to kick his son to the curb.

CHAPTER 10

NEW FACES, PLACES AND SOCIAL GRACES

1984 ARRIVED WITH all the hype George Orwell's *1984* could deliver. Everywhere you turned someone was making the commentary "is 1984 really *1984?*", or comparing and exploiting any ironic touches that could be concocted between the book and modern society. This lasted for about three weeks until society was finally allowed to get back to itself.

As for me, I continued now and then to harbor dreams of nurturing some sort of writing career, but had no clue where to begin. Occasionally I'd dust off a short story that I'd written in college or pen an attempt at some one-act playwriting contest, but eventually each manuscript found its way back into a drawer, along with the accompanying rejection slip. Remarkably, I never felt the desire to complain or suffer "writer's woe." I had my day job to keep me warm. And soon, almost without even realizing it, I gradually gave up thoughts of writing altogether.

Earlier that year we'd welcomed a new client to ITF. Filling the opening left by Billy Mattila was a young man named Alfred Forrest Flynn who, for reasons I never fully understood, went by the nickname of Iggy. He was a small blond fellow with Down syndrome who bore an uncanny resemblance to singer John Denver. He wore large, round glasses, which only amplified his smooth, round face, and was rarely seen without his prized ten-gallon Stetson. (According to his mother, Iggy had a hero-worship thing for Hoss Cartwright on *Bonanza* ever since the episode in which Hoss befriended the leprechauns.) In any case, Iggy was bright and his comprehension was as sharp as his eternal smile. He was able to speak but,

106

similar to Jim, he also possessed a significant communication hindrance. Whereas Jim tended to mumble his way through life, Iggy meowed.

Known to speech therapists and workers in the field, roughly ten percent of people with mental retardation impart a particular speech impairment known as "gliding." The rest of the world knows it as "baby talk." It's a specific speech pattern wherein certain consonants are dropped, giving us "weal" instead of "real," "yeg" instead of "leg," and "too dark to park the car" becomes "too dahk to pahk the cah." It's also sometimes referred to as "Kennedy-speak" in reference to the regional accent of people from New England. Gliding may be caused in part by certain aspects of brain damage, or by physical trappings such as an enlarged tongue commonly seen in people with Down syndrome. However, also like Jim, every now and then an intelligible word or two would break through on its own, punctuating conversations with moments of clarity. Otherwise, Alfred Forrest "Iggy" Flynn didn't really say much – which suited his new roommate, the ever-tranquil Hughie, just fine.

I used to enjoy conducting classes when they included both Jim and Iggy. Though the rest of us often had to second-guess what the two were saying, *they* seemed to understand each other perfectly, and their good-natured jibbing had a certain amount of charm:

"Muh-mo-muh-muh-muh."

"Meow-me-mew-mew-meow."

"Muh-mo-my-bob-bobby-brown."

"Mew-meow-mew-ming-ming!"

"You o'd man!"

"You cwown!"

(I think that last word was supposed to be "clown.")

I could only imagine what they were actually saying; perhaps discussing ways to solve the energy crisis or exchanging hypotheses on how to bring about world peace, or even extolling the very meaning of life itself. Regardless, Jim and Iggy became fast friends. And it was this very disability of Iggy's that awarded me one of my favorite little moments on the job.

One Sunday morning, I decided to take the guys out for breakfast disguised as the perfect excuse to practice their purchasing skills. Hitting the local Kountry Kitchen, the place was packed – just the way I hoped it would be. This particular coffee shop was not one of Sammy's regular hangouts. Instead, it was frequented by the God-fearing, flag-waving, authoritarian zealots of East County's right-wing concourse. The kind of place where patrons sat and bemoaned too many "fags" in the White House, openly discussed gastro-intestinal ailments without shame, and still believed retarded people should be hooked to clothesline leashes.

Over time I'd grown relatively fearless of such situations and had become bolder in taking on the so-called normal folk. But still, I had to keep my methods refined. As the hostess led us to our table, I proudly paraded Sammy's face, Cole's crutches, Owen's coat, Jim's bangs, and Iggy's "Rocky Mountain High" smile past those who dared to look up from their kitchen-sink omelets and home fries. It always amused me how most restaurants would seat people with developmental disabilities in the back – trying to hide us when, in fact, all it did was allow greater opportunity to showcase ourselves in public. Ever so slowly, we scuffled our way across worn-out carpeting, passing scores of wide-eyed children . . . *(Good, I thought. The cute little gawkers will naturally ask their parents about the funny-looking people and their parents will be forced to discuss it with them.)* . . . passing the glares and clenched sphincters . . . *(Ha! People like you need to know we exist and, yes, we even get hungry.)* . . . passing the downcast eyes of people too uncomfortable to acknowledge us . . . *(Serves you right! I hope we ruined your breakfast, asshole.).*

Now, it's important to understand here that from the 1860s until the 1970s, several American cities had "ugly laws" making it illegal for persons considered *"diseased, maimed, mutilated or in any way deformed so as to be an unsightly or disgusting object"* from appearing in public (*Chicago Municipal Code, sec. 36034*). The goal of these laws was allegedly to preserve the pretty facade of the community. Punishment for being caught with your beauty down ranged from fines of $50.00 to incarceration. Chicago was the last to repeal its Ugly Law as late as 1974. And yet, the past incident with Sammy and Mullet Head taught me that we were fated to continually test the public at large.

Settling into our booth, the slack-jawed waitress tending us was clearly someone who still believed in the Ugly Law. By now I could spot a tard-hater at twenty paces: over-protective mothers, garden-variety good ol' boys, teenage stoners, ill-humored waitresses. The only thing that compounded her obvious discomfort at having to serve "those people" was her rudeness. Menus were dropped onto the table from a safe distance above. Enthusiastic greetings by Sammy, Owen and myself were flatly ignored.

"I'll come back and you tell me what they want," the waitress directed me.

As she walked away I was properly pissed. Nevertheless, as I sat there fuming, a disconcerting thought occurred to me: Was I over-reacting to all this? Just because I was a houseparent, did that make me an expert on what an "appropriate" response to a handicapped person should be? Had I, in fact, become a *disability snob*?

During my time in the field I'd seen great diversity in how both "outsiders" *and* caregivers spoke to, acknowledged, or even thought about people with mental challenges. From Michele's first "asshole" assertion to those people watching Jackie have a seizure in the grocery store; from the tentative pity and outright cruelty of the frat party students to Dot's views on rough justice; from the fearful expression on Mullet Head's face to the gentle touch of Mickey Mouse – everything from apathy to advocacy, all from individuals whose responses were as spontaneous as they were extreme.

So then, who was I to rule on how one should address a person with developmental disabilities? Was it fair to mock the reactions of others just because they lack certain social graces? Furthermore, was this undeniably sour waitress actually justified in her own, ignorant, uneducated way? The answer was swift and eloquent.

Hell, no.

Our waitress' attitude was demeaning and discourteous – *no one* could argue that. It would've been considered rude had it been aimed at "normal" diners; the fact that it was directed at a group of disabled patrons didn't let her off the hook. Imagine if she'd displayed the same attitudinal barriers toward a person who was blind. Or deaf. Or in a wheelchair. She let her ignorance and fear color her behavior, when all she had to do was treat the clients the way any fellow human being would like to be treated – clean, straightforward and with *respect*.

No, I thought. *This* fellow human being needed a lesson.

Little did our waitress know whenever I take my clients out for meals I always encourage them to order for themselves. When she finally returned, I purposely let Iggy speak first.

"I wan' may-maw, mew-mo, meow-mew-mew-mew . . . and coffee," Iggy beamed proudly.

Utterly dumbfounded, the waitress turned to me for help in translating this new and frightening language.

I looked at her casually and smiled. "I'll have the same," I said.

TRENT: *Vegas, baby! Vegas!*
– scene from **Swingers**

During the early years of the home video revolution VCRs began to sprout overnight atop TV sets nationwide, and people with limited means were privileged to check out free movies from the local library. ITF was no exception to this great new benefaction. As a result, night after night the clients would gather in the rec room for such classic fare as *The War of the Gargantuas* and *Abbott and Costello's Jack and the Beanstalk*. Over and over. Again and again.

We needed something fresh – and we needed it *asap*.

For a while Dawn had been mulling over the idea that it would be fun for us to take the clients on vacation. She wanted them to get out beyond the confines of fast food drive-thrus and picnics in the park, beyond Wednesday night Square Dancing at the local rec center, beyond the pungent trappings of Sea World, the Zoo and the Wild Animal Park, even beyond the annual amusements of disabled Disneyland days.

I couldn't have agreed more.

When the day came that Shepherd Hills' finance department finally agreed to cover the cost of staff-accompanied vacations, we immediately brainstormed all the ideas we could within our means. First and foremost, the trips would have to be ultra-low budget, as in motels and coffee shops. (Good intentions could only take us as far as The Hills' pocketbook would allow.) Second, we'd have to use the Blue Beast, so trips needed to be within a reasonable driving distance. Beyond that, the only limits were our imaginations and common sense. One out of two ain't bad.

We decided on three trips. Dot would take a four-nighter to Sedona and the Grand Canyon, Anita would escort a five-nighter up the California coast to Hearst Castle, Monterey and San Francisco, and I would motor a three-nighter to Las Vegas.

Dawn presented the idea to the residents at the weekly Tenant Meeting, where it was received with the standard array of whoops, yelps and a round of "*Aw riiiiight!*" Next, we made three separate sign-up sheets. At the top of each we pasted photos of the destinations and posted them in the rec room. The very next day all three were filled with scrawled, overlapping signatures.

The names confirmed for Anita's San Francisco jaunt included Hughie Lamb and Holly Gross. (Have fun pushing that wheelchair over the hills of Frisco, I thought.) Signing on to follow Dot into the Grand Canyon were Cole Petersen, Sammy White and Darlene Beaudine. Lastly, the names for Las Vegas included Owen Van Winkle, Iggy Flynn and Jackie Chuckam.

Only Jim Livingston remained unsigned.

Immediately, I sprang into action.

Knock, knock. "*Coming in!*"

I entered Jim's apartment to find him dressed in a Jack Daniel's T-shirt and jockey shorts, with chocolate stains on his face. (Did this guy have a secret stash of Ding Dongs hidden someplace, or what?) "Whooze 'at?" he said, parting his bangs so he could see. "Oh!" he smiled approvingly. "It's Steeb Gigger . . . Muh-my houseparent."

"Jimbo!" I sang. "My man! You want to go with us to Las Vegas?"

"Mm-hm," he nodded.

Oh. Well, that was easy, I thought. "Okay, then," I said. "I'll add you to the list." I paused, uncertain whether or not Jim understood what I was asking, so to be safe I repeated, "You're *sure* you want to go to Las Vegas with us . . . right?"

No response.

"Me, Owen, Jackie, Iggy? Right?"

No response.

"A vay-cay-shun. Gambling. Buffets. Pretty girls. Lights. *Sabe?*"

At that, Jim answered me. "Muh-muh-mo-me-mo-muh-you-mas-bob-mo-me-mo-muh-muh-muhm-muhm-go-go-with-moo-mo-bobby-bobby-brown!"

Silence.

"Good," I replied. "Just so long as we're clear."

As I left Jim's apartment, I stopped to gather my thoughts: My first trip to Las Vegas. And it's going to be with . . . four *clients*. Hmm. Will it be my last?

In the days prior to leaving my excitement began to grow. I kept picturing the five of us on the town, rolling the old bones, going toe-to-toe with one-armed bandits, walking side-by-side with Frank, Dean and Sammy (the *other* Sammy). *Vegas!* The name rang like music to my ears. *Vegas!* O, you wicked temptress. *Vegas!* And best of all, it was gonna be *free!*

It was then Jackie said something that floored me.

"Hey, S-S-Steve! When we get Vegas, I get *woman?*"

Huh?

Since when did Jackie Chuckam ever show any interest in women? It was a side of him that, frankly, I'd just never considered. But of course it made perfect sense. He *had* to want sex now and then. *All* humans are sexual beings – with normal desires for sexual expression. As it was, the only ones at ITF getting any regular action were Hughie and Holly – and even *that* was questionable. Otherwise, Darlene pretty much took care of everyone else, but only when she wanted it, and *never* with Jackie. So what opportunities did Jackie ever have? Just how much did he already know? What was he doing out there in the big city alone on his bike?

Hey, Steve! When we get Vegas, I get woooman*?*

To be honest, I actually contemplated it. I mean, what the hell? Prostitution was legal in Nevada just outside Clark County, which encompassed the city of Las Vegas. And what's more, Jackle *knew* this. So then, why couldn't I take him out to one of the ranches in Pahrump? When, I justified, is he ever going to get another chance like this? After all, what are big brothers – and big brothels – for?

I ran the idea past Dawn.

"Are you insane?!"

After some sincere debate, Dawn finally said, "Look. I understand your point, but I just can't approve something like that. End of discussion."

Sadly, I had to inform Jackie, "Sorry, Bud. No get woman."

CHAPTER 11

ROAD TRIP

CLARK GRISWOLD: We're from out of town.
MAN GIVING DIRECTIONS: No shit.
– *scene from* **National Lampoon's Vacation**

ON THE MORNING of Sunday, August 12, 1984, in the grand tradition of Kerouac, Steinbeck, Pirsig, and the Ricardos and the Mertzes, we crammed five grown men, five overstuffed suitcases and one six-pack of Mountain Dew into one Blue Beast. Moments later, we were cruisin' the I-15 North. Next stop, Sin City!

It was the same summer that Wham!'s "Wake Me Up Before You Go-Go" was popular, and Murphy's Law dictated it to be the only song we could get on the radio. That inane opening still rings through my head on hot, sticky, scary nights:

"You do the Jitterbug" ... (tick, tick) ... "You do the Jitterbug" ... (tick, tick) ... "You do the Jitterbug" ... (tick, tick) .... "You do the Jitterbug" ...

"AAAAAHHHHH! Make it stop!"

"What's wrong?" Owen said.

"Oh . . . nothing," I said.

Meanwhile, I learned all too quickly that there was no such thing as a non-stop road trip. About every hour on the average we'd have to pull over for at least one or two bathroom breaks . . .

CHALLENGED: A TRIBUTE

"– Can't you guys all learn to pee at the same time? –"
"– Why does James Livingston get to sit in the front? –"
"– Muh-muh, mo mee, bobby-brown! –"
"– C'mon, guys. Everyone can't ride shotgun at once. –"
"– Meow-mew-mew. –"
"– How come you always get to ride in front, Steve? –"
"– 'Cause I'm the one driving. –"
"– That's no excuse. –"
"– Shut up, Oh-Oh-Owen. –"
"– Aw, your head. –"

Just outside Barstow it was finally Owen's turn to sit up front. Owen possessed reading skills at a simple level, which he flexed freely all the way to Vegas by keeping tabs on all the mileage signs – and I mean *all* the mileage signs – with great diligence as in, "Victorville, 44 miles" or "Baker, 62 miles," or "next rest stop, 30 miles."

"That reminds me," Owen chirped, "I gotta pee again!"

"Naturally," I said dryly.

At one point a car went by with a bumper sticker on the rear window. Owen perked up as it caught his eye. "Honk If You're Jesus!"

"What?"

"That sign on the car. It says, 'Honk If You're Jesus.'"

I started laughing. I was pretty sure it probably said "Honk If You *Love* Jesus" – but I kinda liked Owen's version better.

"Wake up, guys. We're here!"

As we pulled into the Motel-6 just off Tropicana Blvd. the large red, white and mostly blue sign was a budget-friendly oasis in the desert. This was my first stay in a motel. Ever. Growing up with my father there were no family vacations, no explorations of the nation's highways, no opportunities to see the world beyond our own back yard. So for me, a free trip to the Vegas Motel-6 was more than an adventure, it was a crusade. The crisp red flash of the "Vacancy" sign. The double storied, gleaming white building that appeared to go on for miles. (I stepped out of the wagon onto the asphalt and continued my admiration.) The cool, blue pool rippling behind its private enclosure. The . . . the . . . what the hell? The *heat!* Jesus! . . . How can it be so damned *hot?* It didn't take long to ascertain that even with air-conditioning, the temperature in Las Vegas always hovered about twenty degrees south of the boiling point.

After checking in, I maneuvered the Blue Beast around the edge of the building and followed the driveway alllll theee waaay dowwwwwn to the end of the complex. Interesting, I thought. Motels apparently put people with developmental disabilities in the back just like restaurants did.

The room was small, but the 19-inch Zenith bolted to the wall offered us the first of what were sure to be many perks.

"Look, guys," I sang. "Free HBO!"

"What's HBO?" asked Owen.

"It's a movie channel. Uncut. No commercials."

"Why don't we have it on our TV at home?"

"Y-yeah!" added Jackie.

"Muh-muh-mo-muhm!"

"Meowm-me-mew-meow!"

Me and my big mouth.

Promising them I'd look into it when we returned home, I instructed everyone to pick their spots and claim them with their suitcases. With five of us sharing one room – two double beds plus one roll-away – I was prepared for things to be pretty confined. Still, I felt it best – and safest – to keep everyone together rather than split them up.

Jim and Iggy grabbed the double bed nearest the "baffroom." Jackie snagged the side of the other bed next to the window – and no one was going to dispute him. The roll-away next to the air-conditioner was mine. That left Owen to share the remaining double with his favorite roommate.

"Don't get any ideas, old man," Owen quipped to Jackie. "I already have a girlfriend."

"Aw, y-your head," Jackie shot back.

As everyone began to unpack, Owen asked me what we were going to do that evening. Now, I had painstakingly planned a kick-ass itinerary that I thought everyone would enjoy: Circus Circus where Sean Connery as James Bond gambled in *Diamonds Are Forever*; the neon signs along Las Vegas Blvd. a.k.a. "the Strip"; the downtown district where Sean Connery eluded the cops while driving sideways on two wheels in *Diamonds Are Forever*; the fountains at Caesars Palace where Evel Knievel almost splattered; the Hilton Hotel where Sean Connery watched Plenty O'Toole get thrown out the top story window in *Diamonds Are Forever*. (Did I mention I'd recently watched *Diamonds Are Forever*?) In short, all the essentials. I was going to be the best tour guide ever. But Owen had a certain little hidden talent – which I didn't realize at first.

When he asked what we were going to do, I happily answered, "Well, first I thought we'd take a drive up and down the Strip and check out the town."

Owen nodded his acknowledgement. "Or . . . ?"

"Or," I said, "we could do a little gambling. How's that sound?"

Again Owen nodded his acknowledgement. "Or-r-r . . . ?"

"Or-r-r," I said, "we could eat first then gamble later."

"Yeah!" Owen pounced. "That's a good idea. Let's do that."

Next door to the motel stood the Granada Casino and Restaurant, a modest, slots-only grind joint and greasy spoon. *Come and Get It!* invited the sign. *Daily*

Specials! The Granada was my first real taste of Vegas – both literally and figuratively – complete with the chef's recommendation: *Roast Prime Rib Au Jus for only $5.45.*

"Isn't this a great town, you guys?" I declared over and over.

The clients returned a few nods, but otherwise there was no real response. It wasn't their fault, really. I'd learned that most individuals with retardation lack a cognitive sophistication, and often only relate to things that are concrete in nature. Abstract thought is not something they tend to grasp, hence there's little *appreciation* for the concept of things to come. No matter. Once we hit the Strip I was sure they would all perk up.

About halfway through our dinner of fatty prime rib and bottomless pea soup something happened to me. Maybe it was because it was my first road trip, but for some reason I went "souvenir happy." Sitting atop the table next to the Sweet 'n Low was one of those clear acrylic card holders that displays the daily specials: *Monday– Stuffed Pork Chops, $4.95; Wednesday– Shrimp in a Basket, $3.95;* and so on. I was mesmerized. This was the kind of worthless gem you only saw in restaurants. And suddenly, only one thing ran through my mind: *I want that clear acrylic card holder . . . I need that clear acrylic card holder . . . Must have clear acrylic card holder!*

My eyes darted the depth of the room. The moment I was certain no one was watching, I skillfully palmed the card holder from the table and slipped it into my pocket. Looking up ever so nonchalantly, I was met by Owen staring at me in disbelief. "THAT'S *STEA*LING!" he shouted.

Luckily, nobody else was paying attention. The personification of honesty, I told him, "No, it's okay. It's a souvenir. They want us to take things like this."

"BUT THAT'S *STEA*LING!" he shouted again.

Holy shit, I thought. Gimme a break, will ya?

By now people were beginning to glance over, and for a brief second I wished I possessed a keener sense of cunning. But ultimately I remembered that this was a "working" vacation and I was supposed to be a good role model. That and paranoia got the best of me. I returned the card holder to the table and shot Owen the stink eye. "There! Happy?" I then looked over to see Jackie, Jim and Iggy staring at me, puzzled. "Never you guys mind!" I said defensively.

Everyone finished their meals and we rose to leave. Ushering the pack to the door, I doubled back and flipped a few bucks on the table for a tip . . . and once more looked around.

Outside, I fingered the piece of acrylic in my pocket and smiled.

As the sun set in the west, we hit the Tropicana Hotel because it was the closest major landmark within walking distance. The casino was bustling and bright, with multicolored floral carpeting, an exotic, tropical bamboo motif, and a stunning, 4,000-square-foot stained-glass canopy over the gaming tables. Festive and elegant, it was a lasting tribute to Classic Las Vegas.

I located a secluded bank of nickel slots that looked safe, honest and inviting; bubbled windows of cherries, Liberty Bells and American flags, all flashing, ringing and crying *"pull me, pull me, win me, win me!"* Upholding my responsibilities as mother hen, before we sat down to play I showed each client where the cashier was and instructed them that if they needed any change to either go there or wait for me to help them. Everyone dutifully agreed.

All seemed well at first. Other gamblers came and went, drifting from machine to machine, carrying scuffed plastic buckets of coins, a nickel here, a nickel there, damn, no luck, moving on. Meanwhile, playing the machine next to Jackie was a nondescript black man in a cheap leather jacket. I didn't think anything of it at the time; the sense of security in Vegas was well ingrained – people openly carrying buckets of loose change, people there simply to have a good time. I'd even go so far as to say there was something *wholesome* about it all.

"You guys all doing okay?" I confirmed.

"Mmmm," came their collective response, hypnotized by the siren song of clinking coins.

Confident that everything was under control, I decided to treat myself to a brief jaunt around the floor to drink in the scene. After all, who could deny anyone the thrill of their first real live casino? Row after row of lights, money, action! Not to mention scantily-clad cocktail waitresses.

I was gone no more than a few minutes, but just as I returned I found Jackie barreling toward me with tears in his eyes.

"Steeeeeve! That black guy stole my twenty d-d-dollars!"

Immediately, I searched the aisles. But the man was long gone. I asked Jackie what happened. He told me the man offered to take his twenty dollars to the cashier for him and get it changed into nickels. And, being the habitually lazy person he was, Jackie willingly agreed. Initially, I'd felt at fault for leaving him alone when I should've been there watching over him. But hearing this, my sympathy for Jackie quickly faded. Jackie was the type of person who would go into the grocery store, hand his list to a box boy, and let the box boy shop for him. It astounded me that people like these box boys thought they were doing Jackie a favor when in reality Jackie was just taking advantage of them. Like so many others, he'd learned young how to pinpoint and use those who would take pity on him. Only this time someone had taken advantage of Jackie. He was the victim of his own expertise in helplessness.

When I asked Jackie why *he* didn't get his *own* nickels from the cashier, he knew exactly where I was going. Jackie hung his head, contrite. "Oh, sh-shit." And he didn't say anything more about it.

Sh-shit is right, I thought. Sh-shit is right.

It was still early when we returned to the motel. I didn't care. I figured we'd had our fill of Vegas hospitality for one night. Jackie was the first to shower and the first to crawl into bed without a word. Seeing him lying there curled in a fetal position, the covers pulled over his head in disgrace, my sympathies returned. Still, despite my feelings, what Jackie did was in poor judgment and he should've known better. In the end I compromised; I decided I would neither excuse it nor scold it. The poor guy'd had enough.

And, apparently, so had Iggy.

"Phew, Iggy! Was that you again?"

"*Hee-hee-hee-hee-hee!*"

Iggy had never been taught proper manners when it came to passing gas. Even though he was well into his twenties, when it came to farting he behaved like a little kid. It didn't matter where he was, be it private or public, to him it was always a big joke. In fact, I often wondered if Iggy's patented "Meow-mew-mew" wasn't actually code for "pull my finger."

Back in orientation we were taught that people with mental retardation do not have the "mind of a child" as many believe. But behaving child*like* is an entirely different matter. It's a trait that many clients not only project naturally, but sometimes do a little *too* well. After all, some of these guys have had twenty or thirty years experience behaving like an eight-year-old. Regardless, Iggy's farting was getting old pretty fast.

At first I tried counseling him by saying it simply wasn't polite to do it in front of others. When that didn't work I came up with a better solution. I instructed Iggy that from now on, any time he had to pass wind, he was to stick his butt out the door into the hallway so the rest of us wouldn't have to smell it. Sound and logical.

Showers resumed, one client after the other, all settling in for a night of free HBO. About twenty minutes into *The China Syndrome*, Iggy got up, walked over to the door, stuck his rear end out and went *brrafft!* He then closed the door and climbed back into bed.

"Thank you, Iggy," I said. "Much better."

And all smelled right with the world.

The next morning I awoke to the fetid locker room smells of mixed manhood hanging in the air like a wet wool blanket. Five adult males confined to one single room didn't come without its repercussions. Everywhere I looked there were knobby joints, misshapen feet, and varicose veins typically obscured by clothing. There were liver spots. Crusty moles. Clumps of back hair. Skin tags. I'd once thought it was difficult to watch *one* client bathe and dress. That was nothing compared to living with it times four. I had to wonder. Is this what it would've been like if I'd grown up with brothers?

"What are we doing today?" Owen asked.

"Today I thought we'd do a little sight-seeing," I said.

"Orrr . . . ?"

"Or, we could check out the buffet at Circus Circus. I hear it's pretty good."

"Yeah!" Owen pounced. "That's a good idea. Let's do that."

As each of us greeted the day to give Vegas another chance, I noticed that Iggy was already dressed and ready to go. And, no surprise, he had to pass gas again. *Jeez*, I thought, *what'd this guy eat in another life?*

Iggy opened the front door and let loose his gastro-turbulence, grander than I'd ever heard him fart before. *BRRRRRAAAAAAAAAFFFFFT!*

This time, however, as he finished, Iggy glanced behind him, as if something had caught his attention.

"Uh-oh," he said, and ducked back inside.

Slowly it dawned on me. "Iggy . . . was there somebody out there in the hall?"

Iggy nodded. "Uh-huh." And burst out laughing.

Hm, I thought, maybe my idea wasn't such a good one after all. I rushed to the door and looked out into the hall – and there, boarding the elevator a couple doors down, was a mother, a father, and three little girls dressed in matching summer outfits.

"Uh . . . Sorry 'bout that," I shrugged.

The family didn't say anything back. Each member simply returned a disgusted frown.

Later that morning I still couldn't shake the embarrassment I felt for Iggy. He was still such a kid at heart, it made me want to teach him a sense of grown-up dignity that much more. But then, the more I thought about *that*, I finally just had to laugh. Fact is, mankind has been farting successfully since the Stone Age. And, no matter how you may try to reinvent the wheel, it always seems to roll back on you. Besides, it was just plain *funny*. Think about it from the perspective of the family. What *they* saw, basically, was a door open, a butt thrust itself into the hall, fart, and then promptly disappear back into the room. I could just imagine the postcard to the folks back home:

> *Dear Aunt Mabel,*
> *Today we saw eight different men dressed like Elvis, Daddy played Blackjack*
> *at The Dunes, and a butt farted at us in the hallway. Wish you were here.*

Our first drive up the Strip reminded me of Pleasure Island in *Pinocchio*, rhythmically dotted by marquees advertising everything from a wealth of Vegas royalty like Wayne Newton and Keely Smith to nickel slot tournaments, $1.99 buffets and topless revues. It was at once majestic and kitschy, grand and inviting, informal and artistic, all slathered in broad desert daylight, glowing like one big, over-exposed Kodachrome.

"Guys!" I shouted with exuberance from behind the wheel. "Look at this place! Isn't this incredible?"

I turned to see every last one of them, fast asleep.

After queuing up forty minutes for the "all-u-can-eat" brunch at Circus Circus, visions of trapeze artists in *Diamonds Are Forever* gracefully gliding over Sean Connery in his custom-tailored tux were fading fast. Instead, we found ourselves surrounded by what I was sure had to be the same pack of mewling kids and harried parents we'd encountered at Disneyland. Circus Circus was the only hotel at the time that dared utter the F word. *Family*. Still, I had no right to complain. For me, at least, it was free. And so in due course, we came, we ate, we conquered.

After brunch I checked the itinerary to see what was in store. "How about we cruise the downtown area?"

"Or . . . ?"

"Or, we can . . ." I slowly trailed off. What happened to that great itinerary I planned? Why weren't we following it? That's when I finally realized Owen's "little hidden talent." And I'd been falling for it, hook, line and –

"*Wait* a minute!" I shouted. "No 'or!' There is no 'or!' We're going downtown! Got it? That is what we are going to do!"

Owen shrugged. "'Kay. Can I bring my tape recorder?"

Downtown Las Vegas was like the Strip's sleazier, wheezier, Good-Time-Charlie brother, a place where nudie-club barkers badgered passersby and Asian hostesses stood in casino entryways hawking chances to win "velly big money" with one free spin. Stale smoke shrouded desperate gamblers under claustrophobic ceilings. Carpets were encrusted with chewing gum, coffee stains, cigarette burns, and other unidentifiable blotches beneath two-dollar tables defended by locals who looked like the crew off a ship stricken with scurvy. And yet, roaming Fremont Street dressed in our own line of Goodwill fashions, damned if we didn't fit right in.

After a well-heeled day of gambling, gorging and palming a Binion's souvenir ashtray, that night we drove back to our motel via the Strip for a nighttime view of this world-famous neonopolis. The entire 4 1/2 mile stretch flickered, flashed, glowed and gleamed in a voluminous brilliance of illumination. Neon is a Las Vegas religion; a synthetic, raw beauty of hypnotic inorganic animation worthy of canonization. (Forgive me as I utter a small prayer.)

Lining up for showers in summer camp fashion, the gang crawled over one another in our cramped little room, suitcases flipping open to retrieve the necessary toiletries and bedtime medications. It was during this regime I observed certain habits by Jim that apparently came from years of institutionalized upbringing. Rituals like aligning his shoes and tomorrow's change of clothes next to his bed, and hiding his wallet inside his pillowcase as he slept or showered. It was the same as he ate his meals one food item at a time, never mixing them together, as if they were still compartmentalized on his plate the way food is served in prisons and hospitals. And though it was presumptuous, I couldn't help but wonder how controlled – and humbled – his past life must have been.

Sitting on the bed next to Jim, I engaged him in a bit of small talk to pass the time, figuring full well that I'd do most of the talking and he'd do most of the muh-muhming. It was here I inadvertently unearthed the secret to finally conversing *with* Jim, not *at* Jim, like so many others seemed to do. The topic was nothing special, just a recounting of the day's events and the sights we'd seen. I asked Jim several questions, and offhandedly found myself whittling down his responses by process of elimination. In other words, I would repeat what I thought Jim had said, then ask him if it was indeed what he meant to say. It was through this casual series of yes's and no's that I was able to slowly crack the Livingston code. But more importantly, I was rewarded with the discovery of a hidden enthusiasm at the center of Jim's heart, eager to share the good time he was having. It was a small victory we would quietly celebrate together.

Meanwhile, complimentary HBO entertained the room by continuing its Jane Fonda marathon. The clients were currently in the middle of *Cat Ballou.* Finishing my turn to shower, I exited the bathroom dripping wet with a towel wrapped around me and took a quick head count. Someone was MIA.

"Where's Jackie?"

"That clown?" Owen said. "He went outside for a walk."

. . . *"Hey Steve. When we get Vegas, I get* woooman*?"* . . .

"Oh, shit! No!"

Instantly, wet skin was met by a dirty T-shirt and sweat pants. I ran outside into the parking lot, jutting between cars, scanning the horizon. There in the distance, standing out on Tropicana Blvd., I spotted two figures illuminated by a shimmering neon radiance. I almost fainted. One was Jackie, silhouetted by his trademark slouch and bushel of hair. The other was a woman dressed in a red halter top, Daisy Dukes, spiked heels and a platinum blond flip. Nice to see the classics never go out of style.

Even from that far away I could see she was doing all the talking while Jackie stood there, eagerly nodding his head. With their verbal transaction complete, the woman took Jackie by the arm and together they began to walk off.

"JACKIE! NO!"

I ran towards them. Jackie looked up and saw me coming – a deer in the headlights – and bolted the other way. Halfway to them, I stopped short. The woman's make-up began screaming at me five minutes before the woman did. Screaming. Cursing. Something about an impending disembowelment. The next thing I knew she was coming after me, appearing to make good on her promise.

I doubled back as fast as I could and barreled straight for the room. Meeting Jackie at the door I hollered, "Open the door! Quick! Get in!"

"It locked!" Jackie shouted.

"Bang on it! Open it! Hurry!"

The two of us banged on the door. The smell of AquaNet was right on top of us. Finally, the door opened – and a butt farted as us. I shoved Iggy back inside

CHALLENGED: A TRIBUTE | 121

and Jackie and I tumbled in on top of him. Door, *slam!* Lock, *click!* Drapes, *swoosh!*, closed. "Everybody keep quiet and maybe she'll go away," I whispered.

Whack!

Something hit the window – I think it may have been a high-heeled pump, but I couldn't be certain.

For the next several minutes we listened to a blizzard of cuss words rage outside the door as the woman darted back and forth. It took that long before I realized Jackie was patting me on the back repeating, "I sorry, I sorry, I sorry . . ."

Eventually the woman gave up and wandered off. Looking into Jackie's face, the angst, the shame, the confusion, I didn't say anything. I didn't have the patience to counsel him, nor the heart to yell at him. All the poor man wanted was "woman." And stronger men than Jackie will always succumb to their temptations in Las Vegas. (And yet, I couldn't help but wonder, what would Sean Connery do in a case like this?)

We finished off the evening with a showing of *Klute* and turned out the lights. In the end, the only prostitute Jackie got to spend the night with was Jane Fonda. Still, I drifted off to sleep appreciative for the knowledge that if I learned anything this trip it was: When in Vegas, never *ever* come between a hooker and her John.

Click!

. . . *"You do the Jitterbug"* . . . *(tick, tick)* . . . *"Wake me UP before you go-go –"*

"Will someone please shut off that damn clock radio?!"

The morning of the third day began like every other morning.

"Hey, guys. Whaddaya say today we check out the action at Caesars Palace?"

"Orrr . . . ?"

"No 'or!' We're going to Caesars Palace!"

"'Kay."

The decor of Caesars Palace was almost too pretentious for its own good, with vaulted ceilings, classic statuary, and graceful arches atoned in marble, black and silver. All the dealers wore tuxedos and all the gamblers remained dead quiet – apparently there were some serious-ass bets going on here. As for us, we decided to make a go at one more round of nickel slots. Learning from my previous mistake, this time I stayed put and watched the clients play – if not for security's sake, then simply for the sheer enjoyment.

Over the last couple of days I noticed that Jim had developed a very specific system for winning – or so he thought. He would start out with a $10 bill and feed it into the machine. Once registered, he would then hit the "cash out" button and the entire amount would come spilling out in nickels, plinking gaily into the silver tray below. Jim would then scoop all the nickels into a plastic coin bucket provided by the casino. Then, and only then, would he begin to play – plunking one nickel at a time into the machine and pulling the handle. Anytime one of those pulls registered a win, be it two, three or ten nickels, Jim would once again push the button to cash out. However, this time he would purposely leave *those* nickels in the tray. Once his bucket was empty, Jim would scoop whatever nickels he'd "won" from the tray. So in Jim's mind, he was always a winner. It didn't matter to him that he may have put ten dollars in and only received a total of three dollars back. Jim didn't comprehend this – nor did he care. In the mind of Mr. Mouth, he hadn't lost seven dollars, he'd won three.

Once I figured out what Jim was doing, I had to marvel at its logic – no matter how illogical. Jim's system was Jim's system. No one taught it to him or tried to make him change it. He came up with it all on his own – all with the goal of always beating the house. And to that end, James Livingston was a mathematically-challenged genius. His own sure thing. Who was I to burst his bubble?

As it was, I didn't have to.

On that same afternoon as I watched Jim unknowingly kid himself, karma kissed him on the other cheek. It happened when he plunked one of his nickels into the machine and pulled the handle the exact same way he'd done every time before.

Thunk . . . Thunk . . . Thunk!

Triple Bar, Triple Bar, Triple Bar!

To the shrill din of a fire bell, the machine registered a win of *one thousand* nickels. Fifty dollars, free and clear. This time Jim knew he really had a winner. Without hesitation, he pushed the cash out button – and in a melodious rippling stream, one thousand nickels poured out of his machine.

A crowd began to gather. The other clients looked on, pie-eyed. Two elderly ladies who'd been there all morning fluttered over Jim and cooed their congratulations. Seeing that he was disabled, their kind words rang sincere to his good fortune. Still, this didn't stop me from squeezing in between them, just to make sure the nickels remained with their rightful owner.

One thousand nickels. Plunk, plunk, plunk! One thousand nickels. Man, oh man! Jim would have a story to tell when he got home – anyway, as best as he could convey.

With the last nickel scooped and secured in his bucket, I escorted Jim to the cashier. Together we watched as the silver discs were channeled into a chute and the total slowly climbed to register exactly $54.15. I pooled the cash and beckoned Jim to follow me off to the side. But just as I began to recount the money, Jim said something that made me stop.

"You lucky, Steeb. You lucky."

The articulation of the words should have been enough to impress me – and any other time that might have been the case. But what made me stop and turn cold was the fact that Jim thought this $50 was *my* money. Not his. He was congratulating me on the money that I would be pocketing, not him. It was this level of trust, of naiveté, compounded by the realization of just how easily a client could be exploited that stirred me. I could've easily slipped those bills into my pocket and no one would be the wiser.

It made me feel sorry for Jim. For all my clients. Standing in the middle of one of the world's most famous casinos, designed to manipulate and exploit our greed, it made my clients, my friends, instantly all the more vulnerable.

"No, Jim," I said softly. "This is *your* money. *You* won this money. It's yours to keep and do anything you want with. You understand?"

Jim stared at me blankly. As I handed him the wad of cash, quite possibly the most money he'd ever seen at one time, I watched his face register surprise, then joy, then gratitude, and finally understanding. Of course it was his money. Of course he would take it. And, of course, he would guard it with his life.

That I would see to.

Our last night in Vegas had to be a memorable one. More than just casino neon, bad buffets, smoky grind joints, coffee shop specials, and lost wages. I wanted us to go out on a traditional Vegas high. A *show!*

"Ya goin' to Vegas?" people would say. "Oh, ya *gotta* see a *show!*"

But which one? Taking into consideration our budget, the appropriateness of content, and the overall amount of required glitz, I opted to take the gang to see the famous, world-renowned revue "Nudes On Ice" at the Union Plaza in downtown Las Vegas. Not only did there promise to be air-conditioning (which was worth the price alone), but also dancers, skaters, ventriloquists, comedians, production numbers, headdresses, and best of all, showgirls.

Topless showgirls.

Again, *top*less. *Topless* showgirls. On *ice*.

It was the least I could do seeing as how Dawn wouldn't allow me to take Jackie to a cathouse. The *very* least. Here I was in Las Vegas with what essentially amounted to four adult males harboring the sexual curiosities of four 13-year-olds. Okay, make that *five* 13-year-olds. What am I, made of stone?

(Note: What may have seemed the obvious choice to some, namely a strip club, was out of the question. First there was the price to consider – out of our reach. Then there were the live girls to consider – perhaps not far enough out of our reach. I didn't want a repeat of Jackie's street-side interlude. Lastly, there was Owen's mouth to consider. No matter how stealthily we may have attempted a visit to a strip club, there would always be Owen to rat us out – complete with tape recorded evidence.)

And so, for a mere ten dollars a ticket, all that represented Vegas – glitz, grandeur and cheap erotic thrills – would be ours to take home in our minds.

That evening, everyone dressed in their best digs; a collection of paisley neckties, Payless dress shoes, and polyester shirts that came three to a package. Bottles of Aqua Velva were freely exchanged. Owen, naturally, wore his magenta corduroy jacket, while Iggy donned his ten-gallon hat and a bolo string tie with an Indian head nickel slide. I even got Jackie to slick down his fright wig with a healthy fistful of Thrifty Drugs-brand mousse. For a group of out-of-towners, I had to admit, we looked pretty okay.

At 8:05 p.m. the lights slowly dimmed. A hush fell over the adequately-drunken crowd. The announcer's voice filled the room.

"Lllllllladies and gentlemen . . . please welcome . . . all the way from the French Riviera . . . Nudes On Ice!"

A single spotlight hit the stage. A pre-recorded orchestra sounded a fanfare. Suddenly, out of nowhere, six athletic, rhinestone-trimmed female ice skaters took to the stage, nipples to the wind. Their feathery headdresses fluttered wildly as each one gained momentum. *Zip! Swoosh! Whoosh! Screeeeech!* The bosomy sextuplets shifted their hips deftly in overlapping circles with flawless execution. The music swelled and a pre-recorded chorus sang their praises, confirming them to be:

"The fabulous, fabulous Nuuudes . . . On . . . Iiiiiiiiiiiice!"

Even with the mousse, Jackie's fright wig stood on end.

The stage was the size of an average coffee table. A single pair of speakers flanked either side, cranked for maximum feedback. A track of disco lights hung just beneath the proscenium arch, high enough so as not to melt the stage but close enough to light the bare essentials. True to form, when we first came in, the maitre d' sat us at a table in the back. (Again, why buck tradition?) In this case, however, the back of the room turned out to be in our favor. Not only was the showroom so small that *every* seat felt like a front row venue, but as the skaters skirted and skeetched about the frozen platform, shaved ice chips shot from their blades and landed in the drinks of those sitting up close. Now *that's* service, I thought impressed.

Suddenly, the music shifted.

"Get down, get down . . . Get down, get down . . . Jungle boogie – Arrrooooh!"

At that, two more topless ice skaters appeared and joined the first six to fill out the ensemble. Two final, athletic, rhinestone-trimmed, topless *males*. Glitter to glitter, all eight of them ultimately commingled conjointly atop the coffee table and struck a final tableau in glorious, nudie 3-D.

TA-DAAAH!

I never applauded as heartily as I did that night.

What followed next is best described as competently-choreographed pandemonium. There were dance routines, musical renditions, lighting effects, and an abundance of areola. At one point the lights dimmed to a frosty shade of blue as a spangled topless couple performed a classically-rendered, Winter Olympian pair-skating routine – complete with overhead lifts, butterfly jumps and death spirals – set to the scratchy-vinyl vocals of Steve and Eydie.

"It seems we stood and talked like this before . . . We looked at each other in the same way then . . . But I can't remember whe-e-ere or whe-e-e-en . . ."

And with each new refrain, the entire front row would bob and weave as the naked blades of glory came within inches of slashing their throats.

CHALLENGED: A TRIBUTE

I never laughed as heartily as I did that night.

When it came time for the comedian to do his segment I sat back with little anticipation, sensing this might be a good time to mentally catch up on my laundry list. (Hmm, are there any "Nudes On Ice" souvenir ashtrays around here? . . .)

"Ladies and gentlemen . . . the world famous Nudes On Ice Revue *is proud to present the comedy stylings of Irving "Crazy Man" Finklestein!"*

A seaweed-haired man dressed in a ruffled tuxedo circa 1973 staggered onto a wooden plank at the front of the stage with a Highball in his hand. His voice sounded like a trumpet with adenoids. Flashing a plastic grin that was only slightly smaller than his paunch, he greeted the house.

"Evenin', folks! How ya doin', how ya doin'? You all havin' a good time? You all winnin' big? Who's not havin' a good time? Who's not winnin' big? Tell ya what. On the count of three, everyone yell and cheer as loud as you can. Ready? *Onetwothree!"*

(Audience screams and cheers.)

"You know what's great about that? The people out there in the casino. They hear you all in here cheerin' and havin' a good time while they're losin' all their money. *Pisses 'em off!"*

(Appreciative audience laughter.)

Then came his opening joke.

"You know, I went to Denny's the other day for breakfast. I ordered the Number One – and the waiter *PEED* on me!

Rim shot.

Now, this joke was odds-on meant to suffice as his grabber. But in our case, it became both a grabber and a turning point. As soon as he delivered that first punch line, all four of the clients burst out laughing. Then came his follow up.

"Boy, howdy! I tell ya, whatever ya do, *don't* order the Number *Two!"*

Rim shot.

Our table erupted. Jim and Iggy threw back their heads and howled with delight. Owen pounded the table and wheezed a series of raspy chest chortles. Even Jackie let fly a solid and sustained belly laugh. *"YAH-HA-HA-HAAAAAR!!!"*

Must be a proud night for this comic, I thought. He's finally found his core audience.

The routine continued pretty much in the same vein as those first two gems. A mix of drunk jokes, bad-in-bed jokes, observational humor and political incorrectness. What surely had to be the low point of his act came when he spotted a table of Asian-Americans sitting down front.

"Hey, would'ja lookit what we got here? What happened, d'ja all just come in off da boat? *Huh?!* Hey, I think I just met your cousin from Vietnam in the lobby. Sum Dum Fuck! I kid, I kid. But seriously . . . wash-ee clothes-ee? *HUH?!"*

Holy shit, I thought. Is this guy kidding?

But still, the clients roared on. They loved it. They laughed hard and loud like drunken hyenas or – dare I say – mental patients. Whether or not the Asians met him in the back alley after the show, I've no idea. But for that instant, Irving "Crazy Man" Finklestein was a hero. Apologizing for nothing, it made me feel good to see my guys so happy. Especially Jackie. After what he'd been through, he deserved a good laugh.

For the grand finale, the audience was treated to the hypothermic reviviscence of all sixteen nipples in a full-blown, fur-trimmed tribute to *Doctor Zhivago*. No expense was spared. From the tips of their Russian dancing boots to the tops of their bearskin caps, the titular ensemble twirled, leapt and squat-kicked their way through a topless "Somewhere My Love"-ified extravaganza of Bolshevik rebellion on skates. It was enough to turn your ushanka on its ear flaps.

After the final curtain fell, our table was the last to leave, still reeling from the thrill of it all. A night like this was rare for us – the sheer act of dressing up!, to go out on the town!, to order nightclub-style Cokes garnished with maraschino cherries!, to see nipple after nipple after nipple! – sending us off fully satisfied with the free show that only cost $10. It was the best $10 I never spent.

That night, before bed, I noticed everyone took just a little longer to shower than usual. I also noticed everyone slept just a little more soundly than usual, too.

I guess my work here was done.

The next morning, we packed our bags and loaded up for the long drive home. I should've been ashamed that my sports duffel included one clear acrylic card holder from the Granada Casino, two Motel-6 bath towels, a two-week supply of complimentary Motel-6 baby soaps, three ashtrays from the Tropicana Hotel, Circus Circus and Binion's respectively, a stack of flyers for the Liberace Museum, a book of 2-for-1 buffet coupons due to expire in a month, a stack of flyers for strippers, and a rock from the motel parking lot. I should've been ashamed – but I wasn't. When I first arrived in Las Vegas it had engaged me like Pleasure Island in *Pinocchio*. In *Pinocchio* kids act like adults and turn into jackasses, whereas in Vegas adults act like kids and turn into jackasses. I had gone bat-shit souvenir crazy. It was clearly time to leave.

As we hit the highway, the sound of worn radials on desert asphalt cast a tranquil purr. I checked the rear view and noticed Jackie in the back seat brooding. Suddenly, he leaned forward and said with determination, "Steve, that black guy a fuckin' liar, huh?"

Before I could catch myself I shot back, "Yeah, but whose fault was it?"

Jackie slumped back and hung his head. "I know, I know."

I instantly regretted what I said. Jackie was right. That guy *was* a fucking liar. He was the worst kind of vermin that preys on the innocent; someone who just didn't play fair. And the fact that Jackie brought it up a full three days later made it obvious that this was something he was going to carry with him for a long, long time. But, I thought, how else is he ever going to learn? How else is he going to realize the "natural consequences" of independent living? Back at ITF, Cole Petersen was considered by everyone to be the brightest resident of the group. But Jackie was every bit as bright as Cole. Jackie had potential, *true* potential to one day make it on his own. If only he'd stop being so lazy. If only he'd start taking responsibility more seriously. If only he'd apply some common sense. If only he'd . . .

If only.

If only he hadn't been dropped as a baby.

I reflected momentarily back to something that was said to us in orientation:

Our role is far past the diagnostic stage. We're past the parental decisions of what to do with their broken child – we just get the pieces.

What the instructor forgot to mention was that it's up to us to supply the Krazy Glue.

"San Diego, 300 miles."

Owen's voice returned me to the present, and hearing him report the miles in his own regular sort of way invited a welcome and soothing wave of comfort to wash over me. I thought about the last three days and had to smile. Like most of society, I never really saw the clients as "regular" people before. It's something our culture has never embraced, nor, it seems, has the patience to seek. *Regular* people, you say? Don't be absurd! Of course they're not *regular* people. Everyone knows they're saints and angels . . . Aren't they?

Just then I felt a tap on my shoulder from the back seat.

"Hey, Steeb," Jim said with a devilish grin. "You a o'd man."

Like a naughty six-year-old, Iggy echoed, "Whooooo! You hear he caw you? He caw you *o'd man.*"

One by one, the entire crew – Jim, Iggy, Owen, and last of all Jackie – burst out laughing and cackling. And in that, I realized it was a good thing. The last four days – hell, the last *two years* – the clients had confounded me, moved me, amused me, even angered me, just as real and as "regular" as it was natural. But when they teased me the same way they teased each other, it meant they had accepted me into their game, into their world, with an entirely different kind of trust. And that, I told myself, was pretty damn cool.

Angels or devils? I suppose it depends on how you glue the pieces together. Either way, it was one hell of a road trip. Either way, I couldn't wait to return with my boys again next year.

CHAPTER 12

THE OTHER SIDE OF THE FENCE

ALL SHEPHERD HILLS employees were required to punch a time clock located on the main campus in a small, separate alcove with a cigarette burn-marred couch, a small card table with two mismatched chairs, a bulletin board cluttered with outdated union notices, and a blessed Coke machine that only charged fifty cents per can. The time clock room was, in essence, a silent oasis plopped in the middle of bedlam. For some it was a place to sit quietly and gather your thoughts before your shift, for others it was a sanctuary where you could gripe about the union, vent about your clients, bitch about your troubles, and churn the gossip mill with rumors of your colleagues. Often I would arrive early to work and wait patiently for the witching hour to arrive, punch my card, then hurry across the grassy grounds to the back gate, across the parking lot, and into glorious oblivion – at least as far as the main campus workers were concerned.

Working in ITF Village felt as far removed from the rest of The Hills as being a castaway in the middle of the Pacific. In fact, by the summer of 1985 I'd now gone three years knowing barely a wit about the main campus, which loomed across the back parking lot less than a hundred feet away. And yet, there were still moments of crossover with the main campus staff while waiting to clock in that forced me to associate with the bitchers and moaners who worked in the units. In other words, I'd heard the horror stories.

Stories about employees enduring such hardships as biting, pinching, scratching, kicking, hair-pulling, snot-flicking, jizz-whizzing, feces-smearing, public nudity, public masturbation, and an endless swell of wet sheets and diaper pails – all punctuated by bouts of aggression and self-injurious behavior. Yet even though I was three years into the job, I was somehow always treated differently. Each encounter with a main campus employee was invariably the same:

"You new?"

"No. Been here three years."

"*Three years?!* How come I haven't seen you around? What unit you work in?"

"ITF."

And that's when the eyes would roll.

"Ohhhhh, no *won*der. You're way out back there."

"Yeah. Guess so."

Beat.

"So . . . ITF, eh?" (Scoff.) "Your kids are *easy*."

There it was. Easy. The word was as demeaning as it was ignorant. It was a direct reflection, as in How Do *You* Rate? How did *you* get such easy, high-functioning clients who take their own baths and wipe their own butts? You got it easy. I got it HARD! I work in the *REAL* units. Where the kids smear their shit and piss their beds. The *REAL* units where they flop their dicks out and wag 'em in your face. The *REAL* units where we have to lift 'em outta wheelchairs and change their dirty tampons. The *REAL* units where they all share one giant toilet and fifteen people have to go *at the same time!* I GOT IT HARDER THAN *YOU!!!*

Or, at least, that's the way it felt.

But I *didn't* have it easier. I was a fellow party member just like them. True, maybe I didn't have to actually put my back into my job – but I sure as hell had to put my *brain* into it. So what if my clients didn't require diaper changes or transfers to and from bath chairs? My clients were thinkers. Manipulators. Mental mind fuckers. They were – what's the word? – *smart!*

If I'd wanted to, I could've just as easily dismissed the clients in the units as no more complex than a bunch of drooling, gibbering two-year-olds. I could've just as easily dismissed the main campus staff as nothing but glorified babysitters. Meanwhile, *my* clients were smart enough to *question* their emotions. Imagine that kind of daily struggle – for both them *and* me. Many were the nights I'd drag my butt up to the time clock room physically tired by way of emotional exhaustion. Many were the nights it'd take a good hour after a shift just to decompress, to worry whether or not I had covered all my bases or left myself vulnerable the next day to a client's master plan to overthrow me, to remember *not* to take things personally, to forgive and *forget.* I GOT IT HARD, TOO!

Or, at least, that's the way it felt.

One day, I arrived earlier than usual to work for no other reason than the wind just happened to be at my back. Sitting alone in the time clock room, it wasn't long before I was joined by two forces from the front lines, busily relating battle tales about client bodily functions. The first employee was a lifer from Unit 3. She was dressed in scrubs and bore the posture of a grizzled prospector. The other, from Unit 7, was only in her mid-thirties, but already sported frazzled gray curls. As Grizzled and Frazzled each gathered their hair in a mop and proceeded to braid it behind them, Grizzled began to spin a yarn about how her twelve-year-old daughter had recently volunteered to help with a client's birthday party at the Family Fun Video Arcade.

The way she detailed it, a group of eight plus her daughter were exiled to the back room, which was designed to handle multiple children's birthday parties. According to the arcade's policy it was easier to keep track of everybody that way, with less chance of them disturbing the patrons out front. After a fair amount of sheet cake had been consumed by all, Louie, one of the clients, began to grow antsy. When the group didn't move fast enough for Louie's liking, he reached into his pants, pulled out a clump of poop and threw it across the room – indicating he was ready to leave. Unfortunately, the brown grenade landed near a *NORMAL* child's birthday party, causing all the other parents to go ballistic. Screaming, yelling, swooning.

Frazzled was howling. "So what'd you do?"

Grizzled shrugged. "I just walked over, scooped the turd into a party hat and tossed it in the nearest toilet." Grizzled paused to snort. "And I'm like, you're *parents.* What, you never had to clean up your kid's *poop* before?"

"Amateurs," said Frazzled, shaking her head.

Grizzled finished her story with the fact that when they got home, her daughter vowed *never* to volunteer again.

Right then and there I had no qualms about awarding Grizzled first prize for most humiliating moment on the job. And yet, all through the story, Grizzled and Frazzled's conversation had been punctuated by shrewd grins and knowing guffaws. For them, stories like these were all in a day's work if not badges of honor.

The exact second the time clock hit 2:00 p.m. both women bid each other "see ya" and strolled off to their respective units to face another shift in paradise. Though neither of them acknowledged me with more than a passing nod, somehow I got the distinct feeling Grizzled's close encounter of the turd kind was meant for my benefit. I just didn't realize it would be an omen of things to come.

Heading into the ITF office I was met at the door by Dawn. "They need you to work in Unit 2 tonight," she said.

"Wait . . . *What?*"

"They're short-staffed, so the on-grounds manager called and asked if we had any extras."

I was confused. "But . . . I work in ITF."

Dawn went on to remind me that while ITF was my "home" department, when an employee is hired at Shepherd Hills they can be pulled to any unit at any moment when needed. Slowly, a vague recollection of this rule trickled back to me from orientation – a bit of info I'd conveniently forgotten over the last three years. Apparently it was only by the grace of good fortune that I'd never been called to leave my comfort zone. Until today.

"They need help with an outing," Dawn finished. "Meet them out back by their van at six o'clock."

I was embarrassed to ask Dawn this next question. "Um . . . where exactly is Unit 2?"

At ten after six I located a small woman dressed in sweats standing watchfully next to Unit 2's van. She couldn't have been more than eighteen or nineteen. Seated inside were three clients, two females and one male, ready to go. Immediately, I could tell they were clients of a much lower functioning level than those I was used to working with simply by their flaccid body language, like wet raincoats slung over a chair. One of the women looked like a life-sized bobble-head doll. The other was a dead ringer for the throat-slashing dwarf at the end of *Don't Look Now*, red pixie hood and all. The man wore dark glasses and held a white cane with a red tip.

I was dutifully informed by the girl that Unit 2 had been the recipient of some donated Padres tickets, and I was to escort the three clients, Jane, Emily and Patrick, to the stadium. "Don't worry," she said, "they've all been toileted." She handed me the keys, a mileage log, and an envelope with the tickets. "Have fun."

"Wait a second. You're not coming with me?" I said.

"Can't. Too busy."

I glanced once more into the van window. "Um . . . Is that guy blind?"

The girl cocked a half smile. "Yeah, but he still likes to listen to the games. Is that going to be a problem?"

"No, but –"

"Don't worry, you'll be fine." And with that, she turned and shot back through the gate.

I eyed the three clients warily and sighed. They might as well have been from another galaxy. Gradually my skin began to crawl with that old familiar, *too*-familiar, first-day-on-the-job anxiety.

Our tickets turned out to be a set of donated nosebleed seats, bestowed by some altruistic dumbshit who knew nothing of this population, I'm sure. With one arm linked around Blind Patrick, the other around Slasher Emily, and Bobble-Head Jane trailing behind with her hand firmly grasping the back of my belt, we inched our way toward the fourth level, one step at a time. Without even looking, I could already feel the entire stadium watching the freak show. And who could blame them? If I were in the stands I'd probably be watching us, too. But that was just the teaser.

Halfway to our seats Emily began to scream in the shrill key of a sea gull. "*I don't wanna go! I don't wanna go! Waa-laa-laa-laaaaah!*" This in turn caused Jane to tug sharply upward on my waistband, reintroducing me to The Art of the Wedgie. But instead of turning around and going home – which would've been the *sensible* thing to do – I became so frustrated that I was damned and determined to make it to our seats, if for the sake of anything to prove to the clients – as well as the gawkers – that it could be done.

At last we made it to the top. Literally the *top* of Jack Murphy Stadium. The very last row. Even the peanut vendors didn't climb this high. We were so high up, I could see the parking lot – of *Yankee* Stadium. So high up, an eagle flew by, followed by Superman and a stray UFO out of Roswell circa 1947. So high up, I can't even think of another lame joke to insert here for lack of oxygen.

Just as we began to settle in, Patrick mumbled he had to go to the bathroom. My stomach dropped. "You're kidding me, right Patrick? You're kidding me. Are you kidding me, Patrick? You're kidding me, *right?*" (I hoped that if I repeated it enough, the contents of his bladder might magically evaporate.) Resigned to my sense of duty, I knew there was no way I could leave anyone from this bunch behind to do a bathroom run, which only meant one thing: I was going to have to remake the entire journey *in reverse*. Once again we assumed the position – arm-in-arm-in-wedgie – and began our descent. One. Step. At. A. Time.

When we finally made it to the first landing, I briefly stopped to take stock of the situation before moving on. However, Patrick had a more creative interpretation. On cue, he unzipped his pants, whipped out his business, and right there on the landing, in all its glory . . . he began to pee.

All at once, Emily dropped to her knees and began wailing, the pixie hood falling from her head into the wet puddle. Jane twisted a fistful of my Levi button-flies so tight they cinched around my crotch like a Speedo full of ball bearings. Meanwhile, the people around Patrick started screaming and pointing – but mostly just laughing. Anguished and embarrassed, I looked around helplessly and said, ". . . Does anyone have a cup?"

Taking pity, a scruffy-looking man wearing an Oakland A's cap and a Krazy Kat tattoo on his arm kindly dumped the remainder of his beer and handed it to me.

I poised the empty cup beneath Patrick gingerly.

And he filled it.

(Rumor has it if you look up the word "mortified" in the dictionary you'll find a full-page photo of my face from that exact moment.)

Needless to say, we didn't stay for the game. I got the distinct feeling that no one wanted us around much after that. Besides, the damn Padres lost anyway.

If this incident had happened to Grizzled or Frazzled, I've no doubt the story would've found itself pinned to their chest along with all the other on-the-job medals they amassed on a regular basis. But in my case it had a strikingly different effect. Instead of chalking it up to experience, the whole thing just made me feel . . . *sad*. Sad for the clients in Unit 2, sad for clients like them everywhere. They were a fundamental part of the sub-culture and they would never know it. I worried that this event would become stuck in my head as an ever-lasting image of all the

Patricks, Emilys and Janes in the world – just one, big, scorned mass of peeing, wailing, head-bobbing humanity – and there would be no way to change it.

But even more shameful, I couldn't deny the *fear* it instilled in me. Fear that I no longer had the sanctity of ITF to shield me, and that I could be called back to work in the units – to face all those horror stories head on – at any given moment. The truth is, I *did* want to help. Just not in that way. I was ashamed to admit the last thing I wanted was to *ever* have to work with that level of client again.

If there was ever a time to revisit my original game plan, it was now.

CHAPTER 13

SCHOOL DAZED

B Y THE FALL of 1985, the incident with Patrick aside, the culpability I carried for not yet returning to college made me reevaluate becoming a high school English teacher. I knew deep down it was time to get back on track. But another part of me wasn't ready to completely abandon Shepherd Hills – at least not just yet. So for the time being, I compromised. I took a job as a teacher's aide for the San Diego Union High School District, while still retaining part-time houseparent status at The Hills. I now officially had *two* jobs. Or as Anita wryly commented, "two feet planted firmly in separate graves."

I landed a position at the O'Malley School for the Creative and Performing Arts, a "magnet" high school that emphasized classes in Drama and Music. Thanks to my bachelor's degree, I was assigned to assist in a variety of English classes – most notably the one, single Creative Writing class. The position couldn't have been more perfect. A dream opportunity not only to get my feet wet at the high school level, but a chance to share the very same subjects I loved with the very student body I one day hoped to cultivate and educate; to teach all that I believed was good about the world by way of the written word. The only thing missing was Karen Valentine in a ponytail.

O'Malley was located in the Skyline District of San Diego known for its – as realtors commonly refer to it – "mixed" population. (Translation: poor and ethnic.) Adolescents who wanted to attend yet lived outside the area required special permission. Those who already lived in the area could attend regardless. Thus, a

CHALLENGED: A TRIBUTE

high percentage of poor black and Hispanic students – many with no interest in learning about the arts – sat in on classes. On the flip side, a handful of affluent white students from cities such as La Jolla, the Beverly Hills of the southern coastline, were bused in (or, more typically, drove to school in their own Porches, Beamers and Mercedes). This could have led to a potentially precarious student dynamic but, surprisingly, everyone got along fine. As it turned out there was no racial discourse – because if the students shared anything, it was the color of apathy.

Being a high school for the performing arts, there were no varsity athletics. No cheerleading squads. No debate teams. Not even a school newspaper. Instead, these kids were spoon-fed extra-curricular dreams of super-stardom, and any semblance of school spirit was outclassed by want of global adulation. As for the students who didn't care to act, sing, dance or play a musical instrument, Creative Writing, I learned, was essentially the final dumping ground.

At first I thoroughly enjoyed working with these "normal" kids in opposition to the clients. Working with teenagers always provides a pop-cultural bookmark in time. In 1985 *Miami Vice* was the trend for fashion with white linen blazers layered over tangerine T-shirts. *The Breakfast Club* spawned Judd Nelson wannabes and Molly Ringwald dress-alikes, and Janet Jackson filled the quad at lunchtime by way of boom-box bravado. But it didn't take long for me to become disenchanted with it all. The assignments, the school, the administration, and especially the students. I grew tired watching teachers spend the majority of class time power-struggling with everyone to sit down and be quiet. I lost faith in students who repeatedly churned out flabby Stephen King rip-offs, or tried to palm off Pink Floyd's *The Wall* as original poetry. I became disillusioned by over-crowded classrooms with kids who treated me kindly as an aide, but turned treacherous the minute the teacher stepped out of the classroom. I was appalled to discover the school's principal had no idea his own son was a known drug dealer – known by everyone *including* the teachers – yet no one dared say anything because the principal was more invested in appearances than reality.

Though there was only a 10-year age difference between myself and the kids, I could see that a formidable digression in scholarly evolution had taken place. Granted, selfishness is nothing new for teens – and each new adolescent *zeitgeist* exponentially grows more self-involved than the last. But the true revelation came with the discovery that the vast majority of kids *simply didn't want to learn*. What happened, I asked myself, between my generation and this one? Had I really been so out of touch?

The answer was yes. (Especially for people who use words like *zeitgeist*.) I realized I hadn't been the typical student at all. The comforts I'd felt in the rituals of school life were because I was the kid who buckled. Kept quiet. Attended class. Did my homework. Made decent grades. As it turned out, *typical* students were much different – they just didn't give a shit.

The same patience I had for my clients at Shepherd Hills escaped me at O'Malley. Purely out of spite, I took to calling each of these wasteful kids a "dit" (short for "diva in training") behind their backs, as opposed to my more motivated clients, the so-called "tards." In time, I began to look upon the dits with a mix of disgust, melancholy and regret. They had opportunities my clients never dreamed of, and they were willingly pissing them away, choosing instead to fantasize about Hollywood mansions and New York penthouses filled with free cars, cash and cocaine. Maybe a cross-section was lost somewhere in the mix; maybe some of them would actually become future actors, dancers, musicians, or perhaps even doctors, lawyers and a teacher or two. But I couldn't see them. All I could see were future alcoholics, spouse-abusers, and people destined to travel from street corner to street corner with a cardboard-sturdy promise to "work for food."

It shook me. I thought I'd had the calling, but I was wrong. The realization that there would always be kids who just didn't want help was enough for me to say *enough!* – especially to a gathering of what I ultimately considered unruly little shits. And that's when it hit me. Being a houseparent *already* satisfied my teacher instinct. Being a houseparent gave me small, manageable groups of people who at least *attempted* to give me their attention. It gave me people who actually *needed* to know the things I taught them to succeed in life. Not children weaned on instant gratification, demanding to be awarded simply for existing.

Eventually, I lost all desire to work with the dits. Instead, I wanted to teach life lessons. I wanted to counsel. I wanted to advocate. And I wanted to wake up in the morning and do it all over again. I'd already found my audience – I just hadn't realized it. God bless the American school teacher, I thought – because I knew then and there I could never be one.

But that's not what got me fired.

One morning, I was handed a stack of essays to review pertaining to the play *Cyrano de Bergerac*. As an aide my job was to correct and grade them for grammar. The topic of the assignment was innocent enough: *Do you think Cyrano is a noble character? Explain.*

After shuffling through a mixed batch of indifferent 9th-grade babble, I came across an essay by a young black student. Her opening argument read:

> *Why do Cyrano act the way he do? He should just be tellin Roxanna how he feel bout her. He should NOT be messin with no Christian.*

Now, I ain't never been one to insist on no proper use of English. But the concept of Ebonics begs a second gander. Since the mid-1970's Ebonics has been an on-again/off-again hot-button topic. And at O'Malley, with a black student majority of mixed social stature, it was real and it was substantial and, though it may have had its detractors, it had its place. Hell, even a couple kids on *The Cosby*

Show spoke it. But because I'd already renounced the dits, I just couldn't resist falling back on my jokey urges. In the margin I wrote my reply to her thesis:

Then there be no play.

For some reason the school drug dealer's father failed to appreciate my gift of irony.

And so the way of the future became a thing of the past. At O'Malley I'd crafted myself the mental image of a teacher who wanted to save those who, like me, considered themselves lost. But in actuality my days at Shepherd Hills had created a *better* image, designed to give guidance to those who would otherwise be lost without it. After leaving the school district, I never felt more alive by having one foot still in the grave at ITF Village.

I returned to ITF, reinstated at full-time status, with the plan to continue toward my teaching credential. Only this time it would *not* be in high school English. It would be in Special Education. Next semester. For sure.

PART III

WELCOME TO THE CLP– MAKE YOURSELF AT HOME (WILL YOU BE STAYING LONG?)

CHAPTER 14

1986– BIG BROTHER FINALLY BLINKS

ON FEBRUARY 14TH, Valentine's Day, Dawn rallied everyone into the rec room to share the big news. Shepherd Hills had received a grant to establish a new pilot program. It was to be located out in the community, four miles south of the main campus, in an apartment complex known as Spring Tree. Six clients from ITF would pair up two-by-two to share three 2-bed/2-bath apartments. This meant that each person would now have his or her *very own* bedroom and *very own* bathroom. The whole thing was slated to be up and running by June 1st, with Dawn heading things as department supervisor. It would be called the Community Living Program.

A fourth apartment, a one-bedroom studio, would be designated as a combination rent-free office and living quarters for one lucky "live-in manager." An assistant staff member would help fill the remaining coverage, but only one person would live there, working a four-days-on, three-days-off schedule to oversee the teaching of independent living skills and provide counseling, supervision and support. The job even came with its own pager.

They had me at "rent-free."

Yee-ha! *Rent-free!* Doing a job I already loved, *rent-free*. A long overdue venture into independence, *rent-free*. A personal haven where I could rekindle my writing , *rent-free*. I had no problem combining my work and living environment, as long as it meant the freedom of my own place – and the chance to finally escape the tyranny of my old man. Golden opportunities such as this don't fall into your lap for no reason. And though he and I would be separated by a buffer of only sixteen freeway minutes, that simple, one-bedroom studio would be an oasis of solitude.

More importantly, the live-in manager would also be . . . (wait for it) . . . *in charge.*

I immediately applied for the position and was ready to fight for it, tooth and nail. As it turned out, I didn't have to. No one else was even remotely interested. In fact, no one even applied for the *assistant* position. Much to my surprise, Dot, Anita and *all* of Shepherd Hills chose to remain right where they were, safe within their individual comfort zones. I would be going it alone.

Did I mention it was *rent-free?*

First came the planning stage. With just six openings, this meant three people's hopes for independence were destined to be crushed. When the time came for us to sit down and decide which six of the Notorious Nine would be leaving ITF and which three would be staying, it was done with quiet, serious professionalism. There was no room for personal feelings here, a realization that hounded us all too well.

We considered each client's formal diagnosis, annual progress, functioning-level and general attitude. We considered behaviors vs. skill levels. ADL's. Ability vs. motivation. Training retention. Growth and development. Medication regimes. Mobility skills. Community integration needs. Major health conditions. Client preferences. Family preferences. Likes. Dislikes. General comprehension. All things social, emotional, cognitive, communicative, vocational and educational. In short, potential.

Lastly, the X factor was considered – meaning we didn't know how this was going to work until we tried it. This was the first residential program designed on good intentions and crossed fingers. The Shepherd Hills Community Living Program was going to be a leap of faith.

When all was said and done, the following clients were picked to room together. They would be the ones to head up the new CLP:

Cole Petersen and Owen Van Winkle

Sammy White and Hughie Lamb

Holly Gross and Darlene Beaudine.

Cole had easily made the top of the list. Despite his hippie-dippy quirks, Cole's natural abilities and high score levels made him a houseparent's dream. From there the others fell naturally into place. It was a recipe with all the right ingredients for success. In theory, not much was really expected to change in the way of services other than the dynamics of the complex and the ever-widening road to liberation. But with this also came the burden of making it "out there."

The clients who didn't make the cut included Jim Livingston, Iggy Flynn and Jackie Chuckam.

Jim and Iggy were sure to be fine; neither of them indicated a strong desire to move or reason to mourn. Their world was innately flexible. To them, changes were a way of life; faces came and went, and every new face was an automatic friend. But then there was Jackie. There was no denying we all knew being left behind would hurt him.

Truthfully, Jackie simply was not ready to move. At best he had only "maintained" at ITF. But knowing all too well how poorly he responded to the departure of those who were familiar vs. the acceptance of new faces, this was going to be a tremendous test of Jackie's will. If I were in his position I'm not sure I could handle it. We could already foresee the transition period as being one of the hardest things Jackie would ever have to face.

Once the new Mighty Six had been chosen, I was informed the new CLP would be blessed with its own vehicle. This, of course, was a programmatic necessity shared by all the units for the purposes of doctor runs, errands and emergencies. Immediately, this sent a shiver down my spine because, by now, I'd grown familiar with The Hills' "hand-me-down" nature of filling in the budgetary gaps. I steadied myself. "You're not going to give us the Blue Beast, are you?"

"No," Dawn reassured me, "that'll stay with ITF."

"You mean The Hills is gonna give us our own new van?"

"Er . . . not quite," she smiled sheepishly.

"What, then?"

They gave us the goddamn Sunshine Van.

THAT OLD GUY WHO RIDES A RED BIKE

Jonathan "Jackie" Chuckam was famous. From the stalls of the Lakeside Rodeo to the shores of Mission Bay, Jackie Chuckam was known around San Diego County as "that old guy who rides a red bike." Early in his adult life, Jackie Chuckam had gone prematurely gray, making him the butt of chronic teasing by a lifetime of foster-home housemates. This, coupled with a steadfast distaste for any sort of personal grooming, often left him looking stubbled, gruff and primed for eating those who ventured too close beneath his bridge. But Jackie loved his vintage Hiawatha *Meteor Chief* – it was his confidant and best friend. And so, despite the pleas of the houseparents to take a little pride in his appearance, whenever he could, or just plain wanted to, Jackie would mount his faithful steed and ride across town. And ride and ride and ride.

Whereas Sammy knew the streets of San Diego by way of mass transit, Jackie knew the alleys, back roads, dirt roads and driveways, all by an intimate tangle of bike lanes, which led him to the fringes of the real world. There was hardly a time when Jackie wasn't seen by passing motorists as he investigated curiosities of the day. During the week, Jackie would make his way to local construction sites and inquire what was being built, then return and excitedly report his findings to Dawn. (*"That new b-b-building in Santee gonna be a p-p-pencil factory!"*) On weekends, his excursions ventured farther, over the Grossmont Summit, all the way to the San Diego shoreline, always looking to explore any unusual activity in the expanding neighborhoods, or simply spy on bikini-clad tourists thanks to year-round, sun-dappled weather. In the early evenings he'd park on the sloping hilltops overlooking Santana High School and watch the adolescent purity of football practice, secretly wishing he could've been one of them in his youth, a would-be All-State all-star, instead of segregated to the "slow" trailer clear across campus.

And as he'd pedal his way along the hot asphalt, shock of gray and white hair fluttering in the wind, you could hear the people say, "There goes that old guy who rides a red bike." For better or worse, Jackie was a local legend. It was his one and sacred form of escape; a secret code no one else could crack.

Two days after Dawn's announcement of the new CLP, each houseparent sat down with their respective clients and broke the news of who was scheduled to move and who would be staying behind. Sammy grinned with pride and insisted I repeatedly trade high-fives with him to mark the occasion. Owen, on the other hand, took the news more quietly than I'd expected. Not that he didn't appear happy, but rather oddly pensive. "Can I take all my stuff with me my brother gave me?" he asked.

"Of course," I said. "It'll be your apartment. You'll have your own bedroom and everything."

"My bird, too?"

"Of course."

Then there was Jackie. As I explained the decision for him to remain at ITF, noting and encouraging his future potential to join the next wave, Jackie simply hung his head and nodded. And nodded and nodded. Damn that Dawn! *She* should have broken the news to him, not me. She had the best rapport with Jackie, everyone knew that. Which is probably exactly why she delegated the task to me. Regardless, as I did my best to soft sell the news, it was obvious Jackie'd finally had enough. In mid-sentence he walked out on me, hopped on his bike and took off. I didn't even try to stop him.

For the next week or so, Jackie's daily rides became longer and more frequent. Most nights he'd miss dinner completely, cruising the streets till well after 10 p.m. when he wouldn't have to face Dawn or me. He even began to sneak out in the early morning, out past the back fence with a nod to the cows grazing on dead weeds, pushing his bike around the rear of the ITF complex, then making a hasty break for it, no regard at all for attending his day program. To hell with us, he just wanted to ride. No cares, no guilt, no new faces to get used to. Just escape. Again, I didn't try to stop him.

CHALLENGED: A TRIBUTE

Watching all this I felt I'd lost Jackie for good. Whatever headway I'd made over the last four years was now back to square one, to a time when Jackie The Giant Knife-Wielding Maniac wanted nothing to do with me.

Then one day the unexpected happened. Jackie came home – early. Riding up on his bike fragrant with body odor, I greeted him enthusiastically and, much to my surprise, Jackie greeted me back. Though his demeanor remained static and unmoved, Jackie nevertheless returned home agreeable to his daily responsibilities. Was this a new Jackie, ready to prove himself worthy of joining the new CLP? No, that would've been too much to ask for. Whatever the reason, I was happy to see the old guy back.

"Okay, so what do you want to do first," I asked leadingly.

"I dunno."

"I suppose you wouldn't want to take your bath, would you?"

No answer.

"No, didn't think so. Well, it's too early to start dinner . . . How about you dust the furniture?" At this point I was looking for something, anything, for Jackie to do that would keep him productive – furniture polishing was simply the first thing that sprang to mind. I handed Jackie a rag and the standard client troika of generic-brand cleaning products – a can of generic Endust, a can of generic Glade, and a bottle of generic 409. He took them from me and slowly began to remove random knick-knacks from the end table, exposing silhouettes of shiny wood outlined by a well-ignored layer of grime. Jackie Chuckam? Dusting the furniture? It was too good to be true. Better leave him alone so as not to pressure him, I thought.

"I'll check on you later, Jackie. Good job!"

Jackie shrugged, half-heartedly spritzing the polish. It was a grand sight to behold as I slipped out the door.

After finishing next week's menu with Sammy, I started back across the courtyard towards the office. Lounging on one of the rusty chairs next to the rec room pay phone was Cole, self-satisfied and smoking a cigarette. In the distance, Darlene was making her way toward Sammy's apartment. Cole shouted to her in a lewdly playful taunt. "Hey, Darlene! Your boyfriend wants to stick his dick up your butt!"

"*Oh, Gawd, Co-o-o-o-ole!*" Darlene cackled.

Isn't that sweet? I smirked to myself. These are the people we've chosen to represent Shepherd Hills in the community. The leaders of tomorrow. What's next?

Closer now, from Apartment #5 I heard a familiar squabbling. Owen was home and, for reasons unknown, yelling and cursing.

Knock, knock. "*Coming in.*"

I walked in and found Owen livid, in tears, hoarse from yelling. "*You did it on purpose!*"

Jackie was backed into a corner, wringing his hands. "Owen, p-p-please . . . I sorry."

"You're damn right you're sorry! You'll pay, you son-of-bitch!"

It was a role reversal unlike anything I'd seen before. Owen was ablaze while Jackie cowered from him, like a child about to receive a spanking.

"What the hell's going on here?!" I shouted.

"Look what he did! It's not fair!"

Pointing to his bird cage, Owen dragged me closer. There, lying motionless at the bottom, was Owen's parakeet.

I winced. "Aw, Jesus . . ."

"It was a accident . . ." Jackie pleaded.

"What happened?" I said, barely a whisper.

"I was c-c-cleaning and s-s-spraying this air f-f-freshener and I got t-t-too close to the cage. I didn't know . . . I didn't know . . ."

"What am I gonna tell my brother?" Owen whined.

"It was an accident, Owen," I said. "I'm sure your brother will understand."

"No, he won't!"

"I sorry, Owen . . . I s-s-sorry . . ."

"You bastard!" Owen yelled once more at Jackie. "You Nazi bastard!"

"Owen, stop it!" I asserted. "Jackie said he was sorry. We can get another bird. All of us together."

"No!" Owen insisted. "No! He killed him because he's jealous of me. I'm going to the Special Olympics in two weeks and my brother's gonna come see me. He's jealous 'cause my brother loves me and his parents *hate* him!"

Jackie bolted straight, a nerve struck. "Th-Th-That n-n-n-n-not t-t-t-t-true!"

"He just wants me to get in trouble."

"M-M-My f-f-father, f-f-father, f-f-father –" Jackie was now choking on his own spit.

"Owen, don't!" I begged.

But Owen was determined to twist the knife one last time. "His father never calls him because he doesn't *lo-o-o-ve* him."

And that was all it took.

The sleeping giant erupted, now rudely awakened.

"*EEEEEAAAAAAAAGGH!*"

Jackie plowed past me and into the bedroom, slapping the walls as he went. Fueled by sheer rage, he swept his mammoth, fisted arm across Owen's dresser, sending his roommate's stereo and family photos airborne. Smashing, pounding, shrieking. Jackie tore into every last one of Owen's greeting cards, postcards and Special Olympics certificates, ripping them down off Owen's half of the wall till it was as bare as his own.

"*AAAAAGH! . . . NYAAAARGH! . . . AAAAUUUUGH! . . .*"

CHALLENGED: A TRIBUTE | 147

My mind raced. What little I recalled from MAB training was lost in the chaos. But it wouldn't have mattered. Jackie's fury was too great – a runaway train on icy tracks. Instead, I put all my effort into shielding Owen in the corner, safe from harm's way. As the two of us looked on helpless, Jackie let go an anguished caterwaul and toppled Owen's massive TV to the floor with a sickening crash.

And then, there was silence.

Heavy breathing. Whimpers.

I looked to see Owen, quaking like a frightened animal. Then I looked to Jackie.

Jackie was gone.

The last I saw of him was his back as he stood on the pedals of his bike, hoofing and pumping up the driveway as fast as he could, across the parking lot, gone.

The police report indicated that Jackie had apparently ridden his bike into the crosswalk against the light, less than a mile from ITF Village. As he bore his way across the busy street, witnesses said a panel truck saw Jackie and stopped just in time. This blocked the view of a sedan passing on the truck's right, which met Jackie just as he cleared the truck's front end. He was knocked clear of the bike and flew twenty feet into the intersection. He landed on his head and was killed instantly.

Word spread quickly across the East County that "that old guy who rides a red bike" had died. Had Jackie been wearing his helmet, could this have been prevented? No one could say for sure. Three days later a service was held in the Shepherd Hills auditorium, normally reserved for Sunday church and Friday night dances. It was presided over by The Hills' chaplain, Rebecca Lloyd, a kind-hearted woman with a Lamb Chop sock puppet haircut. Somehow I managed to squeeze into an old dress shirt and black pants I hadn't worn since high school. It was the first time in a long time I showed up to work in something other than baggy jeans.

A number of individuals, clients and staff alike, took turns stepping forward to share their wishes and prayers for Jackie. Rebecca spoke of how God had "called Jackie home." Meanwhile, I stood in the back with nothing of value to say, hiding behind a pair of dark sunglasses. *Mother*fucker, *mother*fucker, *mother*fucker . . . were the only words that rang through my mind. *If only I hadn't given him that motherfucking air freshener. None of this would have happened.* I never shared that part of the story with anyone. It was a measure of guilt I was burdened to carry alone.

As the service drew to a close, those in attendance moved onto the front lawn of Shepherd Hills where Rebecca and a few community volunteers handed out balloons on strings to the crowd, instructing each of us to hold onto them tightly. The chaplain then asked if there was anyone else who wanted to share a few final words about their good friend Jackie. Most heads turned to look at Dawn, who up till now hadn't said a word. It was clear she was on another plane. Dawn lidded her eyes, struggling to helm her love for Jackie in quiet, dignified silence, with volumes to share but not the capacity to share it.

Rebecca then gestured for Owen to stand next to her. "Owen has requested to recite a prayer," she said. "As he does, we'd like to ask each of you to release your balloon."

With a gentle count of three, the entire crowd lifted their balloons high and watched the glorious, multicolored wave float into the sky, floating and dancing and drifting free over the hills of East County, with a casual wink to wind-torn clouds, almost too beautiful to bear. Owen's voice was profoundly human.

May I be no man's enemy.
May I never devise evil against any man.
May I love, seek and attain only that which is good.
May I never fail a friend in danger.
May I always keep tame that which rages within me.
May I always know good men and follow their footsteps.

Neither Jackie's mother nor father attended the service.

Back at ITF Village the atmosphere remained somber. The emotional fulfillment of the balloons had given everyone a way, both tangible and symbolic, to say good-bye to Jackie. And yet, as the clients mourned and sobbed the remainder of the day, not one allowed Owen to hug them. Not one offered him any comfort, no matter how hard the tears coursed down his cheeks. I remembered what Michelle told me my first day on the job. Amazing, I thought. Nobody really did like him.

The next day the question arose of how Jackie was to be buried. He'd had no burial plans that we were aware of. What do you do in a case like this? The death of a client was something I'd not foreseen. Immediately, the staff volunteered to pitch in for burial costs. But it wasn't our decision to make. Not long after, Dawn informed us that burial was going to be handled by Jackie's parents. As is customary, responsibility legally goes to the next of kin. Regardless of our desires to help, we were out of the loop and unceremoniously disregarded. It was then Dawn informed us Jackie's parents had chosen to bury him indigent. It was the least expensive method available and thus their best option. Jackie's ashes would be disposed of at sea. No markers, no site to visit, no place to lay flowers.

My co-workers and I were stunned. How *dare* they?! How *dare* his fucking parents treat their son this way? Casting his ashes to sea just to save a few dollars? The thought of it was sickening. But Dawn reaffirmed there was nothing we could do. Jackie was gone; his bed stripped, his chart and all identifying information matter-of-factly gleaned and sent to the records room for filing. Remember him with good thoughts, Dawn advised us. Go to the beach now and then and say hi.

And be sure to give Owen a hug once in a while, too.

"I'm not crazy about reality, but it's still the only place to get a decent meal."
– Groucho Marx

Cole Petersen enjoyed a colorful variety of *nom de plumes*. "John Lennon," "Joe Cool," "Mr. Blue" (on the days he wore all blue), and my personal favorite, "Captain Trippendicular." Most people define their lives using other people's terms. But not Cole. And with less than a month to go before the established CLP move date, it would cost him dearly.

It started innocently enough with an episode of bowel incontinence. One afternoon, Cole took a nap and woke up with a smeared mess in his pants.

"John Lennon pooped his pants!" Sammy shouted, bursting into the office with life-or-death urgency. Minutes later I was there to offer help as Cole cleaned himself up. Contrite and embarrassed, Cole refused any assistance and shut the bathroom door in my face. With misguided humor, I quipped through the door that maybe he should "knock off the tofu and bean sprouts."

"I don't eat that shit!" he snarled, unamused.

And nothing more was said about it that day.

The next afternoon Cole's day program called to report an incident. Apparently, Cole punched another client in the throat when that client cut in front of him in the snack line. Rough justice or not, this was unlike Cole and deemed inappropriate. Any further violations like it and Cole would be suspended for two days.

The very next afternoon at program, when Cole was asked to wait to collect his art and ceramic supplies, he threw one of his crutches at a client in a wheelchair, gashing the client's leg. It was seen as "willful aggression." Suspension was enacted immediately.

For the next forty-eight hours Cole hid in his apartment. His stereo blasted day and night. He began to break selected records and chuck the pieces out into the courtyard. In an effort to lighten the situation, when he first tossed out *The Best of the Cowsills* I joked that he'd done us all a favor. But by the time he got to *Abbey Road*, we all knew something major was wrong. He refused any attempts at skill programming, and traditional behavior interventions proved fruitless. Instead, Cole responded with threats to hurt people and episodes of tossing furniture. Surpassing even Billy Mattila for sheer rebellion, we watched helplessly as Cole demoted himself from Captain Trippendicular to Sergeant Fuck You.

The whole thing came as a complete shock. No one was prepared for it – least of all Dawn. At first Dawn was determined to give Cole every last chance – including augmented psychotropic drug therapy and PRN medications to sedate him. (PRN meds were meds to be given "as needed.") But instead, they had the opposite effect. Cole became wired. He didn't sleep, didn't eat, and when he finally emerged from his apartment, he began to drag himself around the courtyard, wobbling and thrashing unsteadily atop those two metal sticks, weirdly obsessed with the false fact that Shepherd Hills was going to close down. "*I have to work to make The Hills money so we don't get kicked out!*' I attempted to reassure him this wasn't true, only to be met with shouts of disbelief. When I tried to redirect him back to the things he enjoyed like music and art, he poised a single crutch at me like a samurai sword.

"Get away from me, man. I'll mess you up good – I swear!"

He didn't need to warn me twice.

On the third morning, Cole abruptly announced he no longer wanted to move to the CLP. Dawn counseled him at length about reaching his potential beyond ceramics and groovin', but Cole remained adamant. Then, that night, he did something I didn't see coming. As I passed him in the courtyard – steering well clear of his swinging radius – Cole suddenly cowered dramatically and shouted, "Don't hit me, don't hit me *again*!" Startled, I approached to ask what the heck he was talking about – which sent him curling into a ball on the cement.

"*DON'T HIT ME!*"

I immediately retreated to the office where I found myself earnestly trying to reassure Dawn and my co-workers that I never touched the man. Although they said they believed me, I was still regarded with a disturbing share of raised eyebrows. I didn't sign on for this, I thought. What do you do when a client *lies* about you? None of us could see or feel or hear the turmoil that was going on inside of his head. And simply saying "he's retarded" is no justification for defense.

Luckily, if not sadly serendipitous, Cole began accusing *everyone* of hitting him, which validated my innocence. And though it gave me a strangely comforting sense of relief, there was no denying the inescapable hopelessness we *all* felt as we watched Cole burrow deeper and deeper into his own inner hell.

By the fourth day, Cole started hobbling around the back parking lot, peering into car windows. When I asked him what he was doing, he said he was looking at the designs of the patterns in the upholstery. "What's wrong with that?" he challenged. "I have the right to do that, *don't I?*" But The Hills' employees weren't so disposed to advocate client rights. They didn't appreciate Cole "stalking" their cars. Curious, I asked him what exactly he saw in the patterns.

"I see salad dressing," came the bizarre reply.

We briefly thought maybe Cole had somehow, somewhere, gotten hold of some hallucinogens in an attempt to try and emulate his passion for '60s folklore, but an emergency blood panel proved him clean. So then, what was it? Were the expectations of the CLP transition simply too much for him to handle? Dawn sat alone at her desk with her head in her hands. "*Why*, Cole?" she asked, as if he were there to provide an answer. "Why *now*?"

Day five, all those sinless episodes of *My Three Sons* and *Leave It To Beaver* I'd invested in as a child didn't prepare me for what came next. Behind our backs, Cole ventured into the residential streets just outside Shepherd Hills and dared wend the same primrose paths as Chip and Ernie and Wally and the Beav. Only Cole's path didn't lead him to the nearest sand lot or malt shop; instead, he tried to touch two little girls on their way home from school in a place where little girls should never be touched. Though they were easily able to outrun him, the creepy *clack-clack* of his crutches trailing them from behind was enough to place a terrified call to 911.

When the police returned Cole to The Hills, Dawn – who'd always had a good rapport with local law enforcement – was able to talk them into letting it slide. After all, he wasn't a criminal, just "*curious*," just "*confused*," just "*mentally challenged*." The two cops went for it, leaving Cole in Dawn's custody – just as innocently as returning a naughty child home to his mother for a good scolding.

As soon as they left, Dawn turned to Cole to deliver that scolding. He heaved a patio chair at her, missing her head by inches.

"*I am bloody Jesus!*" he screamed.

That's when Dawn called County Mental Health.

Cole stood in the courtyard flowerbed, shouting in protest, waving and threatening to hit people with his crutches. He'd become, by all intents, a one-man '68 Chicago Convention riot. All that was missing was the tear gas.

In the midst of the mayhem, I ran to meet the ambulance at the main campus gate to forewarn them about Cole's aggressive condition. Within moments, flashing lights barreled down upon me as I flagged them to a hard stop. I immediately launched into a frantic spiel, defining for them how to do their job (which I'm certain they greatly appreciated).

"Just tell us where he is," the driver said flatly.

At that, I hopped in the back of their van. My heart pumped furiously as I guided them down the driveway into the back lot, all the while continuing to spew forth instructions on how they needed to be ready, that Cole was combative, that they might even – "*get ready, now, I'm not kidding*" – have to *restrain* him.

As we drove up the ITF driveway, a small mob stood interlocked in a circle just outside the rec room the way kids encircle a playground fight. Holy crap, I thought, who did Cole attack this time? Are they okay? Is anybody hurt? *We gotta stop this!* That's when the mob parted to reveal Cole . . . lying on the grass, all alone, snoring peacefully. Apparently, five days' worth of PRN meds and pure exhaustion had finally taken their toll.

The two ambulance medics eyeballed me with a smirk. It didn't matter when I tried to explain that Cole *had* been out of control – the pair simply, mechanically, lifted him onto a gurney like a wad of crumpled Kleenex, slid him through the back doors of their van, exchanged a few why-and-wherefore words with Dawn, and drove away.

That night, the courtyard went quiet. No more stereo, no more angry shouts, no more creepy *clack-clack*.

Everything happened so suddenly, there hadn't even been time to contact Cole's family. Ultimately, that job was left to his social worker. It didn't take long afterward for it to become official: Cole had suffered a psychotic break. He would not be returning to ITF Village anytime soon. And he certainly would not be moving with us to the new CLP.

The meltdown of Cole Petersen was so unexpected, so disturbingly random, it capsized our entire workplace. Not one of us had seen it coming. What's more, no one could comprehend *why* it had come. Was it a bad side-effect to meds? A fit of separation anxiety? Destiny? Perhaps Hughie Lamb surmised it best as the ambulance drove away:

"Dat hippie *crazy.*"

That hippie crazy had been our number one pick to do the Community Living Program proud. Besides his potential for success, everyone *liked* Cole. And for that reason alone I would miss him. But there was still no getting around the fact that we'd lost our best prospect, our golden boy. Suddenly, just a couple weeks shy of the move date, the highly-anticipated CLP project found itself one very important client short of a green light. Losing Cole was like suffering a small explosion that left a gaping hole in our own little Walden II.

After all that happened, I began to reevaluate things. What exactly was I to make of our mission to provide "quality of life?" Did these people really *want* to move, or had they just been taught to think it was something they *should* do? How natural was their quest for independence? Was it something they desired, or had they simply been conditioned by the concept of normalization? Did they even understand what the word "independent" meant? Did I?

An emergency staff meeting was called.

Dawn gathered all the houseparents from all three shifts. The agenda: To brainstorm a way to *save this project.* Moving ahead with a one-bed opening was proposed, but immediately dismissed. In order to implement the program, the grant required a minimum of six clients. Asking Regional Center to fill the position with an outside referral was also rejected, as it could prove too risky to introduce a new, unknown personality into the mix at this stage. So then, what was the solution? That's when I said:

"Why not move Jim?"

(It was here in the conversation I was forced to wait for the laughter to die down.)

"I'm serious," I said.

"But he can't talk," Dot said.

"No, but he can *communicate,*" I shot back. "People who can't talk or see or hear live on their own all the time. How are they so different?"

"C'mon," Anita tossed in. "Can you imagine James going to the store by himself? Or even catching the right bus?"

"In time, sure," I said. "So I might have to go with him at first. So I might have to go with him a *lot.* He learned how to dress himself every day, didn't he? Bathe himself? Even if it's by rote, why can't he learn to shop and clean an apartment and pay bills – by habit?"

CHALLENGED: A TRIBUTE

I continued my bleeding-heart tirade, taking jabs at the concepts of "Normalization" and "What Are We Here For, Anyway?" I scolded my fellow co-workers for dwelling on what Jim *couldn't* do, rather than what he *could* do. It's not that I professed to know Jim better than they did, but something told me there was more going on behind those sheepdog bangs of his than meets the eye. Besides, *I* was the one slated to be the live-in manager. Ultimately it was my ass on the line, not theirs.

Up to this point Dawn hadn't said anything. I met her eyes with a surge of enthusiasm. "Dawn, you *know* Jim's percentages are just as good as Hughie's. Doesn't he at least deserve a chance?" It was another TV movie-of-the-week moment in the making. The only thing missing was a close-up on Jim's crooked grin as he crossed the finish line dead last-but-proud.

Dawn's lip curled a half smile. "Actually, I'm thinking it might not be a bad idea."

And so it was decided. Jim Livingston would round out the CLP pilot team. Jim Livingston, an otherwise easily-dismissed pawn now elevated to the rank of rook. Suddenly, I felt like Bobby Fischer squatting before a novelty chess board of slightly damaged pieces, contemplating his endgame technique. All I had to do now was make the first move.

Then I remembered. I never learned to play chess.

CHAPTER 15

NORMALIZATION NATION

"**YOU'RE** *WHAT?!*"

My father's face lost all color the day I broke the news that I was moving out.

The old man was speechless. No more accusations of financial affliction. No more verbal whipping post. No more "you're lucky to be living here." The coop was about to be proverbially flown. I honestly don't think he ever thought he'd see the day. I was certain I *never* would.

And still, the only response my pop could muster was: "Who's gonna cut the fucking grass?"

Throughout my whole childhood my father remained a confusing, snarled knot of provider, role model and opportunistic monster. It wasn't until I grew old enough that everything would finally begin to untangle and I would come to a simple, sudden insight: *The less I saw of my old man, the better.* Working for Shepherd Hills afforded me that very wish. Whereas most people long to hear the five o'clock whistle so they can rush home to loved ones, I inevitably found myself drawn toward those same creature comforts as far away from Dad as I could get. In other words, home became work, and work became home. And though I fought endless guilt over leaving my mother behind with Mr. Personality, she assured me she would be all right. In some ways I even hoped that maybe the two of them would rekindle whatever they had when first married now that the kiddies were gone. But I suppose parents just don't see the world through the same rose-colored specs as their children, no matter how old either generation grows.

Maybe I should've been more considerate of my father's disposition, but the truth is I no longer gave a damn what he thought. In my mind I'd already given up on him because, in my imagination, I'd never really accepted him as my father at all. I gave up on him the day he missed my high school graduation, opting instead to stay home to watch a double-header on TV. I gave up on him every time he forgot my birthday and then stupidly laughed about it. I gave up on him the day he told me that the world wouldn't miss me when I was gone. I gave up on him the very first moment I felt his fist in anger. I'd already given up on him *over and over* again – but just never fully estimated the worth.

In the special-needs field, for those clients who are able, a move to an apartment, even a supervised one, is seen as an *"age appropriate"* step towards independence. But I discovered that age appropriateness transcends well beyond those with cognitive challenges. Standing side by side with my clients, I began to appreciate a sort of camaraderie. After all, this was the first major move – for *all* of us. *Our* first apartment. *Our* first shared taste of independence – that is, if independence can indeed be shared. This move was the chance to explore our place in the world; to finally take ownership of our lives.

My stuff was packed and ready to go in less than two hours.

SPRING TREE, THE PLACE TO BE!

On June 1, 1986, the Shepherd Hills' newly-prized pig at the fair – otherwise known as the Community Living Program – was let loose from the barn. Ready or not, the Mighty Six had been winningly coached that living independently was their destiny. Independence! The single greatest buzzword known to the D.D. sub-culture. And so the exodus lumbered onward. After three days of furniture dollying, pizza delivery, sore backs and a disgruntled Shepherd Hills maintenance crew who complained they had better things to do like unclogging toilets, the moves were completed.

The Spring Tree apartment complex was kin to every other Southern Californian family complex – a standard series of beige-on-brown stucco buildings, rec areas and laundry rooms broken up by patches of lawn and curvy cement walkways, playground equipment, and a pool. It many ways it was Shepherd Hills' architectural cousin, without the locked gates.

Much to everyone's surprise, Dot volunteered to take charge of furnishing the clients' new digs with economical elegance. All of the furniture was purchased at a warehouse outlet just north of the Mexican border, custom-made to suit our miniscule budget, while all the accessories came by way of Target and K-Mart. By the time everything was functionally-if-not-fashionably furnished, each place began to look like a home anyone could be proud of, right down to your basic newlywed sets of kitchen cutlery, toiletries and linens.

But where Dot truly shined was in finding a theme to go with each apartment. Sammy and Hughie's homestead took on a Western theme, complimented by throw pillows of sage and muddy brown, and a few panoramas of Sedona from the local swap meet. Darlene and Holly were invited to live in an English tea party. (Amazing what a few doilies can do, I thought.) With a small tea cart for their living room end table, it became the perfect spot for Darlene to lay her Chuck E. Cheese cap after a hard day's work. Lastly, Jim and Owen bagged themselves a duck hunter's theme, with soft marshy tones and oak-framed pictures of mallards gracefully in flight. Additionally, tending to Owen's personal well-being, anything that hadn't been destroyed by Jackie was replaced by his brother with something just a little bigger and a little better, such as a big*ger* big-screen TV and a high*er* high-tech stereo.

Then came the *clients'* turn to decorate.

A fistful of nails and thumbtacks were equally distributed to readjust, re-measure and re-hang a multitude of personal tchotchkes including Special Olympics ribbons, merits of perfect day program attendance, family photos of relatives both dear and unknown, birthday cards, a poster of Heather Thomas (Sammy's) and a poster of Laurel and Hardy (mine). By the same token, Hughie's bedroom became a showcase for his one, true talent: do-it-yourself scenic hook rugs depicting everything from mountainscapes to puppy dogs to the Golden Gate Bridge.

The only exception was Jim. He was more than happy to leave his *Star Wars* paraphernalia behind to embrace the aesthetics of Target and K-Mart. Jim loved his new tasteful pictures of waterfowl. He loved his soft new bath towels and clean, new, germ-free toothbrush cup. He was delighted to decorate his new apartment in something fresh, rather than something Yoda. I took it as a true sign of maturity and growth. I'm certain Jim knew he was on his way to better things.

That night, I felt exactly how Jim must've felt. It was well after midnight, but still I giddily wandered every inch of the 545 square feet of my apartment-*my* apartment-*MY* apartment. Life stretched before me, a vast, unexplored continent of abandon. While The Hills had furnished the necessary office equipment, *I* was left to furnish the "live-in" coordinates on my own. No matter. It was a small price to pay for freedom. I spent the entire first night shifting and re-shifting what few sticks of used furniture I was able to scrounge – one worn-out mattress, one dinged-up dresser, one pitted nightstand, one sagging sofa, and one thrift-store portable TV, complete with rabbit ears – wandering and giggling brazenly at the prospect of making myself a peanut butter and jelly sandwich chased by a shot of tequila, wandering and admiring my beloved poster of Laurel and Hardy from every possible angle, wandering and daydreaming of all that was yet to come, all the potential bestowed upon that celebrated rite of passage known as "the first apartment."

Growing up, straying from rental unit to rental unit, my old man never once allowed us to turn the heater on at night. The highest our thermostat ever read was

OFF. "Kee-ryst, why do youse need the heater on?" Pop would bellow. "That's what *blankets* are for!" That night, I purposely cranked the heater in my new apartment up to 85 degrees. I awoke the next morning drenched in sweat, my head pounding in agony from breathing in a full night's worth of dry, stuffy, hot air.

I never felt so refreshed.

With Jim's unforeseen change in status, this meant the mass migration to the CLP had left one last chess piece back in the box. Alfred Forrest "Iggy" Flynn was left behind to pass both expertise and wind upon a new generation. Once the familiar faces of ITF moved out, a new group of dream-chasers rotated up from Unit 8 to replace them. A new group of gawky gaits, drooping smiles and challenged temperaments who had proven to be cognitively ready to endeavor a "less restrictive" setting, eager for the chance to learn how to live independently. But more than that, as far as this new group of clients was concerned, living in ITF meant you had to be *smart*. And the fact that Iggy *already* lived there made him, in their eyes, King of Smarts. Long live the king.

Meanwhile, being that I was the only staff member to make the move to the CLP, Dawn quickly hired a new worker to assist me. Irma Fritts was a second-generation empty nester, meaning she had now seen both her children and grandchildren grow up and move out. The best thing I can say about Irma is that her heart was in the right place. Unfortunately, it was buried deep within 300 pounds of flesh. Irma possessed the kind of body an insult comic would personally invite to sit down front at one of his concerts, and then mercilessly fire into with a barrage of time-honored fat jokes. It was a girth that caused her to move and think slower than a turtle with a head cold. At the end of her shift, she would sit for two hours charting the day's data and progress notes. Not a day went by that didn't start with questions about her routine or end with complaints about her iron-poor blood with an iron-poor voice – a drawling, nasal monotone vexingly reminiscent of Jon Lovitz's "Annoying Man" from *Saturday Night Live*.

But the most frustrating quirk Irma possessed was that she always started a conversation in the middle of a sentence – typically a complaint of some sort – and you'd have no idea what she was talking about. Perhaps this anecdote characterizes Irma best:

One evening we were sitting in my apartment-slash-office and the phone rang. Irma had been waiting for a call back from one of The Hills' nurses so she could get approval to give Holly some Tylenol. When she answered the phone, she immediately began talking mid-sentence.

". . . in her wheelchair and the pedal came loose and it fell off on her other foot and she started to cry and I told her to be careful but she didn't and she never is and I said –"

Suddenly, she stopped. There was a moment of silence as Irma listened to what the person on the other end of the line was saying – to which came Irma's testy and offended reply:

"I *AM* a staff person."

"Why Be Normal?"
– popular bumper sticker from the 1980's

The CLP was born as a microcosm of hope and optimism. Once the six newcomers settled in, I knew the smells of burnt toast, sweaty sneakers, cigarettes and sex would follow soon enough. And even though we were intermittently displaced by the commonwealth of yowling children, bickering spouses, laundry room slobs, nosy solicitors, and dubious Dumpster divers, we did our best to make Spring Tree our home.

In the beginning, my apartment-slash-office was more office-slash-apartment. It was the place the clients came to by default whenever they had a problem, a question, a concern –

> STEVE (*sighs tiredly*): What is it this time, Darlene?
> DARLENE (*panicky*): I can't find my special, one-year anniversary Chuck E. Cheese pin! Should I call 911?

– needed attention, craved comfort, or simply had an urge to talk. To them, my place was a safe haven from self-dependence. And to them, I became a peer. Head peer to be sure, but still a peer. I had to be careful not to assimilate into their world – while fostering their assimilation into the "real" world. As a newly appointed Community Living Counselor, it fell upon me to helm the clients through the unstable waters of the community – and hope the community would excuse their wake.

At first there was a natural honeymoon period; the clients did their own laundry, took their own meds, got to work by themselves. It appeared ITF had been a success. The clients had actually *learned* the basic sensibilities of independence – at least as much as they'd been allowed to. Each individual received a monthly payment from the state called Supplemental Security Income, which guaranteed just enough to cover their rent and expenses, and each individual was accountable for the upkeep of his or her apartment. Meanwhile, it was up to me to ensure all the bills got paid on time, all the necessary doctor appointments were scheduled and attended, all the offers for "free credit cards" were intercepted and found their way into the trash, and all the remaining gaps of everyday living were filled in responsibly. Despite my routine dealings with Irma's not-so-quick wit, the job felt like it was heaven sent.

Our initial strategy was not to lump the clients together in one apartment building and risk being branded "the Retard Annex." Instead, we spaced everyone out amongst the complex to help ease the sting of osmosis into normal society – for *both* sides. I knew darn well going in that the other tenants in the complex, my age or older, had grown up during a time when the idea of allowing a retarded person to live next door was unthinkable. The best way to help educate the community about its new neighbors was for us to first try and meet *their* standards.

Still, the past few years as a houseparent had caused my personal views to change from feeling self-conscious about the clients to believing that the general population needed them. Society, I felt, *needed* the clients as a testament, not only to the importance of communal affiliation, but to the power of transformation. Not that I was asking people to change their minds about disabilities, but I did hope they might change their minds about themselves. I hoped that we could create an opportunity by way of disability for others to express their caring, compassion, respect and nobility of manner.

(Then again, maybe I was hoping for too much.)

CHAPTER 16

PEOPLE LIKE THIS SHOULDN'T BE ALLOWED TO LIVE ON THEIR OWN

D ARLENE BEAUDINE CARRIED a dual diagnosis of mild mental retardation and OCD – a fact that had never been of major concern back at ITF. But changing the environment, changing the "playing field," brought an entirely new set of rules and regulations, of rights vs. responsibilities.

Obsessive Compulsive Disorder presents itself as *"recurrent, persistent obsessions, compulsions, or repetitive behaviors that one feels he or she must complete."* Every once in a while to manage her anxiety, one of the rituals Darlene liked to fulfill was to dance naked in front of her mirror with her fingers twinkling above her head in a frenzied, moose-horn manner. No musical accompaniment. Just bouncing and jiggling and twinkling. It afforded her a certain hypnotic calming effect. An "I'll-show-you-mine-if-you-show-me-yours" alliance meant for one.

To further understand the Full Darlene, it's important to remember the sheer, how should I say this? . . . "buoyancy" that was granted her. Darlene was extr*eeee*mely well-endowed. We're talking enough to feed a family of five in one sitting.

I think I've made my point.

Soon after Darlene moved to Spring Tree, she subsequently discovered that, at night, the indoor reflection of her bedroom window doubled nicely as a mirror – a mirror that nicely reflected her doubles. It didn't take long for word to spread to all the little boys in the nearby buildings about the lady in apartment "42-D" – kiddie code for the size of her chest. Every night, after dinner, a horde of curious hormones would gather outside Darlene's window to watch the free show. None of the boys realized she was developmentally disabled, nor did they care. To a male adolescent, gazongas are gazongas are gazongas – and *free* gazongas are the best gazongas of all.

I think I've made my point.

Ah, but all good free shows eventually come with a price tag. Soon enough, one of the kids' mothers complained to the apartment manager, and the manager complained to me. The night I received a phone call about Darlene came as a shock to say the least.

"She's doing *what*?!"

Grudgingly having to forgo the season premiere of *Alf*, I set my Panda Inn take-out Orange Chicken aside, cinched up my sweats, and hot-footed it over to Darlene's. As I rounded the corner to her building, I spied a small platoon of pubescent tally whackers crouching stealthily amongst the hedges, giggling giddily as only a young penis can, gazing hungrily as if Darlene were dangling two ham sandwiches in front of Mama Cass. Suddenly, one of them saw me and shouted, "Guys – busted!"

Whoosh! – into the night they scattered.

I sighed and re-cinched my sweats. No denying it; it was obvious the moment called for a serious sit down. I entered the apartment and trudged past the tea doilies, into Darlene's room.

For this one I was on my own. I wasn't quite sure how to handle it, but I knew the situation required immediate attention. For the next half hour I explained to Darlene, oh so delicately, that it was okay to dance naked in front of the window if that's what she really liked to do. *But*, I told her, she also needed to be respectful of her neighbors. I walked over to the window to demonstrate. "The next time you want to dance in front of your window," I said, "just close the curtains." In order to drive my point home, I physically *closed the curtains* at the same time I said "close the curtains." Visual aids are vital in teaching things to people with developmental disabilities, and in this case black and white had to be midnight and blizzard. "Okay?"

Darlene watched me the entire time. I could see that her grasp was keen and clear. As I finished the night's lesson on the responsibilities of privacy, she nodded and acknowledged me in a jovial, sing-songy voice. "Okaaaaay!"

Well.

The next night I got another call. It was the manager. Can you *please* do something about Darlene? Once again, I threw on my sweats, jammed on my Reeboks, rounded the corner and the kids scattered. Once again, there was Darlene, shimmying and twinkling in the window. Only this time something was different. Darlene was now standing naked at the window – with the curtains drawn *behind* her. This time she'd positioned herself *between* the window and the curtain, dancing and bouncing and smiling to beat the band.

It took me a moment to appreciate it, but I had to hand it to Darlene. After all, she *did* close the curtains like I'd asked her to do. Who was I to fault her?

Once again I spoke to Darlene and, in the end, it was agreed that if she wanted to watch herself dance naked, it was probably best to do it in front of the bathroom mirror the way she used to do at ITF – behind closed doors.

"Okaaaaay!"

Back in my apartment I didn't know whether to laugh or sigh. The entire affair only reinforced the concept of how easily instructions – no matter how well-intended – can often become lost in translation by a client and taken literally. It revealed to me how functionally stalled the clients could still be while pretending to live the lives of independent adults – no matter how innocently they miscalculated their choices.

I realized then that if I hoped to survive in the field, this concept would need to remain in the forefront of my counseling methods.

> *CHARLES BUSHMAN: So, you were out in the world, huh? What was it like?*
> *KARL CHILDERS: It was too big.*
> *– scene from* **Sling Blade**

The final months of 1986 saw further tests of new-found freedom. There was the time instead of paying his phone bill, Sammy added the Playboy Channel to his cable subscription because it was his *right*, as he firmly proclaimed. And there was the time we took the whole bunch to Mission Beach Park for the day, and Owen ditched us to go buy beer because it was his *right* as he, too, firmly proclaimed.

Regardless of trial and error, it really should've come as no shock that once the honeymoon period was over, certain matters would spark, smolder and scorch the veneer of the dream, as I found myself putting out countless fires. Fires like spending grocery money on candy and Cokes. Stealing from roommates. Cutting day program to hang out at the transit center. Renting porno tapes from the local video store, and then losing them. Once I even spotted Darlene on the Fletcher Parkway meridian, dancing that same frenzied, moose-horn jig – but by the time I hooked a U-turn to double back and stop her, she was gone.

In dealing with "developmental immaturity," it's clinically felt that: *clients require some measure of supervision because of their limited ability to foresee the consequences of their actions.* But to me, the follies of the Mighty Six were a sore indication of how each client, given total freedom, might develop their own street urchin code of ethics to *survive* in the community.

So I wondered. Would the outside world simply turn out to be too overwhelming to master and manipulate. Was it just "too big?"

All of this began to leave me with freshman doubts whether or not I could hack this job – or still wanted to. Nevertheless, pressing forward, the majority of our neighbors remained tolerant of the clients if not supportive – not to mention

CHALLENGED: A TRIBUTE | 163

accepting. (Just accepting the Sunshine Van into the parking lot was testimony enough.) This, in the face of unforeseen dangers, gave me renewed hope for 1987. Until the arrival of spring.

It happened on a Sunday morning, an otherwise typical springtime San Diego morning poised to greet pollen in the air and sunbeams piercing dark, leaden clouds. In the upstairs corner of Building 4, Jim lolled atop his bed jeering at the Padres on TV, while Owen was busy Windexing his little heart out. He'd already tackled his bedroom window, bathroom mirror, and even the chrome on the toaster. All that was left was the living room window. Determined to scrub every last bit of grime set deep in the corners so the sun could shine through, Owen the Crusty Fireplug, resourceful man that he was, climbed up onto the arm of the sofa and steadied himself against the glass.

The woman in the apartment below heard it all. The crash from Owen's arm as it punched through the windowpane in a *ba-room!* of thunder, the crash of the pane as it popped and shattered, the crash of Owen's body tumbling like a soft melon onto the upstairs deck. Instantly, the woman bolted from her apartment and vaulted upstairs to see what happened. She found Owen kneeling in blood, clasping his left arm with his right hand, pale as a ghost. When she asked him if he was all right, Owen removed his hand. His entire forearm was sliced clean from wrist to elbow, like a split fire hose. The woman turned as white as Owen and almost fainted.

Meanwhile, Jim emerged from his bedroom. He took one look at the broken glass, promptly yelled at Owen for breaking the window – "*Mo mah, muh-muhm!* . . . *You cwown!*" – and went back into his room.

Steeling herself, the woman shouted to her husband. Within moments, a towel found its way tightly around Owen's arm, Owen found his way to a hospital bed, and his arm found its way to just shy of a billion stitches.

Hospital rooms are always the same; sterile and white, permeated by the smell of rubbing alcohol, and never anything good on TV. Owen's expression had frozen into one of undying disbelief at what had happened to him; lost and bewildered, as if he'd taken a wrong turn somewhere on the path home. He was confused and for good reason. Why am I in this bed? Why is my arm bandaged and bound to this pole? Why are there tubes sticking in me and machines all around going beep-beep-beep? He would spend the next several days fading in and out of a pain-killing haze, listening to the doctors utter incomprehensible prattle like, *"There were a lot of nasty cuts – but no severed tendons, nerves or anything too vital"* and *"Quite a lot of blood lost, but he'll be okay."*

When I first arrived, Owen didn't say anything, didn't even grunt me a greeting. It was the quietest I'd ever seen him. Instead, he merely gestured to the bandaged mass suspended next to him with that same, unchanging expression, as if pleading for an answer. *Why did this happen to me?* The best I could do was take his good hand and give it a reassuring squeeze. I watched powerlessly as a single tear slid down his cheek, as untouchable as a shadow. Where was the fairness in all of this?

When Owen was released from the hospital, his brother requested an emergency staffing. Those present included Owen, his social worker, a nurse consultant, Dawn and me. Owen's brother, direct from Palm Springs, arrived 40 minutes late and insisted we restart the meeting from the beginning.

Hiram "Sonny" Van Winkle flounced into the CLP office-slash-apartment looking like a demented cherry parfait. He wore white canvas shoes with no socks, bright red linen cargo pants, a white linen blazer over a deodorant soap-pink T-shirt, and saucer-sized, red-tinted sunglasses that would've made Elton John retch in his prime, all crowned by a red fedora. (A-ha, I thought. Suddenly that magenta corduroy jacket makes perfect sense.)

Typically, at any support team meeting, surrounded by all the professionals who encompass their world, the client essentially sits in silence as their aptitudes are splayed across a table and their lives encapsulated in just under an hour. And yet, in a room full of family members and so-called experts, whenever there was a question of what a client needed, I found it amusing that all heads inevitably turned to the houseparent for an answer – the low man on the totem pole, King Lear's fool who ultimately provides the greatest insights, the lowest paid "professional" in the room.

However this meeting was different. It quickly became apparent that my opinions didn't matter. When I attempted to interject on Owen's behalf, his brother silenced me with dual ice picks thrown from icy blue eyes. But even more upsetting was seeing a side of Owen I'd never seen before. When Owen would try to speak, his brother would sternly sweep his hand across his own chin, and Owen would immediately stop talking. With that brief gesture, Owen's voice was denied.

After hearing the facts of the accident, Owen's brother stood and clutched his chest for effect. Taking full advantage of the spotlight, he stated he had come to the conclusion that community living and "*the normal grid*," as he called it, were *NOT* for his brother, and further declared he was *EXTREMLY* dissatisfied with the CLP.

"Can I come live with you in Palm Springs?" Owen asked hopefully.

Chin sweep.

"My poor brother could've been *killed!*" Sonny wailed dramatically. "Why was he allowed to climb on the sofa? Aren't you people paid to *watch over* him? To *take care* of him? Isn't that your *job*? Where the hell were the staff? *How could Shepherd Hills let this happen?!*"

In all my years with the special-needs field I'd harbored mixed feelings about family members. Some, like Sammy's parents, embraced him for who he was, while others, like Jim's, were just names on an admitting form. But most, like Owen's brother, remained a ghostly thorn in a counselor's side. Whether doting too much or loving too little, more often than not, parents and family members forced our clients to tolerate everything from mollycoddling to heartache. To be fair, I can't begin to profess what it must be like to have a child with mental retardation; the overwhelmed feelings of fright, uncertainty, isolation and guilt – that subject alone is worthy of countless volumes by families both accepting and distraught. But that didn't excuse siblings like Sonny Van Winkle. He represented those who felt it their undeniable right to tell us how to do our jobs, and the entitlement to point fingers.

Dawn offered the reality of the situation; the fact that by living independently, Owen was now responsible for himself in new and different ways. Staff were no longer there 24/7. The independence of "the normal grid" comes with the dignity of risk – and accidents are something no one can dare foresee. Unfortunately, these were not the answers Owen's brother wanted to hear.

"*Sis*ter," he said cattily, "there is *nooo* dignity in almost *dyyyyying.*"

And then, the damndest thing happened. After a performance worthy of a front row ticket, Hiram "Sonny" Van Winkle collapsed back into his chair and anchored his chin firmly in his hand. "Oh, what the hell," he said with a puckered grin. "I sup*pooose* he can stay."

The rest of us exchanged dumbfounded looks.

"Just so long," Sonny re-ignited, "that *IIIII* can take him until he recuperates, and *IIIII* feel he's well enough to return. Naturally, I'll pay for you to hold his bed."

"Fine," Dawn agreed. Anything to shut him up.

What the hell just happened? I wondered. Had all this been just a crazy excuse for Owen's brother to audition for Diva of the Year? Who was this bizarre, gaudy man that seemed to command so much power? I'll tell you who he was. He was The Brother. And I was just the houseparent. And that's all I was allowed to know. In that moment I had to consider, maybe there was good reason for Owen's egocentric quirks after all.

Sonny and Owen embraced heartily, and Sonny smiled as if posing for a full-page spread in *Variety.* I, for one, couldn't wait for the *faaaaab*ulous reviews.

The following week a one-pound box of Russell Stover chocolates (with the price tag still on it) arrived at Owen's first floor neighbor's apartment, accompanied by a simple thank-you card signed, "Mr. Sonny Van Winkle."

That's it? I thought. If it hadn't been for this woman Owen would have bled to death. Couldn't his brother see that? As far as I was concerned, this woman and her husband were heroes. No one else had heard the crash – or perhaps if they did, no one else responded. And if that was the case, their heroics just doubled. I smiled sheepishly at the woman, clearly mortified by Sonny Van Winkle's feeble token of gratitude, embarrassed for myself, the CLP, and most of all, for Owen.

The next day, with the permission of the Spring Tree Apartments corporate management, the Shepherd Hills maintenance crew quietly installed safety windows in all three CLP client apartments.

Indeed, that was it.

"Because psychologists have been able to discover, exactly as in a slow-motion picture, the way the human creature acquires knowledge and habits, the normal child has been vastly helped by what the retarded have taught us."
– Pearl S. Buck, American author, 1938 Nobel Prize for Literature

Owen's temporary relinquishment of the CLP left Jim with the apartment all to himself. It would become his private bachelor pad – and his personal testing ground.

Much to everyone's surprise, Jim had emerged as one of the CLP's success stories, demonstrating ever-increasing potential by the day. But Jim had been a success story his entire life, even though none of us realized it until he moved into his own apartment. Jim's path to independence was not an easy one, beginning with a childhood typical for those of his generation born with D.D., a lost generation if ever there was one.

James Cornell Livingston was born in 1951 at a time when people with developmental disabilities were considered a mistake. Cognitive minorities were no longer the gentle simpletons romanticized by Southern literature and cared for by entire communities. In the mid-1900s, the "menace of the feeble mind" was in serious need of lock and key. Terms like "idiot," "imbecile" and "moron" were *clinical definitions*, not just words made up for Bugs Bunny to mispronounce. Subsequently, people with Down syndrome – "Mongoloids" – were seen as one of the worst offenders simply by virtue of their physical trappings. The very day he was born, Jim was placed by his parents – at the advice of his pediatrician – in an institution and all but forgotten.

At age 2 1/2 Jim was placed at the Otsega School in Edmeston, New York, a school for "Mongoloid children." From there he proceeded to bounce across the nation from school to hospital to institution. It was in these settings Jim learned behaviors of self-preservation and surveillance like hiding what few personal belongings he owned in his pillow case at night. In 1968 he was transferred to Camarillo State Hospital in California. He remained there until 1973, following a Writ of Habeas Corpus, and was placed in the Taylor Board and Care foster home in Lakeside, California, with five other male residents. He was twenty-two, the same age I was when I graduated college.

At first Jim refused to speak to anyone. Six months later he had lost 50 pounds. A physical exam revealed him to be "slow-moving," "seemingly depressed" with a "sallow complexion," and a patient that "appeared to be chronically ill." This exam led to the recommendation for a short-term hospitalization to closely monitor his medications, depression and dietary intake.

A psychological evaluation was performed over the course of three visits. Initially, Jim hardly spoke to the psychologist, choosing instead to grimace at

CHALLENGED: A TRIBUTE

him, stare motionless, and hide his face. The second visit Jim was passive, but more responsive. Attention to tasks and testing began with a spurt of interest, only to diminish within 30 seconds. On the third visit, the Draw-A-Person test was administered. When asked to draw a person, Jim first produced a "girl," then a "flower," then a "man with a pipe hat." When pressed to draw a person like himself, he refused.

In his summary and conclusions, the psychologist noted:

> *James appears to have enough awareness to draw these examination sessions out for longer and longer periods of time. He seems to want the contact of the testing visits, and the quality of his performance indicates some appreciable change as more rapport was accomplished.*
>
> *The quality of his opportunities for companionship should be investigated. If James were to have "family visits" in someone's home for the weekend, it might assuage his wish for more personal attachment. His identifications, though weak, are with men. If at all possible, a male companion who would be willing to spend time with him might be supportive toward his progression.*
>
> *All formal testing indicates that James should be able to return to a family care home to continue his plan for participation in the community.*

Soon after Jim returned to the Taylor Home, he slowly began to show promise in his ability to take care of all his own needs with some supervision. I.Q. testing was scored at 50, which classified him as "moderately mentally retarded." He was described as "being cooperative and exhibits no serious behavior problems, though speech has always been poor."

When the Taylor Home closed unexpectedly in 1979, the best option for new placement was a large, gated campus that encouraged independence and self-empowerment known as Shepherd Hills Board and Care. There it became apparent the psychologist's original hunches had been correct. He adjusted well, participating in a vocational workshop and attending summer camp. Within just a few years he proceeded to "graduate" from unit to unit, until finally making it to the Independent Training Facility. All it took was a final little nudge for him to land in the community.

Once he became a member of the CLP, Jim was able to pinpoint the basics of independent living almost immediately. He was able to keep himself groomed, take his meds on time, make dinner, grocery shop, and write checks to pay bills – all with pictorial aids, all by rote and repetition. With these successes we were also finally able to focus in on certain personal necessities such as a long-overdue adjustment to his dentures and a new pair of reading glasses. Even his speech challenges didn't slow him down. Thanks to a habitual routine, Jim was able to befriend local bus drivers, bank tellers and convenience store clerks simply by showing up on a regular basis to purchase his daily paper or complete weekly errands. And before long, his natural, untarnished spirit earned him distinction in the neighborhood. In fact, if Jim lacked anything, it wasn't communication skills, it was good judgment – the single hardest element to teach.

One evening, while observing Jim make his lunch for work the following day, I noticed that he packed his sandwich, apple and chips in a plastic produce bag rather than his cherished *Ghostbusters* lunch pail. When I asked Jim where it was, I assumed he'd answer that he left it on the bus, as he'd done on occasion. However, this time his answer was quite different. And it didn't take a professor of linguistics to decipher. The words were clear:

"Bad boy took it."

From what I could discern, a young man, a "bad boy," had snatched Jim's lunch pail from his hand on his way home from the bus stop and dashed off with it – no doubt hoping to pilfer a bank book or wallet hidden inside. Fortunately, the only treasures the bad boy was able to plunder were some used Baggies, a depleted snack-sized box of raisins, and an empty thermos stinking of souring milk. *Un*fortunately, the bad boy didn't stop there. Jim opened his refrigerator to show me that almost an entire week's worth of groceries he'd purchased were gone. He then took me to his room and showed me a blanket and pillow on his closet floor. "I shleep here," he said. Then he pointed to his bed. "Bad boy, bad girl, shleep dere."

Jim stared at me with an irrefutable intensity I suspect was the exact opposite of what he'd given that psychologist during his exam. Finally, he showed me his lock box. Jim kept his lock box hidden in his bottom dresser drawer, camouflaged by a stack of old *National Geographics*. The box had been pried open and was empty. No cash, no coins, no checkbook or bank book. It didn't take long for me to realize Jim had been the victim of exploitation. It took even less time for me to see red. Had this "bad boy" been present I'm not sure what I would have done. My lifelong contempt for bullies stirred a brutal fury within me to want to force-feed every indignity ever served on the playground or behind closed doors back to where they came from. Short of being held at bay by gunpoint, I would have torn the motherfucker's head off.

Instead, I called the police. A single patrol cop answered the call. Standing in Jim's duck hunter-themed bedroom, the officer stonily took my report. Just then, we heard the front door open. Rounding the corner into the living room, the officer and I came face-to-face with a young couple, both skinny, both blond, both white. The boy appeared to be in his early twenties, the girl, maybe fifteen. They froze. It was the briefest of standoffs – but "bad boys" know better than to run when cornered.

"S'up?" the boy said, extending his hand. "I'm Chris." He had the look and disposition of a drifter, and it was clear by his overconfidence he was about to try to talk his way out of something. Simultaneously, the girl immediately fell in step behind him, trained full well to keep her mouth shut.

CHALLENGED: A TRIBUTE

"What the hell –" I began, but the cop intervened, cool, almost apathetic.

"You live here?" the officer said.

"No," Chris said. "I'm just visiting my friend, James."

"That's not true," I said, seething with contempt. "Jim doesn't have any friends. Not *them*, anyway." I was so mad I could hear the veins in my neck throbbing.

"Mind if I see some ID?" the officer said.

"No problem." Chris whipped out his wallet and flashed a California ID card.

"This your current address?"

"No, I've been meaning to get it updated. Right now we're on the road. Heading for Portland, trying to find my father," he said, managing a casual laugh. Oh, the bastard was smooth.

I watched the officer write down the boy's name. Chris Doyle. Further questioning revealed that the girl had no ID, but said her name was Julie Schlict and she was eighteen. Yeah, sure. And I'm mayor of the fucking Munchkins.

I wanted to jump in, to interrogate my own set of questions, to basically pummel the living shit out of this piece of slime. But the cop maintained order. After gathering all the info he could, the cop alluded to the fact that there was concern they had been taking advantage of Jim.

Jim stuck his head out from behind me. "He da bad boy."

With Chris' overly-generous permission, the cop searched their backpacks, but found nothing. Bottom line, there was nothing more the officer could do. For all intents and purposes, Jim had "invited" them into his apartment and there was little that could be done legally. In the end, the cop asked them to leave and not return. But before he did, he took a Polaroid of Chris and Julie – "for the record" – though, as I was informed later, this was just a formality. A little trick the cops use to intimidate people who hopefully didn't know any better.

Gathering their packs, Chris and Julie left without anything more than the kindest of farewells. They knew to keep quiet and move on – and they knew that by doing so nothing could happen to them. I turned to thank the cop for his help. Much to my surprise, however, he wasn't so polite.

"This is why I think people like this shouldn't be allowed to live on their own," he said bluntly.

At that moment a thin blue line a mile high slammed me in the face. I never felt so ignorant. Here I thought the cop and I were in this together – to protect and serve. But it was apparent those brave words had no meaning in Jim's world. "To protect and serve" obviously didn't apply to retards.

I was appalled. I was furious. Victim to yet another bully – a newly rendered, more frightening, more heartbreaking kind. I looked at Jim – and for a fleeting second I grew angry at him as well, wishing and wondering why the hell he couldn't be smarter-just once-BE SMART-DAMN IT! *BE SMART!* But contrary to the way people with mental retardation are often portrayed in movies, they do not become conveniently wise in accordance with plot points. Instead, the round, innocent, chinless face of Mr. Mouth could only stare back at me. He showed no understanding of what just happened, or what could've happened, other than the ability to identify the stranger as a "bad boy." It would have to be the best I could hope for.

After the cop left I continued to fume at what the officer of the law had said. What's more, I couldn't shake the miserable feeling that maybe *I* was to blame because I'd allowed Doyle to slip in under my nose. As a caregiver, all I wanted for Jim and the others was the same thing I wanted for myself. To live a simple, safe, trouble-free life. But in my haste to promote the almighty independent lifestyle, I'd completely ignored the potential hazards of reality that lie in wait for us all.

I thought about Owen and his accident. About Darlene and her topless window dance. About Jackie and the thief in Las Vegas. Each one trying to invoke their own skewed form of "independence." Then I thought about how vulnerable to exploitation our clients really were. It reminded me of the time in Vegas when Jim hadn't even realized he'd won that $50, and how I could've easily claimed it as my own. Grudgingly, I had to consider that maybe the police officer was right.

But I didn't have to accept it.

The next day I appointed myself as neighborhood watch chairman for the clients. After filing a stop-payment on Jim's checkbook and re-establishing a new account, I printed up a stack of flyers warning others to be on the lookout for Chris Doyle and Julie Schlict, a con team in the area targeting people with developmental disabilities. I fired up the Sunshine Van and delivered flyers to every local day program I could think of. And to those I couldn't get to, I put the word out by phone.

It was the least I could do. And nothing more – as the gentle officer had made so abundantly clear.

CHAPTER 17

TRUE LOVE CONQUERS ALL

ROGER MEYERS: Ginny!
VIRGINIA RAE HENSLER: No babies, Roger. They say we will eat them.
– scene from **Like Normal People**

S OUTHERN CALIFORNIA IS
famous for its May Gray and June
Gloom, overcast mornings that refuse to burn off until well past noon. After all
that had occurred through the gray and the gloom, by the summer of 1987 we
somehow managed to finish our first full year in the Community Living Program
on a high note.

It all started with the death of Hughie Lamb.

Holly and Hughie always believed they were destined for nothing less than
life-partnership, no matter what society may try to dictate. Holly was never thought
of as Holly Gross, singular, just as Hughie was never Hughie Lamb, autonomous.
They were, and always would be, "Holly and Hughie." And they wanted nothing
more fervently than to get married. More than living independently. More than
having a "real job" at Chuck E, Cheese. Marriage was the ultimate dream a client
could dare dream.

Holly moved to The Hills' Unit 8 in 1971. Hughie arrived five years later. It
was by all accounts love at first med pass. Within two years, each in their own
way merited a move to the then new Independent Training Facility managed by
a well-respected progressive named Dawn Barry. "There isn't anything you can't

accomplish," she would tell the clients. It was damn the disabilities, full independence ahead!

Over the next several years different faces came and went – both peers and staff. New skills were explored and higher goals set to achieve greatness. And, despite the dubious nature of sexual curiosities, Holly and Hughie remained fast and bound to each others' hip in a whirlwind courtship that ultimately lasted eleven years.

Meanwhile, Holly's brother and legal conservator remained adamant. Conrad Gross made it clear to his little sister that while she and Hughie could remain a couple, marriage was out of the question. To Conrad Gross, humoring his sister in a relationship was darling and safe. Anything beyond that was unforeseeable. To him, despite any appeals from me or anyone else, the concept just didn't seem – as he once put it – "civilized."

Just the same, marriage between consenting clients was not altogether new. Years before, a couple named Roger Meyers and Virginia Rae Hensler from a facility similar to Shepherd Hills met, fell in love, married and moved out to live on their own. This was famously depicted in the 1979 TV Movie-of-the-Week *Like Normal People* starring Shaun Cassidy and Linda Purl. Like any other teenager of my generation home alone on a Friday night, I watched that film and never forgot Virginia's famous whine of *"Waa-Jah!"* no matter how hard I tried.

Now, in 1987, Holly and Hughie had done what Roger and Virginia had done, only in reverse. They moved into the community and *then* tried to get married. But with each passing day, it didn't happen. Instead, they safely remained "that cute little Downs couple."

On May 1st, Hughie Lamb started his day like every other day with a hot shower. Hughie loved to inhale the steam – it cleared his lungs and helped prepare him for the world at hand. This day, however, as the steam saturated the bathroom, it didn't soothe Hughie's chest as it had most other days. Instead, Hughie's chest began to tighten. He couldn't breathe. Quickly and without repent, a perplexing numbness clutched his jaw and spread to his arms. Hughie's knees began to buckle. More tightening. More numbness. Confused and in dire pain, Hughie pounded on the wall of the shower stall, desperately trying to signal his roommate, a neighbor, anyone, that he needed help. He didn't know why. He just knew he needed it. More clutching. More pounding. Suddenly, he fell to his knees with a wet thud. The fiberglass tub so common to apartment living was cold. With his last few breaths, Hughie slapped the wall with all his might just before he passed out. Hot water continued to rain upon his small, round, naked form, heaped over the drain.

That was how the next-door neighbor found him moments later.

CHALLENGED: A TRIBUTE

THE DEATH OF HUGHIE LAMB
A play in One Act
Scene: A hospital operating room.

*(The doors burst open as Hughie Lamb is wheeled in on a gurney. Instantly, a
crack team of doctors and nurses spring into action.)*

DOCTOR: What've we got?

NURSE: Heart attack. Code Blue.

*(Shouts of "Stat!" and "50 cc's of angio-something or other!" are ad-libbed. Hughie
lies splayed upon the operating table as the defibrillator is readied.)*

DOCTOR: Clear!

(Ba-Zap! Hughie's heart strains. Slowly fading from existence.)

DOCTOR: Clear!

(Ba-Zap!)

DOCTOR: Clear!

(Ba-ZAP! Suddenly, the monitors flatline. Hughie dies on the table.)

NURSE: We've lost him, doctor.

DOCTOR: Not on *my* watch. *Clear!*

*(BA-ZAP! The overhead lights explode in a shower of sparks! Nurses scream
and cower as brave doctors shield them from the danger. Beat. Hughie
Lamb sits up.)*

HUGHIE *(groggily)*: Wha' happened?

DOCTOR: You had a heart attack and died.

HUGHIE: Oh sorry. My mistake.

CURTAIN

In all fairness I wasn't there, so my imagination only goes as far as what I've
seen on soap operas and medical sit-coms. But the truth remains Hughie Lamb *did*
die on the table that day. And he *did* come back to life. We all knew there had to
be a reason.

While death is no laughing matter, rebirth is justification to celebrate. A few
weeks later, Hughie returned home to his apartment at the Spring Tree CLP.
Doctors' orders prevented him from overly-strenuous activities on the heart such
as sex and burritos. But one thing was for certain. Hughie Lamb was very much
alive.

Hughie had been officially dead for almost two full minutes. When I asked him
about his brief detour to the other side, Hughie was unable to remember anything
about it at all. No white light, no choral choir, no ethereal encounters. Nor did he
now possess any life-after-death supernatural powers such as the ability to predict
winning lottery numbers or talk to the horses at Del Mar for the inside scoop on
who was strongest to win in the fifth. Instead, Hughie Lamb returned to us the
same as he'd left, none the worse for wear – which was the best any of us could
hope for. In time, he went back to his old, slow-talking, step-shuffling self, to his

regime of Del Taco and Jack In The Box, to preaching the gospel with zeal, and most importantly, to loving Holly with all his heart and soul.

Meanwhile, during Hughie's absence, the ordeal had left Holly Gross on this side of forever, forced behind a curtain of tears. News of his heart attack, followed by subsequent days of touch-and-go recovery, filled her with enormous strife. Holly may not have understood how to figure a 15% tip on dinner at Denny's, but she sure as hell understood death. Each night that Hughie remained in the hospital, Holly cried herself to sleep, her emotional core wrung dry like a dishrag, anguished that the man she loved might not live through till morning. Each night she prayed for his safe return to her side. At last, when Hughie finally returned home, her heart soared. Finally her life was given the go-ahead to pick up where it had so cruelly stalled.

When I shared the news of the grief she suffered with her brother, Conrad Gross arrived at a turning point and the "legal conservator" inside him melted away. Hearing her voice on the phone, he finally understood how Holly felt, and just how much she and Hughie truly belonged together. "All right," he sighed heavily to his little sister. "You and Hughie can get married."

And so it would be a good year. Until their wedding day, Hughie would remain roommates with Sammy, while Holly would continue to room with Darlene. And in that, the betrothed retained an old-fashioned faithfulness reserved solely for each other. Why, you might even say it was positively "civilized."

June 3, 1987. The sky looked like a child's drawing; curly white clouds doodled over streaks of Crayola blue. Hughie wore a caramel-colored suit, set off by a crimson red necktie and embroidered handkerchief. Holly wore white to represent purity, *not* virginity, which is often the misconception. (The *veil* is supposed to represent virginity – which Holly didn't wear.) She carried a bouquet and wore a matching headband of white daisies. A string of faux pearls were only out-shined by her freshly polished dentures. We even polished the chrome on her wheelchair.

Once the word was out, Holly and Hughie quickly became media darlings, if not downright franchisable. Not only was this an interracial marriage, it was an interracial *Down syndrome* marriage. And in today's society, few things are more monumental – or newsworthy – than two people with developmental disabilities entering into matrimony.

Holly took full charge of the opportunity. A photographer and special-interest columnist for the *San Diego Union-Tribune* were dispatched to capture the happy day – with full permission from Holly's brother Conrad. As for Hughie, the man had virtually no family support. Both his parents were deceased, leaving only a distant cousin acknowledged on paper as "primary contact in case of emergencies." Apparently, neither the aftermath of Hughie's heart attack nor seeing her cousin on the most important day of his life warranted a plane ticket from Ignorance, U.S.A. But Hughie remained unconcerned. His cousin was as foreign to him as the

CHALLENGED: A TRIBUTE | 175

concept of dieting. So while Hughie quietly inhaled an endless supply of Jordon Almonds and got pretend-drunk on Martinelli's Sparkling Apple Cider, Holly held court before a small group of guests, answering the reporter's questions with sweet, charismatic Downiness.

The ceremony took place on the deck of the *Bahia Belle*, a small cruise ship, as part of a three-hour San Diego Bay excursion. Their cake was a 9-inch, two-tiered wedding special from the local Lucky supermarket. Balloons were anchored to the backs of deck chairs in hues of light and dark gray, the poor-man's silver. A small, intimate reception was to follow in the ship's galley, with a much larger cake-and-punch reception awaiting us back at the Shepherd Hills auditorium – open to the entire campus.

Prior to the ceremony, the happy couple had requested that Anita and I stand by them as Maid of Honor and Best Man. Both honored and privileged, at the same time Hughie's request made me feel a little sad. Though Hughie had plenty of friends, certainly ones closer to him than I was, it reminded me once again how clients tend to bond strongest with their direct care counselors, whether by choice or design.

As the boat left the dock the wedding party shuffled and wheeled into place overlooking the bow, where we were periodically treated to the icy spray of choppy waters. Under the delivery of our own Hills chaplain, Rebecca, everyone chuckled as they watched us teeter from side to side in unison upon the high seas. At one point, Hughie stepped forward to intone a few choice biblical quotations. In his own, spiritual fashion, his remarks were a novel if not uncertain hybrid of passages from Corinthians, Proverbs, Mark, John, and the lost Book of Tobias:

> *"Love is patient and kind . . . He who finds a wife finds what is good and receives favor from the Lord . . . They are no longer two but one . . . Love one another as I have loved you . . . That she and I may grow old together . . ."*

There was an awkward pause. Hughie turned and looked at the guests. "Dis where y'all supposed to say '*Amen*'," he whispered.

"Amen," we dutifully replied.

When it came time for the Best Man to hand over the ring, I reached into my pocket and rolled it between my fingers one last time. I admit feeling a pang of envy for the blissful couple, as they had now surpassed me into the realm of Happily Ever After, while I stood sulking on the chilly shores of Singledom. An "I do," another "I do," and a kiss later, Holly and Hughie were husband and wife.

"Yee-*ha!*" shouted Hughie.

Following the ceremony, the columnist and her cameraman trailed Holly like a bird trailing bread crumbs, ardently recording every word. Holly's brother stood by and looked on with moist eyes for the joy his sister capably expressed. She spoke of how she and Hughie met at Shepherd Hills eleven years ago at a Halloween party when Hobo Hughie gallantly offered to get Princess Holly a cup of punch, and accidentally knocked the entire bowl over with his bindle. She spoke of how excited they were to honeymoon at the Disneyland Hotel. She spoke of how they were going to live independently in their own married-couple apartment and all the married-couple things they were going to married-couple do. When asked about the challenges they faced of living on their own, Holly replied with full dimples, "I'm not sure. I guess I have to ask my counselor."

Their first dance was an earnest waltz-like shuffle/roll that I'd tried to teach Hughie at the last minute to the tune of Tom Jones' "What's New, Pussycat." Their first shared sliced of cake was mutually smooshed into each others' faces, then neatly inhaled by both. They were precious, charming, adorable and ultimately iconic.

When it came time for the Best Man to make his toast, I rose and felt all eyes upon me. In that moment my mind flashed on all that was happening, all that I wanted to say. I wanted to berate and belittle Hughie's cousin for not being there. I wanted to march over and flick Conrad Gross between the eyes for all the years he'd denied his sister the joy she sought in marriage. I wanted to declare the immeasurable distance it took to get here, that Hughie had to endure a roundtrip to *heaven and back* before finding his own earthly peace. Thankfully, it was a conceptual rant that only lasted a millisecond. I shook it off. Today was their day – as it should be. "To Holly and Hughie," I said, raising my glass. "I can't think of two people who've waited longer, or prayed harder, to finally achieve the happiness they so richly deserve."

"Amen!" shouted Hughie. And we all drank.

When the story appeared in the paper the following week, Holly squealed with delight as she showed it around the workshop to her peers. There, on the front page of the Wednesday Family Life section, was a suitable-for-framing, color photo of Holly and Hughie cutting their wedding cake; two radiant, raisin-eyed, cookie-faced souls. The accompanying article fulfilled all anyone could hope for; an upbeat, feel-good, inspirational piece about a triumphant struggle to overcome all odds; a commentary to boost client awareness and champion the rights of people with disabilities. To their peers, Holly and Hughie had obtained celebrity status and were lifted to a pedestal usually reserved for the heroic likes of Country-Western singers, Hulk Hogan and KITT, the car from *Knight Rider*. But all that mattered to the Lambs was that they were together at last. In the end, the article went down as a feather in their married-couple cap – and up on their wall in a plastic $1.99 frame from Pic 'n Save. And so the legend of Hughie and Holly, Mr. and Mrs., disabled, against all odds and ultimately victorious, was born.

TRUE LOVE, A REBUTTAL

In the months that followed moving out of my parents' house, I still continued to visit semi-regularly on my days off. I would take my mother out to dinner, shopping, movies – significantly simple activities she relished that my father had no patience for. As for my old man, hell, I even continued to cut the grass.

Back in college, as part of my internal rebellion, I often fantasized about writing a cathartic, tell-the-world, Albee-esque play detailing my parents' marriage entitled *Mouthful of Vomit.* (Thankfully, better taste prevailed.) Over the years my mother, too, had fantasized her own sort of magnum opus – and after a lifetime spent building up enough confidence, the time came to fully realize it. When the day arrived to finally leave her husband, there was no doubt I would accompany her concerto of conspiracy.

Being the good son who loves his mother, I wanted to help and guide her, financially, emotionally, and be the kind of son I always thought I should be, the kind of son I always wanted to be. In the weeks prior to her leaving my father, I stealthily loaded my trunk with what few intrinsic possessions she owned and squirreled them away in my apartment. Meanwhile, awaiting her an hour north was an unassuming little senior condo in Oceanside where the weather was cool, the complex was safe, and the cost was easy on the pocketbook.

The morning of her escape, while my father was at work, my mother effectively packed the last of her essentials and bravely finalized her plan. When Pop arrived home to find her half of the closet empty, all hell broke loose. Enraged, he immediately phoned my sister, Carolyn. She offered little condolence. He then demanded to know who was going to make him dinner. (Mind you, my sister now lived 200 miles away.) When Carolyn explained she couldn't help him in that department either, he bellowed, "But all I know how to make is sandwiches – and *that's* not healthy!" All the things he had taken for granted were suddenly dumped in his lap like a pot of boiling hot coffee – hold the sugar.

Throughout their entire marriage, while my father huffed and puffed and blew the rental units down, my mother, like so many women of her generation, had actually been the one to run the household. Surely it was a blow to his manhood that he was no longer wanted as a partner, and no longer needed for what he felt was an irrefutable wisdom in the ways of the world. The fact that he was left confused and furious came as no shock – but the fact that he was left in total desperation did. Only later did I realize what we'd done was cruel if not malicious. It never occurred to me how much the son-of-a-bitch actually *needed* us.

No one had ever taught my father the basic skills to survive on his own – and it quickly showed. My old man didn't know how to cook dinner, couldn't write a check, stood dumbfounded in the shadow of a washing machine – tasks he'd always dismissed as "bitch work"; tasks that, for a man, bore the crown jewels of sissyhood. Conversely, once I needed to learn those skills, my mother taught me them to me and more. Skills that not only aided me toward my own independence, but which I was ultimately able to pass on to my clients. It was realizations like this one that continued to interweave my clients, my father, and my own struggles. For the first time since working at The Hills I saw not just the merit in what I'd been teaching them, but the *value* of it.

If anything haunted my mother, though, it wasn't that my father broke down, but that he broke down far beyond what she'd anticipated. He was left completely shattered. All because he never bothered to learn the simple daily skills I and my clients had learned. He was, for all intents and purposes, *independent*ly retarded.

By the end of the year, Dad filed for divorce from Mom. Thirty-six years of marriage and they finally – officially – divorced. Hindsight told them they probably should've never married in the first place. But my parents came from a generation where they didn't make their lives, their lives made them. Unrealized dreams and lost chances were a given. They were simply two more victims of the wrong place-wrong time-wrong marriage blues.

Between my mother's meager Social Security benefits and what little I could contribute, we were able to scrape enough together to make payments on her new condo. It was there she learned to breathe again. At last, the once-upon-a-time Daddy's princess, exiled by marriage and forced into servantry, was allowed to regain her rightful place as queen of the castle, otherwise known as Oceana South, Development 3, with a small dog named Cookie for companionship and a devoted son who would visit regularly. In time, our mutual independence became sanctuary, whereas my old man became little more than an angry-eyed memory. Nevertheless, I took pride in knowing that if it hadn't been for my own foray into independence, my mother would've probably never followed suit.

Forced to remake his life, my father moved to Oklahoma to track down an old girlfriend and start anew. Once there, he refused to pay my mother alimony in a twisted game of "Gotcha!" To her credit, my mother didn't care. To her it was just one less reason to have to remain acquainted with the man.

When it came to true love I couldn't help but think that Holly and Hughie got it right. They didn't allow themselves to become distracted by the traditional despair, woe and resentment that often seem to complicate so many a "normal" romance. What's more, they *didn't know how*. And it was that very lack of distraction which made them happy. Theirs was an ability to overlook such downfalls and simply bask in the blissful uncaring of how society thinks we *should* behave. Theirs was a purer view of things. *We got to get married! We got our picture in the paper! How awesome is that?* It seemed to me like maybe Holly and Hughie had a better grip on what's important in life more than anyone else. Certainly more than my parents, anyway.

I should learn to be so lucky.

PART IV
NORMAL NOTWITHSTANDING

CHAPTER 18

THE ONE-TWO GUT PUNCH

NOT LONG AFTER the nuptials of Mr. and Mrs. Lamb, the Community Living Program withstood a brief restructuring. Holly and Hughie relocated to their own one-bedroom honeymoon nest, permitting Sammy White and Darlene Beaudine to each graduate to their own individual studio apartments, while Jim Livingston and Owen Van Winkle stayed together as roommates. With our freshman year now complete, in spite of the transitional seesaw between fortuitous charity and near disaster, the Mighty Six remained intact.

In time, life at Spring Tree stabilized into a very comfortable state of affairs, and the routines of everyday living fell readily into place. As far as programming went, there continued to be moments of success . . .

> STEVE: How're you doing with that list of new food words, Owen?
> OWEN: Great! I learned three.

. . . and moments of nonsuccess . . .

> STEVE: How're you doing with that list of new food words, Sammy?
> SAMMY: Crappy! I learned three.

In fact, except for the mandatory monthly staff meetings back at ITF, any remaining ties to the Shepherd Hills main campus began to feel non-existent. The clients remained surprisingly, refreshingly, adept at running their lives with what little supervision Irma and I needed to provide.

From 1987 to 1995 the years passed quickly and effortlessly, as if time had collapsed in on itself; a time when Madonna and O.J. surfed the Internet superhighway wearing Doc Martens and drinking Appletinis before joining Jerry Seinfeld on *The X-Files* to get their tongues pierced at a day spa. Little by little, with each passing year, any real thought of returning to college slowly faded into the sunset as my job, my convictions, and my life settled into a nice, dependable pattern of contented community integration with an abundance of San Diego sunshine. This is the life, I thought. If only the rest of world could be as uncomplicated as this.

THE INCREDIBLY STRANGE TALE OF MANDY MECKEL

In 1995 that abundance of sunshine was briefly interrupted by the storms of El Niño. By year's end, unusually heavy rains had flooded San Diego's valleys, while its hills were left green and dressed for life; an odd paradox of devastated and lush. Meanwhile, two major events occurred that proved to be much more damaging – a one-two gut punch that would uproot my entire, cozy existence. The first punch came from a girl.

It's always a girl.

After nine years with the CLP, depleted and burned out, Irma Fritts finally threw in the towel. Though we'd never been particularly close, she'd always proved a reliable assistant, and at a small going-away party held in the Spring Tree Apartments rec room I wished her well with a warm hug good-bye.

As for me, those same years had been spent carving a niche deeper and deeper into my little unspoiled corner of the universe. Socially, however, this meant one thing:

No steady girlfriend.

I'd long since given up hope of meeting the girl of my dreams in line at a book store, bakery, or art-movie revival house, or even by accidentally knocking over a punch bowl with my bindle. Once in a while there was the cordial lunch date with a considerate colleague, and even the occasional romantic rendezvous, but nothing meaningful, nothing ever-lasting. At times I even found myself browsing the personal ads, daring myself to submit some shy witticism of my own . . .

> *If you hate these things as much as I do, if you feel just as uncomfortable searching for your soul mate amongst ads for pearl cream and hormonal-laced cologne, if you just want someone to laugh with, then call me. Humping optional.*

. . . but never followed through.

CHALLENGED: A TRIBUTE

Consequently, I began to grow pessimistic, fretting that my lifestyle wasn't exactly prime date bait. Friday nights revolved largely around ABC's *TGIF* line-up, mollified by the wisdom of Steve Urkel and the Thighmasterful ass of Suzanne Somers. Taking stock of my existence, I basically lived in a one-bedroom office with no other prospects on the horizon, resigned to twinges of loneliness each time I observed a couple walking hand-in-hand. I was, by my own design, for better or worse, alone.

Irma's replacement was a young woman named Mandy Meckel. Mandy was a classic Plain Jane with tortoise shell glasses and smooth, ivory skin. To me she was the most beautiful woman in the world. Mandy Meckel was also deaf. This didn't matter, however, because she was masterful at reading lips. It also didn't matter because we instantly became lovers.

Now, I admit there are few things more dangerous than two co-workers entering into an affair – especially with an office that neatly doubles as a bedroom. But I was foolish and horny. Make that horny and foolish. I craved some form of passion in my life, something to remedy a decade of isolation and a lifetime of injured worth. In Mandy I found those elements. She was as upbeat and optimistic as they come, someone who awoke each morning ready to take on the world. As to her disability, it was that very vulnerability which also made her shamelessly attractive. Mandy had one of those distinguishable deaf-person voices made seductive in my generation by the striking beauty of actress Marlee Matlin. A voice both violated and self-assured, as if it rolled off the back of her tongue grappling to break free. I loved that voice, and the way she batted her eyes bashfully when she used it, suggesting a hidden modesty. I won't deny there was also something *cool* about having a deaf girlfriend; it was alluring, it was exotic, it set me apart, and it made me feel strangely superior to others. As if to say, imagine! Of all the people Mandy chose to trust, she picked *me*.

But there was more. I also truly *admired* Mandy. Not only was she great with the clients, but her energy and enthusiasm seemed to touch everyone. She shared stories of overcoming her deafness by teaching herself to read lips. Stories of overcoming an oppressive father similar to my own. Stories of ultimately finding her spirit. Stories that were inspirational – and sexy as hell. Such *character* she had. Such *candor*. Such *charm*. Being with Mandy was a natural high.

As our love blossomed, soon Mandy was teaching me basic American Sign Language; signs for "I love you" and "fuck you" – two of the most sought-after phrases by anyone learning a new language, second only to "where's the bathroom?" We'd lie in bed together at the end of our shift, fingers dancing as I mimicked her graceful traces of the ASL alphabet. Each day our love grew deeper and deeper. At one point we even went so far as to tiptoe around the prospect of marriage and kids. At last, I thought, I've found my soul mate. My one and only. My destiny. And so I spent the next three months happy, relaxed, self-satisfied and secure in a serious and loving relationship.

And that's when small clues began to surface.

At first it was nothing major. Odd little moments when Mandy would remark how funny a comedian was on TV, or how a certain singer was unique. When I asked how she could tell these things if she couldn't hear them, Mandy was always quick to counter with an explanation. The comedian *must* be funny "because he *looks* funny," or the singer is unique because "she *looks* unique." Such comments were easily regarded and dismissed. Soon, our conversations became exceedingly casual to the point where I'd accidentally find myself talking to her from across the room. And yet, Mandy was somehow always able to catch the gist of what I was saying. Still this was nothing unusual; I simply chalked it up to her impressive lip-reading skills. Mandy was just that good.

Then one evening, as I passed Holly and Hughie's apartment where I knew Mandy was working, I thought I'd swing by to say hi (and maybe steal a kiss when the Lambs weren't looking). About to knock, I glanced in through the open front window and saw Mandy facing the other way. Sparked by a bit of schoolboy giddiness, I thought it'd be funny to hide from view and pop up playfully to scare her when she turned around. As I squatted silently beneath the window screen and waited, I realized Mandy was talking to someone. I peeked in, but neither Holly nor Hughie were to be seen. Who the heck was she talking to? It was then I realized Mandy was engaged in a one-sided conversation – a conversation *on the phone*. But . . . Mandy doesn't use the phone because she's . . . *what the hell?*

I remained still and listened. The receiver finally dropped into the cradle with a plastic *thunk*. "Hey, Holly," Mandy casually called as she headed into the bedroom, "ready for your bath, hon?" She hadn't seen me. Slowly, I cupped my jaw from the ground and backpedaled an escape to my apartment. There I sat with the curtains drawn, paralyzed. Is what just happened what I *think* just happened? Naw, no, nuh-uh, couldn't be, no way. Wait-wait-wait-wait-wait . . . All this time, had she been lying? To the clients? To me? Lying about being . . . ?

There was no skirting the facts.

Mandy.

Meckel.

Could.

Hear.

The next two days I called in sick and sought sanctuary at my mother's condo. It took me that long to process the sheer *weirdness* of it all. My stomach churned like I'd swallowed a hot rubber glove. What the hell was I going to do? Should I confront her? Should I turn her in? Should I remain silent? What about our relationship? What about trust? I mean, who does something like *that?* I replayed the moment a zillion times in my head, always coming to the same conclusion. Mandy Meckel, in advocating for people with disabilities, lied about a disability she never even had.

But how do I prove it? Not just to others but to myself?

CHALLENGED: A TRIBUTE

Two days later, I got an idea.

I debated fiercely over what I was about to do. But the fact remained that I felt so violated, so foolish and so angry, I knew in order to catch her at her own game it had to be something big.

"Are you sure you're not over-reacting?" my friend Marc from the frat house said.

"It's something I have to do," I said. "Will you help me?" When Marc agreed, I picked my spot and bided my time.

That Friday, after work, Mandy and I went for a drive. Our destination, the top of Mt. Diablo Poquito overlooking San Diego. It was a secluded place, a place to park, unwind from a day's drudgery, and pitch a little old-fashioned woo with your best beau. I also liked it because there was no one around for miles.

As we pulled off the small access road onto a patch of gravel, I applied the parking brake. I turned on the radio and hit the pre-set button to KPBS, the local SDSU station. College deejay, Marc Upcott, was manning the mike for the weekly 2-hour set of light jazz. Mandy rested her head on my shoulder and together we contemplated the honesty of the sparkling city lights. Closing in on the midnight hour, Marc spun a "special request." His voice rang soft and mellow. "This radio dedication is from Steve to the love of his life, Mandy." On cue, "Cast Your Fate To The Wind" by Vince Guaraldi floated from the speakers, a gentle jazz piano combo for star-crossed lovers. Marc continued. "As the couple now sits high atop lover's lane, overlooking the glow of the city, Steve has asked me to relay a very special message: 'To Mandy, I love you with all my heart . . . *will you marry me?*'"

Mandy bolted upright and gurgled, as if she were about to choke. She threw herself on me, covering me in kisses, her eyes welling with tears. "*Yes*," she cried joyously, "*yes, I'll marry you!*"

Hard as it was, I didn't budge an inch.

Suddenly, Mandy tensed and sprung away from me like I was on fire. Our eyes locked. I simply stared, a mix of betrayal and undeniable distress. Mandy withered into a silent haze. All at once, her eyelids fluttered like the wings of a dying butterfly pinned to a science fair project. "I-uh-wa-uh-er-um-my-er-uhmn-I . . ." was all that she could muster.

"I think it's best if you get out," I finally said.

Mandy's face was as pale as a boiled onion. As she stepped onto the gravel I gestured behind her. "Down that road's a pay phone. Here's a quarter. You might want to call a taxi. That is, unless you're really deaf. In that case . . . 'Sorry. My mistake.'"

As the piano on the radio faded to silence, Mandy stared after me pie-eyed, cast in the red glow of my tail lights.

That night Mandy got home just fine. The next day I didn't speak to her any more than I had to. The next *week* I didn't speak to her any more than I had to.

The next *three weeks* I didn't speak to her any more than I had to. The friction was painfully obvious. The clients picked up on it right away. A few, like Sammy, even quizzed me about it. "Why are you mad at Mandy?" he'd ask.

"I'm not," I'd answer with a smile that could freeze beer. Then always, always changed the subject.

In the eight years since Holly and Hughie so effortlessly defined true love, I'd often reflected on whether I might be allowed to one day put those same simple values into practice. With Mandy I thought that maybe now I was finally being given that chance. But in hindsight, I'd given her my heart all too quickly if not foolishly. Whereas before Mandy came along I'd grown pessimistic about love, I'd now graduated with honors to cynical.

In my mind, what Mandy had done was despicable. For years I'd watched people struggle with disabilities that made their lives more difficult while she *faked* a disability to make her life easier. Her deception, essentially a unique form of bullying, was something I couldn't forgive. To me she walked the same filthy plane as those two young grifting punks. And even though I wanted to forgive her, even though part of me imagined there must have been something unbearably sad deep within Mandy for her to do what she'd done, it didn't take much soul-searching before I finally decided to report the whole thing to Dawn. The only questions that remained now were how and when?

It turned out I didn't have to worry about either.

At the next scheduled monthly staff meeting, suddenly – in front of Dawn, myself, and all the houseparents of ITF Village – Mandy broke down. Tears spilled from behind those immense tortoise shell frames as she publicly announced she could, in fact . . . (insert sob for full effect) . . . *h-e-a-r.* I leaned forward with great anticipation, awaiting the final confession. But instead, the way Mandy told it, it wasn't so much a confession as a bona-fide miracle. As Mandy laid down a performance worthy of a thousand Marlee Matlins, she explained that she'd attended a "laying on of hands" at her church, and with the congregation's strength and prayers – Halle-*freakin'*-lujah! – she was now cured. But that wasn't the most astonishing part of the story. The most astonishing part was – *everyone believed her.*

One by one, the entire bunch rose to encircle Mandy in a group hug of comfort and congratulations – leaving me alone on the other side of the room, my mouth hanging open in utter disbelief. What the hell's *wrong* with you people? I asked myself. How could you fall for this? Is mental retardation *airborne?*

No, Mandy Meckel was just that good.

There must be some way out of here
Said the joker to the thief
– Bob Dylan, "All Along the Watchtower"

The second punch came from another girl.

It's always another girl.

The time had finally come for Dawn Barry, our beloved founder and supervisor of the Community Living Program, to retire. Riding in on the same ravaging gales of El Niño as Mandy Meckel, her successor was the devil by way of designer nails, washed ashore by a tempest's rage without intermission. Her name was Sissy Cain. But in my mind she became Sissy Shithead, the proverbial Boss from Hell.

Living the Life of Riley since '86 in my rent-free apartment-slash-office, my entire, stress-free lifestyle was snuffed out the day Shithead took charge. In an effort to cut CLP expenses, the live-in manager position was immediately and unceremoniously axed. I was told I had less than two weeks to move out. Suddenly, with no place to live and unable to afford both my own apartment *and* help my mother with her condo payments, I found myself forced to move in with Mommy and commute from Oceanside – one full hour each way.

On the bright side, it brought my mother and I closer together. I did the cooking and cleaning while she did the relaxing – a privilege she'd earned and a right she deserved. But even this small joy was lost in the wake of despair. In quick succession, Shithead turned the entire Community Living Program inside-out with a series of sweeping changes that made her look good by making the rest of us look bad. We'd heard that before she got into the special-needs field, Shithead used to be a manicurist. One could only imagine the agony she must've inflicted on countless cuticles. Hours providing client services weren't just clipped, they were hacked. Staff hours, even staff *wages*, were stripped away like ugly, unwanted hangnails.

Before long, each member of the Mighty Six found themselves without the extra support they needed. Skill levels declined. Outbursts increased. Any sense of community was gone. Confusion left the clients unsure of who to turn to for help or how to define boundaries – evidenced by the troublesome voicemails left for me by Shithead on my pager:

> *"– James is bringing rotten food to work in his lunches. Fix it! –"*
> *"– Holly keeps setting off the smoke alarm in the middle of the night. Fix it! –"*
> *"– Hughie's lying on the floor of the bank refusing to get up till they give him more money. Fix it! –"*

Whereas Dawn had been someone who'd devoted herself to the clients' welfare, Shithead couldn't care less. She represented all the faceless, upper-management cretins who, with a simple swipe of a red pen, hold our lives in the balance. At our first staff meeting together I innocently remarked how much fun it was working with my clients. Shithead looked at me as if she'd been sucking on bruised lemons. "You're not paid to have *fun* with your clients," she spit. Right then and there I thought, *how can anyone work for someone like this?*

But the Powers That Berate showed no concern. Despite my attempts to complain to the Executive Director, as far as Shepherd Hills was concerned Shithead was infallible. The clients had become an afterthought.

Shithead was also a thief. When asked to give input to re-master the CLP, every suggestion I made was rebuffed with such bullying tactics as "No, we're not going to do *that*," or "That's a *terrible* idea!" However, two or three months later, the same ideas – *my* ideas – would magically resurface as new policy, and I was expected to applaud them. *Bravo!* the Executive Director would praise her. Bravo for your intelligence and insight!

I never felt more powerless.

Meanwhile, as a result of being cut from full-time to part-time, in order to make up for lost wages I was forced back to the main campus where I was reassigned as a floater, subject to any unit they wanted to put me in. This time around I thought I was prepared for it. But instead, I was treated to the same rites of initiation all over again, and this time my initiation came at a much harder cost. The first day I reported to the on-grounds supervisor for an assignment, I asked if they needed a hand in ITF, figuring that at least maybe I'd get the chance to see Iggy again and be on familiar turf. Instead, I was gleefully assigned to:

UNIT 5

The "challenging" unit. The "icky" unit. The worst unit on campus.

The first thing to hit me was the smell. A sour potpourri of urine, feces, mucus, drool, dandruff, cum and germicide. Inching my way across the threshold, I found myself in the midst of fifteen of the most profoundly retarded human beings I'd ever seen. Clients draped on the sofa staring vacantly at a mute TV; clients rocking cross-legged in large chairs of ruptured vinyl; clients sprawled on the floor blowing bouquets of saliva bubbles. Four of them wore scuffed seizure helmets. Three had noses caked in dried snot. One squatted against the wall with both hands down his pants, grunting. Another had a flipper for a left arm. It was as if I'd landed in the eye of a hurricane; still and airless. I knew then the fear I'd once felt working with Patrick, Emily and Jane hadn't been real fear at all.

The one thing I didn't see was any houseparents.

Peeking into one of three bedrooms, five beds lined a cold linoleum floor, side by side without privacy. A petite female client no more than nineteen or twenty swept into the room. She looked directly at me, then directly *through* me. I froze. Her face was that of a China doll, round and bone white with two black eyes. Suddenly, she stripped stark naked in front of me without expression, climbed into bed, and pulled the covers tightly over her head. The entire exhibition lasted no more than a few seconds – a flash of black pubic hair on porcelain skin, of pert breasts with pink nipples – but the initial sight was so jarring I felt insecure and ashamed, like a Peeping Tom viewing something I shouldn't.

CHALLENGED: A TRIBUTE

Wandering further, I pushed through a swinging door and was met by the putrid stench of a forgotten campground Port-A-Potty. Contrary to ancient rumor, there was not "one giant toilet" they all had to share, but rather a lineup of six toilets, each affixed with grab bars and separated by doorless stalls. At the far end were two stand-alone showers, also without privacy. Not since grade school when the boys' bathroom had no doors on the toilet stalls had I experienced the humiliating potency of mass facilities. Even now, just looking at the sheer bareness of it all took me back to a time of daunting, inhibiting effect.

Back in the dayroom the clients still hadn't moved, and there was still no sign of any staff. I casually slipped my hands into my pockets. Slowly, one by one, each of the near-comatose residents rose and began to close in around me like a low-budget zombie flick.

"*Mmmmm . . . Mmmmmmmmm . . . Mmmmmmmmmmm.*"

Shit. I froze, not a clue what to do. What the hell were they up to? Why had they suddenly taken such an interest in my presence? Were they going to attack me all at once or in tag-teams? *Is this the end of poor Steeb Gigger?*

"Take your hands out of your pockets!"

"What?" I said.

From the other side of the room, a woman sporting a throwback perm and carrying a cracked plastic laundry basket had emerged to see what was happening. "Take your hands out of your pockets," she repeated. "They think you've got candy."

I pulled my hands freely into the open and held them palms-up for the foreboding crowd to examine. In unison, the entire bunch turned and shuffled away.

"It's an old habit a lot of them picked up in the mental hospitals," the woman explained as she approached. "Nurses used to reward the patients for good behavior by popping an M&M in their mouths." The woman stopped before me, her face cold. "You working here today?"

"Yeah. I guess."

"Follow me."

I heard a distant *phhhhhtttt!* from the far corner. It was the sound of a pressurized hose coming from the unit's laundry room. There, a second female staff with her hair pulled back beneath a scarf like a milk maiden was busy hosing large brown flakes of sludge off adult cotton diapers, into a drain in the floor before slinging them into a bleach-filled pail to soak. It was only then I recognized her, albeit older and chunkier, as the same young high school cheerleader whom I'd gone through orientation with. The former pepster had traded her pom-poms and pleated skirt for overalls, a padded plastic apron, and rubber gloves. Her face was clean, not a lick of make-up; perhaps she'd sweated it off. We greeted each other with co-worker congeniality, but it was obvious she didn't remember me, and that made me feel a little sad – though not nearly as sad as when she stripped off her gloves and handed me the hose, right before she and Throwback exited for a cigarette break. It didn't matter to Throwback that I was a seasoned employee going on fourteen years, and it sure as hell didn't matter to Cheerleader, who had the same amount of years under her belt as I did. To them I was a new recruit in a time of war, giving entirely new meaning to the battle-torn phrase "in the shit."

Later that same evening, though I didn't think it possible, the lowest point came when one of the clients, a large, muscular man-child not unlike Jackie Chuckam, was denied a second cup of coffee. Coffee and sodas were the staple rewards for many a client in the units, almost to the point of addiction. Staked out next to the half-empty pot in search of an angry fix, the man refused to budge. As I approached to try and talk to him, the man howled and screamed like a tortured animal, and began punching himself in the face. Somewhere, a stat call was immediately sounded.

Having cut my teeth on the other side of the fence at ITF Village, I'd often ignored the distant, garbled echoes of *"Unit 5 – Stat!"* over the P.A. system. Little did I realize a "stat call" meant the convergence of any nearby male employee dog-piling atop a client who had escalated out of control, like something out of *The Snake Pit*. The only difference was, now I was forced to be party to it. Within seconds three other male staff burst upon Unit 5. More screams hit me. Confusion turning to astonishment, to fear. I was being pulled in to help wrestle an unknown body to the ground; his limbs pinned in dramatic fashion, his face pressed into the carpet to muffle the screams. I was horrified. *Is there any way to stop this? The moaning. The gurgling. Dear God – Is that the client or is it me?*

I stared at the other staff standing around watching; some smiling and smirking as if it was funny, others blank and robotic as if they regarded the shrieking man with strict indifference and disdain for all. But there was no expose to be had here, no unwarranted abuse to report. Prone containment was standard practice in the units. It was just the way things were done.

From that point on, aside from the minimal duties I was still expected to fulfill at the CLP, I became permanently assigned to Unit 5. Day after day of acrid smells, brute force, and diapers, diapers, diapers filled with coils of shit. Not a shift went by when I wasn't surrounded by grumbling, pinch-faced co-workers who barked orders to gain behavioral control, only to cause a ripple effect to the opposite. I tried to cope with it by telling myself that a place like Unit 5 had its purpose. It was that necessary place that harbored unspoken trouble and mayhem; the Hills' unofficial, institutionalized dumping ground. I tried to cope with it, but I couldn't. And for that I started to despise everything.

What the hell happened? What happened to the job I used to love? Where did the old CLP disappear to? How did I let Shithead coerce me into an agonizing game of "Keep Away" with my dignity dangled inches beyond my grasp? Throughout my childhood I had listened to my father harangue me as worthless until I was left with no choice but to believe it. Now, underfoot to a new dictatorship, it was all happening again. At thirty-seven years old I felt like a dinosaur of an industry past – seized by an inner panic that I had nowhere else to go.

CHARLY GORDON: I was wondering why the people who would never dream of laughing at a blind or a crippled man would laugh at a moron?
– scene from **Charly**

In the fall of 1996, Shithead announced she was engaged. Astounded, I stood by and watched as she threw herself an engagement party using the CLP Special Use Funds – funds meant for *client* use. Her justification was to allow the clients a chance to wish her congratulations, regardless of the fact that not one of us had been invited to the wedding. *At last!* I thought. Now I have something formidable to catch her with. But by then I'd grown so distraught, I knew full well that no one would listen. No one would care. So instead, I kept my big dinosaur yap shut.

And so the days rumbled onward. Every nerve in my body shredded, every muscle tightened by a torque wrench. Dumbly, I shifted into auto-pilot – beaten, embittered and perpetually pissed. What's worse, I grew resigned that it had been *my* fault. I had allowed my job to become the all-encompassing element that defined me, only to watch it dry up and blow away. If I had any hope of surviving, my newborn hatred needed a means to thrive. And the easiest targets were the people who trusted me the most – my clients from the CLP.

It started slowly. Spiteful mutterings under my breath at the slightest annoyances. Whereas in the past I may have *thought* a client was an asshole, I now found myself mumbling it aloud in their presence. Not loud enough for them to hear, but loud enough to physically unload it from my chest. And it felt *good.*

Teasing followed next. Seemingly harmless ribs such as telling Sammy he didn't have enough in his budget to buy cigarettes just to watch his eyes widen in angst before I burst out laughing, or telling Darlene the cops were coming after her for indecent exposure anytime a black-and-white passed us on the street. Heh-heh-heh. Funny stuff.

Soon I began to openly ridicule them to friends at parties. It was as if the clients had become unwitting characters in my own, sinister stand-up routine. Sammy's lazy eye inspired the alias "Clock and TV" because his divergent gaze made it appear as if he could watch both at the same time. Holly's incontinence was a surefire winner with the toilet-humor crowd. Hughie's exploits of stumbling through everyday life fell prey as buffoonery fodder. At one point I even went so far as to snidely categorize my job as "tard wrangler" just to get a cheap laugh. It wasn't that I had lost respect for the clients – it was that I had lost my *ability* to respect them.

Then there was the Happy Hearts Day incident. By now trips to Disneyland had become annual rituals; fun for the clients, but of little meaning to me. Browsing an Adventureland gift shop, I lazily dug through a barrel of rubber snakes and wiggled one of them playfully in the air.

Jim screamed in horror.

What should have ended there instead turned into depraved torment. "Hey, Jim," I shouted, "wanna pet the . . . *SNAKE*?!" The next thing I knew I was chasing a mentally-challenged grown man around a Disneyland gift shop brandishing a black rubber python as he fled in terror out the door and into the arms of Baloo the Bear.

To me the whole thing was no more harmful than extending a hand in friendship, only to deliver the hidden shock of a dimestore joy buzzer. Cruel? Perhaps. But funny? You betcha. So what if my impishness was at the expense of someone's disability? My ridicule was easily justified. Practical jokes were as fundamental to comedy as pratfalls or slipping on a banana peel. But what I didn't realize was that the resentment I'd incurred, the sheer cynicism, sparked by Mandy and fanned by Shithead, had left my chest hollow and become the foundation for achievements in malice. I now officially hated my job – and that hate had become my own "normal grid." And no one could tell me different.

CHAPTER 19

REDEMPTION 101

CREATURES OF HABIT, even after moving into the CLP, Darlene, Hughie and Holly remained faithful members of the Wagonmasters Society, a club that sponsored weekly square dancing for people with developmentally disabilities. It was an association run strictly by well-meaning volunteers, because – as I considered it – no one else but a well-meaning volunteer would be dumb enough to waste their time on such a thing.

Once a year, the club subsidized a public demonstration in Balboa Park. Amateur groups from all over San Diego County would converge for an all-day event. In their philanthropic fog, the club reserved mornings for people with D.D. so that no one would be left out.

On this particular day I was ordered by Shithead to transport the clients to the event, never mind it was my day off. Furthermore, she'd made arrangements for me to pick up another client to ride along with us. This particular client lived at home with his mother, completely separate of Shepherd Hills. Bad enough it was already an hour's drive to Balboa Park and this guy's house was an additional forty-five minutes out of the way, it also meant suffering additional time stuck behind the wheel of the Sunshine Van. Needless to say, I forged a reasonable resentment about the whole damn thing, but there was nothing I could do about it – it had already been dictated by Shithead.

When I finally found the guy's house – no thanks to Shithead's incoherent directions – he was sitting out front, dressed like a country-Western ragamuffin.

193

As he lumbered into the van, I looked in the rear view mirror and was met by the meanest, nastiest-looking scowl I'd ever seen plastered across a kisser. It was the face of a bulldog. *Grrrr, woof-woof!* And I thought to myself, I don't care if this guy's retarded or not, he's a smirking little shit and I don't like him.

The drive to Balboa Park was only made worse by 90-degree heat and a broken air-conditioner. After jockeying yet *another* half hour to find a parking space big enough to hoist Holly's wheelchair up and down, the clients finally spilled from the van to execute their presentation for a whopping crowd of eight lousy people. Dressed in garish emerald green vests and frilly polka-dotted petticoats, the southern-fried clan meandered about the floor in a graceless, hulking mass of stooped shoulders and unsyncopated gaits, made even *more* ridiculous by Hughie thrusting Holly in and out of the fray in her chair at specified intervals. The few onlookers applauded weakly, and the self-important president of Wagonmasters spouted a lengthy fuss about how wonderfully everybody had performed. But for me, the whole morning was an annoyance – worse, an embarrassment.

Back on the freeway and heading home, Bulldog Boy never once gave up that nasty, snarling grimace. This only burned my butt more. When Holly and Hughie attempted a conversation, I snapped at them to hush up because I needed to concentrate on driving. The five of us rode home in silence, the clients basically allocated to cargo.

When we finally made it back to Bulldog Boy's house, for no reason other than spite I said, "You got any money to pitch in for gas? We're not a damn *taxi* service, y'know." Granted, I knew it was a shitty thing to say, but I had taken it upon myself to decide that this guy didn't deserve a free ride. I had taken it personally simply because of the way he looked and nothing else. In effect, it was something my old man would say. He'd taught me well.

And that's when it happened. When I asked the bulldog for gas money, in this sweet, earnest, childlike voice, he answered:

"I can ask my mommy for some money, if you want."

And just like that, everything stopped. It was a voice that was unbearably innocent. Moreover, unbearably *vulnerable.*

All this puppy wanted was to be a good boy. He wasn't angry at all; the snarl on his face was simply the way his face was "set" and nothing more. But it was his voice that brought it all crashing home.

Immediately, I was back in Jim's apartment the day we caught those two young grifters systematically robbing him blind, the same day an officer of the law scorned his ability to live alone. All I could think was how easy it would be for someone to take advantage of this little man, the same way they'd taken advantage of Jim. He was an innocent child stuck in a grown man's body – and this time I was the one taking advantage. *Me.* The same bastard who'd devoted his life to *helping* people like him. It made me worse than any of the liars and thieves and opportunists I'd ever tried to protect them from.

In truth, his voice was so pure and so human it broke my heart. And in that moment I felt like a failure. I had failed not just in doing my job, but failed the very people I had come to care for. I looked in the rear view mirror. His bulldog expression still hadn't changed. But I had. "No, that's okay," I finally replied. "You don't need money for gas. You're our guest today."

With that, he bounced out of the van and shouted, "G'bye, g'bye, thanks," and ran into his house, Hughie and Holly and Darlene shouting their own childlike good-byes after him. It was as if I'd just dropped off the Beaver after football practice – except the little boy running back inside to be greeted by milk and cookies was a full-grown retarded man.

To this day the chilling, innocent inflection in his voice with just that one sentence still strikes a profound chord in me. *"I can ask my mommy for some money, if you want."* It reminds me how unprotected our clients really are. And how lucky I am to be allowed to be a part of their lives.

Hell, I don't even remember the man's name.

That night, as I drove home in the gathering gloom, I reflected long and hard about what my life had become. It seemed that everything around me was telling me to quit. Was this job really what I wanted to do the rest of my life? If I left Shepherd Hills now, who would I be? Was it too late to return to school after all these years? What was I to make of my anger, of my confusion? Today I'd crossed paths with a forgotten man who had unknowingly spun me around and around till I was lost. Where do I go from here?

My mother always told me that she would be happy as long as I remembered just two things: "Always take a jacket when you go out" and "Always be nice." The day I first interviewed for my job, Dawn had asked me if I'd had any prior exposure to this population. In my answer I hadn't been completely forthcoming. The truth is I *did* have experience with individuals who were considered less fortunate by society's rules. Experience I'm not proud to admit. My encounter that morning jarred loose an emotional tie to the past, which I'd long since suppressed.

It's said that kids can be cruel. And while the first instinct is to think of schoolyard beatings, it more often refers to pre-adolescent verbal warfare. But what's often overlooked is that kids can be *cleverly* cruel. My father's method of spoken sadism was oafish at best. But from it I concocted my own formula for success.

One day, purely by accident, I discovered how easy it was to make other kids cry. Simply by rattling off a slew of insults about one's fragility, poor hygiene or untraditional taste in clothes, other children would curl up like pill bugs and sob. Something inside me felt terrible for doing it, but in a struggle for kiddie domination it was simply too strong to deny. I had to destroy my opponent. I had to win.

Because my family moved every few years, as a means of survival against New-Kid-In-Townism I became the clever cruel kid. In early grades, put-downs were as simple as rhyming someone's name with a naughty word or embarrassing body part, all in an effort to instill prepubescent shock value. Hence, Harold Watkins became Harold Twatkins, Lisa Kitsuta became No Titsuta, Walt Lerwick became Walt Queer Lick, and – my personal favorite – Bob Simek became Snob Slime Crack. Ah, but when you *really* wanted to deliver the final deathblow, branding someone as

RETARDED

always guaranteed victory.

As a result, no one would sit with my victims at lunchtime, invite them home after school to listen to records, or offer to share Popsicles. They were never picked for Heads Up-Seven Up on a rainy day, or asked to trade Hot Wheels. In effect, my evil spirit had the ability to take on a life of its own. It was both sinister and golden.

By age eleven my family uprooted once again, this time landing in a rented shack on the border of Brentwood. By virtue of jurisdiction alone, I was lucky enough to attend Taft Elementary, an affluent grade school brimming with snooty offspring. It was there everything came to a head in Grade 6.

Clara Welch had the face of a toad and the body of a frog. She was gaunt and sickly-looking, with spindly legs and thick, cracked lips. The fact that she also wore gaudy *Laugh-In* style flower-power dresses with white knee socks didn't help matters. Clara *looked* retarded, hence she must've *been* retarded; that was the logic of the day. Either way, there was definitely something "slow" about her that made us all uncomfortable.

As a fat kid growing fatter by the day, my best defense was to create a diversion. It didn't take long to float a few nasty-isms across the playground before the entire student body of Taft treated Clara as if she had the plague.

The sad thing is, I didn't even know her. No one really did. We didn't give her the chance, all because of sheer ignorance compounded by survival of the meanest. Day after day, throughout the course of the school year, Clara sat in the front of the class, victim to sniggers, spitballs and flying boogers. Piggish girls would throw mud on her. Brutish boys would fart at her. One time in the hall someone reached out and tore her dress in passing, "just because." Another time someone left a turd in her locker. At recess, "Turd Toad" sat dejectedly across the blacktop, far from jump ropes and games of Four Square, alone and unwanted, dragging her toes in the kindergarten sand box. It was enough to shatter your heart – if any of us had had one. Meanwhile, I stood by helpless, unable and too cowardly to stop what I'd started. I felt like a monster.

On the last day of the school before summer vacation, the principal passed out copies of the sixth-grade class photo glued to pieces of yellow cardboard that bore the crest of Taft Elementary. Stapled to the back was a tablet of blank pages intended for classmate signatures; a poor man's yearbook. Rah. In a gesture of generosity, the entire graduating sixth-grade student body was released early so we could mingle about the playground, exchanging monikers and sentiments of classroom camaraderie. Gems of childhood wisdom like: *To a cool dude, have a bitchin' summer* and *2 cute + 2 be = 4 gotten.*

Enter Stone Stillwater, the coolest kid in the sixth grade. When the rest of us thought it was cute to say we were voting for Snoopy in the 1968 presidential election, Stone professed support for Pat Paulsen from *The Smothers Brothers' Comedy Hour.* While the rest of us had worn plaid shirts and dress slacks for the school picture, Stone fashioned a Nehru jacket. In my yearbook, Stone wrote: *"Roses are red, violets are purple. Give me a dime and I'll scratch your ka-nurple."* Stone Stillwater was the flagship for eleven-year-old hip. And it was Stone Stillwater who changed my outlook forever that day when he did the unthinkable. As Clara Welch silently began her way home, zigzagging stealthily through scores of classmates, Stone stepped forward and asked her to sign his yearbook. The crowd fell silent. It wasn't a joke. He meant it with all sincerity – a small, genuine and truly heroic gesture that reconditioned everything. Never before had I seen such a look of pure joy overtake a person's face.

One by one the entire sixth-grade class gathered around Clara in a whirlwind of remorse, and one by one we, too, requested her autograph. Cries of "Thanks, Clara," "See ya next year, Clara," and "Have a bitchin' summer, Clara," echoed out onto the kick ball court. All to say how sorry we were for the way we'd treated her. All to hopefully make things right. All because one kid stepped up – proving that the innocence of an eleven-year-old could be equally wise.

I wish it had been me, but I wasn't nearly popular or courageous enough to lead such a revolution. I didn't possess the ability to clean up my own mess. Yet the thing I recall most is how *easily* we all followed suit. We knew all along that what we'd done to Clara wasn't kind, and simply needed someone mature enough to teach us that she deserved respect. Stone Stillwater – long lost to the lonesome winds that cleanse our nations' schoolyards – was a man of distinguished valor. It was a wind that spoke clearly. From that day on I never took the initiative to heartlessly tease anyone again. Instead, I adopted an inner sympathy for people who appeared terminally vulnerable, and at the same time dismissed a childhood filled with countless victims of verbal torment. It was as if I wanted to do penance for all the infantile disrespect and misery I caused – no matter how childish or childlike. My behavior had been unconscionable. But most of all it hadn't been fair – a direct opposition to my core belief.

That summer, my family moved yet again, this time to Orange County where I officially began the fresh hell of adolescence and a new, more subdued and introspective life. I wasn't there to see what became of Clara, but I like to think she went on to become class president, most popular, perhaps prom queen or winner of a Drama scholarship, and grew to achieve every dream she ever had. I like to think that wherever she is today, she's cherished. Still, to this day, that image of Clara's shadow across the playground where we'd exiled her continues to haunt me.

Why did I do it? Were my taunts inherited directly from my father? The moment it all rang clear just how hurtful I'd been to so many classmates, how *intentionally* hurtful, made me sick to my stomach with shame. I wish to God somehow I could go back in time and beg their forgiveness, to offer them Popsicles and records and Hot Wheels. But the best I can offer is that my childhood callousness stopped with them. I can only hope in another life they'll absolve me.

As I pulled my car into the dark, claustrophobic garage of my mother's condo, I sat there overcome with defeat. Like Clara Welch, the clients' vulnerability was unshielded, at once exposed and imperiled, and what little protection I'd tried to provide in the past had all but slipped away. Then I asked myself, just what was it that brought me to Shepherd Hills in the first place? In the beginning I was motivated by a desire to be closer to Michelle, but after she left it was *my* decision to stay. *Why?* Was it all a cosmic coincidence or had I been subconsciously looking for some sort of self-preservation? While I thought I wanted to educate and safeguard the clients, the truth was I needed them to do the same for me.

Whenever people remark that my job "must be very rewarding," I cringe. I never wanted a job that *rewarded* me, I just wanted to be happy while doing it. But that night, when I realized this was no longer the case, I reached my breaking point. It made me understand that people like Sissy Shithead will always define people like me if I let them.

Michelle once told me *"this job is what you make it – so make it matter."* It was time to take back what I'd allowed to be stolen.

The next morning I went into work early and met directly with Shithead's supervisor, the Director of Residential Services. Candid, brief, and to the point, I reported that Shithead had robbed the clients of their money – knowing full well nothing would be done. But I no longer cared about that. Unable to stand Shithead's tyranny any longer after one agonizing year, I decided the best way to move beyond her was to step over her. Laying my soul to bear, I appealed for some relief, some way out. Something, *anything*. Doing my best to mask an inner suffering, I boldly asked what it would take to move beyond my current position. What could I do to start liking my job again? What could I do that would best serve the clients?

Within the hour I had my answer.

JOB DESCRIPTION
Job Title: **Qualified Mental Retardation Professional/Administrator**
Department: Residential Services

Primary Purpose: The QMRP/Administrator has 24-hour responsibility for the health, safety, programs and services to clients residing in assigned house(s).

ESSENTIAL JOB RESPONSIBILITIES:

Responsible for a variety of duties which include but are not limited to:

2. Coordinate client services including schedules, assessments, staffing and individual service plans.
3. Design, implement, and monitor delivery of programs.
4. Provide direct supervision of direct care staff.
5. Ensure compliance with agency's policies and procedures.
6. Ensure client rights and advocate accordingly.
7. Conducts self in a professional manner in all forms of communication with the clients, support staff, family and outside agencies.

QUALIFICATIONS:

Education: BA in Social Work or field related to developmental disabilities (*or substantial experience in related field*).

Experience: One-year experience working with people with developmental disabilities. One year supervisory experience preferred.

By the month's end I left the Community Living Program – and Unit 5 – for a promotion to full-fledged supervisor of three Shepherd Hills' community group homes. After fourteen years of servitude and good faith, I quietly slipped into the ranks of management, as if it had been waiting there for me all along.

In my years as a worker in the special-needs field I've seen people apply for positions with the greatest intentions and highest expectations that they were about to make a difference in the world – and then quit the very next day. In time, they all come and go: wannabe pedagogues, empty nest syndromers, hapless disciplinarians, power strugglers, Pollyannas, assholes and, every now and then, people who truly care. But sticking it out for the long haul, that's a different animal to feed. It's more than just a matter of seeking a career. To attain longevity comes down to a question of work ethics, a belief in inevitability, and a whole lot of hope.

Shortly after I left the CLP, Sissy Cain was fired for misappropriation of funds. In the end, my final stab at thin air apparently made contact after all. As vile and incompetent as she was, it was the greed of a few dollars that ultimately brought her down.

I remembered back to the very first staff meeting helmed by then newly-hired Shithead when she promptly declared: "There is no such thing as job security – *any* of you could be replaced tomorrow." For me her demise was a small but sweet victory; for the clients it meant the inevitable restoration of their very spirit.

Last I heard Shithead went back to doing manicures – for the C.H.U.D.s where she belongs.

PART V

WELCOME HOME– SET A SPELL,
TAKE YOUR SHOES OFF.
Y'ALL COME BACK NOW, Y'HEAR?

CHAPTER 20

THE DAY 10,000 CLIENTS DISAPPEARED

"Those who can, teach. Those who can't teach, become administrators."
– H.J. Peebles, high school English teacher

MY NEW TITLE was now "Qualified Mental Retardation Professional/Administrator," a.k.a. "QMRP," a.k.a. "Q" for short. It caused me great heartache to leave my CLP clients, and to leave an entity that I had essentially built, nurtured, and ultimately watched crumble. I felt as if I'd climbed a 10-year ladder and pulled it up behind me. But the full-time hours and the free apartment-slash-office of the old CLP were now long gone. The time had come for me to move on. In the end, despite constant threats to close down due to low funding and the damage inflicted by Sissy Shithead, the CLP survived. It survived by virtue of the *clients'* success, by their tenacity to rebuild and stabilize.

All that was left for me now was the survival of sanity.

In the late 1990s, the entire special-needs field underwent a change in both mission and philosophy. "Normalization" had been a noble cause, but was now regarded as just another excuse to make the clients fit in rather than call attention to their uniqueness. And so it was replaced by a new fundamental principle:

"Active Treatment"

Whereas normalization had been defined as *"a process by which persons with developmental disabilities are given the opportunity to live and act more like their non-disabled peers in the community,"* active treatment was succinctly defined as *"finding teachable moments."* Everything a client sees and hears should teach them something.

It was also about this time a new terminology for the word "client" itself was instituted. We were all formally informed that from now on, clients would be referred to as "consumers."

Consumers? we asked with furrowed brows. As in people who buy cars, refrigerators and televisions? Where the heck did *that* come from? It all began with People First.

For the record, I always liked the term "client." I always felt it was a show of respect, as in "Jim is my client. I work for him." But in perspective, admittedly, that put me in charge, in that Jim was *my* client. In direct response to this, People First – an international self-advocacy organization for persons with developmental disabilities – decided they no longer liked being someone else's "client." Instead, they decided upon the term "consumer" because it put *them* in charge. Strictly speaking, the people served by the special-needs field are "consumers" of a product in that they "purchase services" from us. Residential services, medical services, vocational services, recreational services. Therefore, they became "consumers" of our product.

That's not to say "client" suddenly became taboo. In fact, both terms remain interchangeable in the field today. Nonetheless, the terms "active treatment" and "consumer" marked a formidable changing of the guard patrolling the euphemism treadmill. Even the name "People First" became its own characterization. Consumers were no longer developmentally disabled individuals, they were individuals *with* a developmental disability. People *first* – that is, *people* who happen to have *disabilities* – with disabilities a distant second.

In addition, we were presented with a list of "People Firstspeak– Interacting with and Etiquette for People with Disabilities":

> Say *"person who has"* instead of *"afflicted or suffers from"*
> Say *"a disability"* instead of *"disabled or handicapped"*
> Say *"without speech or nonverbal"* instead of *"mute or dumb"*
> Say *"deaf or hearing impaired"* instead of *"hard of hearing"*
> Say *"visually impaired"* instead of *"sightless"*
> Say *"non-disabled"* instead of *"normal or healthy"*
> Say *"developmental delay"* instead of *"slow"*

So then, why is all this meaningful? Because in light of this new philosophy, Shepherd Hills Board and Care suddenly and unexpectedly found themselves cast as a waning fixture of an institutionalized age.

CHALLENGED: A TRIBUTE | 205

This caused The Hills to implement a massive transformation. In 1997 the Board of Directors announced the decision to begin closing down the main campus. With it would recede all the aspects Shepherd Hills had taken for granted over the last 30 years. The main kitchen would be auctioned off piece by piece. The wheelchair-accessible pool would be dug up. Each separate unit would be bulldozed into one, big, collective pile.

As an alternative plan, all the consumers would partake in an unprecedented emigration. A total of 27 federally licensed, ICF/DD-H (Intermediate Care Facility for the Developmentally Disabled– Habilitative) community group homes would now establish residency by 2002 amongst the varying neighborhoods of San Diego's East County. The ultimate goal of each home would be to develop each consumer's "quality of life" so they may live as independently as possible – with dignity, choices, and the least amount of restrictions.

This meant challenges. ENORMOUS challenges. It meant consumers learning how to live without fences or locked refrigerators. To share two bathrooms with one toilet each rather than one bathroom with six toilets. It meant family-style, serve-yourself-dining, not pre-portioned plates. No sequestered nurse's station or staff office in which to seek shelter during outbursts. No soda machines inside the time clock room. In fact, no time clock room at all. It meant hands-on, down-sized, six-people-to-a home microcosms. In essence, a monumental change of lifestyle for 150-plus people. For me, it meant the end of one era and the beginning of another.

Because of my experience in the CLP, I was put in charge of three of the first experimental satellite group homes. By now I knew all too well that moving quasi-institutionalized consumers into the community was customarily met with a mixed bag of allegiance and apprehension. There were neighbors, notable and kind, who welcomed us with cheerful smiles, and a few who openly sneered and forbade us from parking in front of their homes. But the majority just kept to themselves – perhaps an indication of society's enlightened tolerance, or perhaps forever fearing one day they might wake to find a deranged freak scratching at the window chanting "one of us, one of us." Either way, we were now all part of the same neighborhood – like it or not.

Little did I realize when I became a Q that very few people had faith in me. Even I caught myself now and then questioning whether or not I belonged here, in this new position. Despite having over fourteen years experience, I was immediately a target of doubt because I'd just spent ten years out in the CLP – all but completely removed from The Hills' main campus, or by everyone's else's mindset, the *real* Hills. And now they were giving me *three* houses with a caseload of *eighteen* brand new consumers? What were they, *nuts?*

Eighteen consumers, each with an entirely new set of quirks and challenges. Eighteen consumers, and not one of them with a diagnosis higher than "Severe Mental Retardation." Whereas the consumers from ITF Village and the CLP had been classified as "high-functioning" and labeled as "Borderline," "Mild" and "Moderate," this crop descended from "Severe" to "Profound." Clinical diagnoses included heavyweight phrases like "hyperactive chronic paranoid schizophrenia," and "major depressive disorder." Common behavior modification plans included "Self-Injurious Behavior," "Destruction of Property," "Aggression," and the great catch-all, "Inappropriate Social Interaction." On top of that were the medical conditions: hypertension, sleep apnea, hiatal hernia, thoraco-lumbar scoliosis, erosive esophagitis, hyperlipidemia, congenital cytogenesis, seborrheic dermatitis, hypothyroidism, transcient ischemic attack – and a whole bunch of other fancy words I knew nothing about. These were consumers who inhabited a completely different corner of the sub-culture that was far more emotionally driven; who needed help but didn't *realize* they needed help; who unknowingly accepted their dependency.

Providing "quality of life" was a buzzword philosophy I'd heard preached since day one on the job – a philosophy affirmed wise enough to mandate *anyone's* life. But over the years I'd grown to feel that it was just as important, if not more so, to provide them with a "quality of *living*." While quality of life fulfills wants, needs and services, it also requires measurement, steeped in the design that a consumer forever has to "achieve" something. But quality of living looks at a person's *day to day* existence. In my mind we needed to look more passionately at a person's *life-pace* and respect the way they step through time. "Active treatment" and "teachable moments" are all well and good. But sometimes we all like to simply *exist* just for the sheer joy of it.

As a newly trained Q, the primary focus of my job changed as well. Whenever people would ask me what I did for a living, I no longer categorized myself wryly as "home economist, Miss Manners and shrink." I now explained it by telling them to imagine they're a parent with a sexually-aware, unruly teenager who cusses, gets into fights, steals people's stuff, refuses responsibility – you know, the usual juvenile delinquent fare. Then I tell them to imagine they can't be parental. They can't scold their teenager, spank them, ground them, send them to bed without supper, or do anything punitive, *but* . . . they still have to figure out a way to stop their child from exhibiting those negative behaviors. "*That*," I tell them, "is what I do for a living." And so, rather than run from it all, I embraced the diversity. I was determined to help teach, support and advocate for each and every consumer the best way I knew how: On paper.

Forging my own transition, I found myself growing exhilarated by assembling new tactics for behavior management strategies and putting them into practice. It was as if I'd accidentally discovered *an entirely new type of creative writing*. To design a successful behavior plan required getting deep into a person's head, generating ten times the character development I'd ever accomplished as a fledgling playwright. And in this I discovered enormous satisfaction – and enormous relief. At long last my writing aspirations, what few there had been, found new definition as a Q. I had kept myself inactive too long. And damn me if that didn't mean one thing: *school was finally back in session.*

CHAPTER 21

GET UP, STAND UP,
STAND UP FOR YOUR RIGHTS

IN THE YEAR 2000 something startling happened. I caught on fire.

Maybe it had been a long time coming, but the thrill of a new job, a *career* no less, lit a blaze under my butt hot enough to ignite my life with new meaning.

It began gradually as I found myself volunteering to help teach orientation classes to new hires. Next, I volunteered to head a drive for the United Way. After that, I formed a task force with other managers to brainstorm solutions to The Hills' "invisible" problems like how to improve employee job performance and increase staff morale. This lead me to step up and offer suggestions on how to reformat and refine the Shepherd Hills Policy and Procedures Manual – ideas I'd withheld from Shithead and only now felt confident enough to share. Before I knew it, I was coordinating monthly Q meetings and facilitating our Human Rights Committee, even sitting in now and then as the Behavior Specialist. (Imagine, me a *specialist!*) What it all came down to, basically, was the desire to teach – vintage Hawaiian shirts and Birkenstocks notwithstanding.

My next quest beckoned the day I was asked to represent Shepherd Hills as a member of the planning committee for the Annual People First Self-Advocacy Conference. This was the same group that had redefined consumer rights, fostered active treatment, and flourished the language of People First philosophy in an effort

208

CHALLENGED: A TRIBUTE

to move beyond the stigma of cognitive disabilities and actively confront them instead. It was an honor I couldn't turn down.

The event was scheduled to take place on Mother's Day weekend at the San Diego Marriott Hotel. Attended by people with developmental disabilities from all over the state, the two-day conference offered workshops ranging in everything from dating and relationships to self-directed services. The first night would be capped by a formal dinner/dance, with the second day ending in the ever-popular open-mike session. This was a convention unlike any other – an indisputable guarantee to lift your spirits.

As a committee member my actual part was small as I found myself assigned to help advertise the already well-known and duly-respected affair. But I didn't mind, just to be a part of such a prestigious group was reward enough. Besides, I got a free T-shirt.

Still, I couldn't avoid the conviction that my interest in joining was largely to compensate – if not overcompensate – for the lingering guilt I still felt leaving my CLP consumers as abruptly as I did. Though comfortable with my career as a Q, I found myself looking for something meaningful again, something personal in the lives of the consumers – *any* consumer. I craved to see those of the "higher-functioning" order stand up for themselves, not just simply follow daily schedules, and hoped People First could quench my thirst.

And boy-howdy, did it ever!

That Mother's Day weekend I was witness to a unique consumer self-realization of rights – and it didn't come from any workshop.

That same year, Chris Burke was scheduled to be the keynote speaker. Burke was a young man with Down syndrome who played a kid with Down syndrome named Corky on the '80s TV show *Life Goes On*. Naturally, this was a *momentous* occasion to all the attendees, to meet one of their own, a fellow human being with cognitive disabilities who had ascended to the level of TV stardom. They were his fan base, his core audience. And Chris Burke knew it. To him it was – *cha-ching!* – time to cash in!

Burke and his entourage arrived in pure Hollywood style. Their entrance to the hotel lobby was like something straight out of *Reservoir Dogs* – complete with slow-motion swagger and sunglasses for all. Walking directly past the check-in committee, Burke refused to speak to anyone who wasn't a reporter. He went straight up to his room and never came down until it was his time to speak.

The next morning after breakfast, when Burke finally sauntered into the main conference room, the place went wild. He spoke briefly about how talented an actor he was, and about the many challenges he had overcome to get where he was today. (Okay, I'll give him that one.) Next, he presented a lengthy compilation of clips from *Life Goes On*. After finishing his speech with a few token, inspirational *bon mots* like, "If I can do it, you can do it too" (which in itself is a highly irresponsible thing to say to a roomful of easily manipulated, star-struck, developmentally disabled people), he *then* proceeded to hawk his book for sale in the lobby – where he would be signing autographs at $5 a pop.

Of course it came as no surprise when scores of consumers lined up with cherished hopes for autographs and "meet 'n greet" conversation. But as each approached their turn, fingers tightly grasping book covers in anticipation, I watched in dismay as Burke wouldn't talk to them, wouldn't even look them in the eye, as he curtly scribbled his mark over the title page. Instead, he directed his "representatives" to shuttle each consumer past the table faster than the candy assembly line on *I Love Lucy*. At one point a young girl with Down syndrome approached him from the side, out of line. As she began to gush praise and delight, Burke raised his hand to her face and refused to acknowledge her. Crestfallen, she was brusquely escorted away.

It gets worse. That night, at the conference dinner/dance, none other than – surprise! – Mister Chris Burke provided the entertainment. It turned out he had his own 3-piece folk band – and they were selling CDs for that, too! Nevertheless, the consumers lit up like they were in the presence of royalty. And, no doubt, to many they were.

The entire matter left me torn. But for me to say anything against their chosen guest of honor would've been sacrilege, taboo, and just plain out of line. I won't deny the virtue in consumers having a positive role model, but I was still appalled to see Burke exploit his fellow individuals, allowing them nothing more than the privilege of being fleeced by an arrogant, self-appointed disabilities guru. And the fact that I couldn't say anything frustrated the hell out of me.

Then I noticed a group of consumers gathering off to the side. Like many, they had each endured the long line for autographs and CDs – and they didn't appear too happy. Inching over to eavesdrop, I could feel the venom coursing through their slurred and personalized phrasings:

> "– *What a fuckin' rip off!* –"
> "– *What a jerk! What a jerk! What a jerk!* –"
> "– *Do you believe dat guy?!* –"
> "– *How rude! He waz so ru-u-ude!* –"
> "– *What a jerk! What a jerk! What a jerk!* –"
> "– *He sings like shit!* –"
> (And maybe the single greatest comment of all):
> "– *Corky a* ASS*hole!* –"

O, gratification, sweet and delicious! I could barely contain myself. Listening to this meeting of the minds I thought, you can have your Active Treatment and your ISPs and your program implementation and all the service analysis you want. *This* was something no training program could teach. *This* was self-actualization in the making. I was proud of those consumers because they came to those conclusions on their own. They *themselves* were able to identify Mister Chris Burke for the sell-out he was. Not only was it revitalizing and transcendent, it made me feel there was hope for true independence after all.

CHAPTER 22

HEY KIDS, LET'S PUT ON A SHOW!

BY YEAR'S END, with all the various task forces and committees I'd piled on my plate, I found myself left with just one last item I wanted to sink my teeth into: A return to the theater.

In the year 2000, before the main campus was due to be completely vacated, there still remained access to the auditorium, which had been left available for Sunday church services. The Hills' resident chaplain, Rebecca Lloyd, the same woman who'd resided over Jackie Chuckam's funeral and Holly and Hughie's wedding, was one of a rare breed who had just the right touch with our population. Her sensibilities were patient and forthright, with a voice of warmth and rejuvenation – and enough moxie to keep the rowdier consumers in line. Once a week she'd open the auditorium to anyone who wanted to attend, and there was never a shortage of those who would flock to hear Rebecca tell Bible stories. The Hills was lucky to have her.

Each year Rebecca organized a small Christmas pageant with a diminutive choir of consumers who did their best to warble a smattering of carols. But this year would be different. This year I stepped forward, seized with a bold and ambitious idea. Instead of the usual sing-along, I proposed we stage our very own version of *A Christmas Carol.*

In part, my idea was fueled by a longing to relive my college Drama days and, in part, I'd been roused by the spirit of Christmas. But the main reason actually stemmed from a much more personal realization. Despite a year of earnest volunteering, I realized that since becoming a QMRP, I'd lost a certain emotional tie to my consumers. Any consumers, all consumers, old and new. The reality of my new position – a position of pen against paper far removed – had caused me to think of my job as dispassionately technical, if not strictly clinical. More often than not, I found myself staring starchily at blank form after blank form, waking from daydreams of good times gone by.

In retrospect, my involvement with the People First conference had been born out of a desire to reconnect with consumers *similar* to those from the CLP. This time I wanted to take that desire all the way. This time my aim would focus on both my current group of consumers and the ones I longed to see again. In short, I missed the old gang. Essentially, they had been the closest thing I ever knew to a family. Still, as I pulled up and parked outside the Spring Tree Apartments to meet with them, I couldn't help but wonder if they missed me as well. Would they forgive me for leaving them four years ago? Hell, would they even *remember* me? Within minutes my fears were put to rest. With the innocence of childlike alliance, each member of the CLP greeted me as if I'd never left. To them, friendship wasn't governed by time. When I asked them if they'd like to participate in the show, every one of them immediately said yes. It was testament to our kinship and I never felt more esteemed.

"Can I bring my tape recorder?" Owen asked.

"Aw, yer head!" Jim chided him playfully.

Some things never change.

For the next several evenings I sat beneath a 40-watt dining room lamp in my mother's condo and wrote feverishly. It was the most sincere attempt at playwriting I'd done in nearly twenty years. I was amazed at how easily the concept fell into place. Borrowing reverently from *Mr. Magoo's Christmas Carol,* I developed a bare-bones structure wherein a brief – *extremely* brief – scene of the classic storyline would be performed, shuffled between songs rendered by the Shepherd Hills choir. Meanwhile, Rebecca would act as narrator to link everything together.

We originally considered calling ourselves The Shepherd Hills International Theatrical Society – that is, until someone pointed out how inappropriate the acronym might look on a flyer. Instead, we dubbed ourselves The Shepherd Hills Famous Players. Not since Fred and Barney's Loyal Order of the Water Buffaloes had there been a title so majestic.

Those consumers who simply wanted to sing – regardless of appreciation for tone or timbre – were designated to the choir. Those who simply wanted their moment on stage were granted the role of townspeople en masse. Over the course of extensive rehearsals we were joined by an array of closet thespians and "look-at-me" divas who were promptly inserted judiciously to help maintain some semblance of a genuine production. Bottom line, no one was left out. Our meager little theater group became a motley mix of consumers, staff, and community volunteers that Rebecca pulled together. But it was the final casting of the main characters that proved most inspirational.

In the lead role of Ebenezer Scrooge I assigned none other than Owen Van Winkle to conquer the task – a role that was tailor-made for his bravado. As Marley's Ghost, Hughie Lamb was only too eager to strut his theatrical stuff. The Ghosts of Christmas Present and Yet To Come were easily filled by Darlene Beaudine and Holly Lamb, respectively. For the Ghost of Christmas Past I tracked down Iggy Flynn, still going strong back at what was left of ITF Village before he was destined to join the CLP once the main campus closed. Adding Iggy to the ensemble was a gladdening I hadn't originally planned on, and a delightful way to welcome him back into the ranks.

The crowning achievement came in the casting of Tiny Tim. The role of the infamous urchin was awarded to Jim Livingston, trademark sheepdog bangs, chocolate mouth and all. Last but not least, Sammy White consented to play Bob Cratchit. Hearkening back to the time I first discovered Sammy's ability to sing (and my inability to operate a simple hearing aid), I was determined to work his talents into the show. After a great deal of pleading, wheedling and a large sausage pizza, I was finally able to appeal to Sammy's ego and he agreed to do a solo of "O Holy Night."

With a budget of exactly zero dollars, what soon formulated could best be described as hypo-community theatre. At first, most of the volunteers showed up for a day or two then disappeared, only to be replaced by another well-meaning yet ultimately disinterested few. Little by little, we managed to layer in a supply of props and costumes – a scarf here, a length of chain there, a box of broken ornaments, some plastic poinsettias, a desk and inkwell for Bob Cratchit, a ball of tangled Christmas lights, and one, used, artificial tree. One donor even delivered us a black top hat for Scrooge – which Owen took to wearing with enough zeal to rival Darlene's Chuck E. Cheese cap.

Meanwhile, women from the local Rotary Club offered to help style hair and assist with make-up. Fabric remnants were draped and safety-pinned to replicate period attire. A local kindergarten teacher conducted the choir. A shy, obese, first-year employee stepped forward to play piano. Even a couple of Shriners showed up with their own horse costume, asking if they could help. (Never one to look a gift horse costume in the mouth, I vowed to somehow find a place for them.) As for me, I was dubbed stage manager and director. Behind the scenes, once again – just the way I liked it.

Our stage design was dictated by a matter of circumstance. Assembled on the main stage were the sets for Scrooge's bedroom, delineated by a single bed and sparse nightstand, and the Cratchit family home, represented by a small dining table. The floor in front of the stage was split in half for the choir and townspeople. The main stage was where the leads would perform, while the floor was left for the supporting cast. Unfortunately, this did not sit well to everyone's liking. During

CHALLENGED: A TRIBUTE | 215

rehearsals it quickly became apparent that the most popular place to be was up on stage. Each time we tried to run the show, there were always a few stray consumers who would try and wander their way into the spotlight. This ultimately prompted Rebecca to make a stern announcement.

"*NO* one is allowed on stage unless they're supposed to be there. Is that *understood?*"

A disappointed collection of consumers, staff and volunteers nodded and mumbled that it was. Still, I wasn't completely convinced.

Something told me it was going to be a night to remember.

Opening night (of a whopping two-night run), everyone took their places in full, festive wardrobe, armed with a couple of hand-held microphones to be passed back and forth at appropriate intervals. I settled in backstage to run the show, with a bargain-basement sound system, and a special effects arsenal that consisted of a sheet-metal thunder board, a recording of Big Ben striking twelve, and an on/off switch to flicker the house lights in order to signify lightning. Playing to a standing-room-only audience – which included the Mayor of Santee, the Santana High School Winter Prom Queen, a reporter from the *Santee Shopping News*, various parents, neighbors, co-workers, Shepherd Hills board members, and other consumers – at exactly 7:05 p.m. (because, as I'd dutifully learned in college, no self-respecting stage show – even Nudes On Ice – *ever* begins before five minutes past the hour) the curtain rose.

"Welcome!" Rebecca greeted the curious crowd. "Thank you for coming. Tonight we would like to dedicate our annual Christmas pageant to all the people who've made Shepherd Hills a success over the years, as we present to you our version of *A Christmas Carol*, freely adapted from the Charles Dickens' novel."

"*EEEEEYYYAAAAAAACCCHHH!*"

On cue, somewhere in the back of the room, a stray consumer brayed his disapproval and began beating his head. As he was briskly escorted outside by a staff member, the audience rumbled uneasily.

Rebecca shook her head. "Everybody's a critic," she quipped, and the room was restored with a laugh.

"Cue the music," I said.

As "The Holly and the Ivy" tinkled from the piano, Rebecca went on to set the scene in grand, yarn-spinning fashion:

"It's Christmas Eve in London, 1834. The townspeople are out and about doing a little last minute shopping, on their way home to their families, and singing the songs of the season with joy."

To a coarsely off-key rendition of "Caroling, Caroling," the coffee and soda-pumped choir and townspeople entered from the back of the room. In the programs, we'd included the words to all the songs and encouraged the audience to join in as they saw fit. As the cast took their places in front of the stage, I peered out from the wings to survey the audience's reaction. Not a single lip was moving.

From there, the choir slipped into "Deck the Halls." On the final "Fa-la-la-la-la," Owen entered with characteristic indignation. "*Bah, Humbug!*" he roared. "If I could work my will, every person who goes about with 'Merry Christmas' on his lips should be boiled in his own pudding, and buried with a stake of holly through his heart!"

I beamed. Owen's reading was flawless. And yet, only light applause rippled through the auditorium. Jeez, I thought, rough room. Probably thinking if they left now they could still make it home in time to catch the last half of *Sabrina, the Teenage Witch*.

"Cue 'Silent Night,' *quick!*" I whispered.

At the same time the choir began to sing, Owen took his place on stage, donned his nightcap and gown, feigned a dramatic yawn, and crawled into Scrooge's bed.

"Cue Hughie."

Chains a-rattling, Marley's Ghost entered to interrupt Scrooge's slumber and warn him of the impending nocturnal visit. Hughie Lamb immediately crossed center stage – directly in front of Owen – and delivered the menacing threat "*Three ghosts!*" repeatedly, as it was the only line he could remember. Miffed at being upstaged, Scrooge gave Marley a sharp poke in the ass with his cane. Nevertheless, Hughie refused to budge, bitten firmly by the acting bug.

Having rendering her narration of the now-famous scene, Rebecca attempted to cue Hughie's exit. "And with that, Marley disappeared."

"Three ghosts! Three ghosts! *Whooooo . . .*"

"I *said*, 'And with *that*, Marley *DIS-A-PPEARED!*"

"Three ghosts! Three ghosts! *Whooooo . . .*"

If this had been a vaudeville review, right about now a giant hook would've bobbed from the wings and snagged Hughie by the throat against his will. Instead, our production only had my arm, which promptly reached out and grabbed Hughie by the chains, yanking him off to a hearty crowd response. Finally, the audience seemed to be warming up.

Next up was Iggy as the Ghost of Christmas Past. Because the part called for a white flowing gown, we dressed him in Holly's wedding dress with her jolly approval. For a brief moment I found myself back on the *Bahia Belle* as a member of Holly and Hughie's wedding party, listing from side to side at the social event of 1987. A testament to Iggy's good nature, he thought dressing in drag was hilarious – but it was the addition of his ten-gallon hat that really gave the costume its pizzazz. And then he farted.

"Cue the choir!"

"The First Noel . . . the angels did say . . ."

As the Ghost of Christmas Present, Darlene and her enormous assets lorded over Scrooge. Suddenly, Darlene broke into her famed moose-horn bop – but

CHALLENGED: A TRIBUTE 217

thankfully left her shirt on. At the same time, Mr. and Mrs. Sammy Cratchit danced around their scant dinner table, leading Tiny Tim Jim through the traces of "The Christmas Song."

"Chess-NUTZ roasting on an o-pen fire . . ."

". . . Mack mah muh-muh-muhn yer nose . . ."

Despite their meager lifestyle, the Cratchits relished their family values, and to prove it we hung a large cardboard sign around Jim's neck that read "God Bless Us, Everyone" – just so no one would miss the point. When it came time for Tiny Tim Jim to deliver his crucial line, Sammy leaned over, poised a microphone under Jim's chin and whispered in Jim's ear. The entire exchange played out over the speaker system:

"Okay, Jim, say 'God bless us, everyone.'"

"Huh?"

"Say 'God bless us, everyone.'"

"Me?"

"Yeah, you."

"Muh-muh-muh?"

"Say 'God bless us, everyone.'"

"Huh?"

"Say 'God . . .'"

At last Jim diligently repeated. "God . . ."

"Bless . . ."

"Bess . . ."

"Us . . ."

"Us . . ."

"Everyone."

"Huh?"

"Everyone. Say 'everyone'!"

"Me?"

"Yeah, you! Say it, blockhead!"

"EVY-WHAHN!" shouted Jim.

The crowd cheered!

By the time we got to the Ghost of Christmas Yet To Come, the audience had fully loosened up. *Cue* the metal-sheet thunder and flickering-lights lightning! *Cue* the sound effects of wind and Big Ben striking twelve! Enter little Holly Lamb – unlike any Dickensian ghost the world had ever seen. Thanks to the last-minute craftsmanship of Santana High School's wood shop, Holly's wheelchair was transformed into a colossal, Big Daddy Roth-influenced rendition of The Grim Reaper on wheels. Attached to the back of her chair rose a seven-foot-tall class project of miter joints and cross beams shrouded in black velvet, complete with a blood-stained scythe and rubber Halloween "Death" mask with flashing red eyes. It was a truly ominous construction that undoubtedly earned an A+. When Holly wheeled herself precariously toward Scrooge, the audience gasped with a collective shiver that passed through them all at once. Scrooge feared this spirit most of all as it towered above him, for this ghost showed Scrooge his destiny – and worst of all, the grave of Tiny Tim. (Not to mention the fact it could topple over any moment and crush him to death.)

"Cue 'The Midnight Cry."

The choir rang out with reverence.

When Jesus steps out on a cloud to call His children
The dead in Christ shall rise to meet Him in the air
And then those that remain shall be quickly changed
Will be changed in a moment
At the Midnight Cry we'll be going ho-o-o-ome

How can I possibly begin to describe the sound; a sound so passionate and pure and genuine that it makes the hairs on the back of your neck stand up? Anyone who's ever heard a gospel choir, *any* gospel choir, can attest to the chills they inspire. There were cheers. There were tears. There were shouts of unabashed exultation. To call it magical wouldn't begin to do it justice. For the humble Shepherd Hills choir, it would be remembered as the night they brought down the house.

Heading full bore into the climax, the room was now ablaze with holiday spirit. Awakening from his nightmares, Scrooge excitedly called out from his bedroom window.

SCROOGE: You, there! What day is it?
TOWNSPEOPLE: Christmas day!
SCROOGE: Christmas? YIPPPPEEEEE!!!

"Cue the horse!"

Enthralled, Scrooge gleefully rejoiced with the realization that he hadn't missed the Yuletide after all – and the audience was right there with him. Grabbing the reins of his faithful steed Midnight the Horse (I *told* you I'd find a way to fit that damn horse costume into the show), Old Ebenezer, dressed in nightshirt and top hat, proceeded to flounce his enthusiasm up and down the aisles, tossing chocolate coins covered in shiny gold foil to the crowd.

This brought us to Sammy's solo.

From my unique vantage point backstage, I was able to survey the entire auditorium. It was at this point I noticed a consumer who wasn't in the play named Kevin Maltz slowly meandering up the aisle from the back of the house. Kevin was non-verbal and autistic, floating about on his own little cloud.

Sammy vaulted onto the stage and planted himself beneath the spotlight. Meanwhile, as Scrooge continued to chew the scenery with melodramatic glee, no one noticed Kevin fluttering his way through the audience to the front of the room. Once Scrooge concluded his exhibition of generosity, Rebecca quieted the crowd so that all ears were now concentrated on Sammy. By the time Sammy began his solo, Kevin had just made it to the forefront of the stage – the one place Rebecca had warned everyone was off limits. Consequently, Sammy's much-anticipated solo went a little something like this:

"*O Holy Night . . . the stars are brightly*" – (sees Kevin) – "YOU GET THE FUCK OUTTA HERE, KEVIN MALTZ! YOU GET AWAY FROM THIS FUCKING STAGE!! DON'T YOU COME UP HERE!! DON'T YOU COME UP HERE!! GODDAMN YOU!!! –"

Now, as stage manager, I figured I'd better do something quick. I ran out on stage and charged my way to Sammy's side. "Sammy, Sammy!" I whispered urgently. "It's okay! Kevin's not coming up here. Just keep singing, okay? *Just . . . keep . . . singing.*"

On cue, Sammy immediately resumed the voice of an angel.

"*. . . It is the night, of our dear Savior's birth . . .*"

Realizing I was now completely exposed like a deer in the footlights, I smiled sheepishly to the crowd and dashed back into the wings. It turned out to be the biggest laugh we got all night. Safe behind the curtain leg, I peered outwards into the darkened room. Kevin was nowhere to be seen.

Sammy finished his song to a rousing ovation. It was then he looked over to me squatting in the wings . . . and tossed me a wink. Just like he'd done with Mullet Head years before. I had to give ol' Sammy credit. He was a pro.

As the cast assembled for their curtain call, the Shepherd Hills choir sang true and proud, mustering enough energy to pull the crowd to their feet.

"*Joy to the world . . . The Lord has come . . .*"

It was also about this time the consumers in the audience figured out the secret beneath the shiny gold wrappers. Their cries went out almost simultaneously.

"*CAN-DEE!!!*"

Overcome with cocoa bean avarice, an assembly of consumers erupted in a mad scramble around the floor, biting and scratching each other over stray morsels, cramming their mouths full of foil-wrapped goodness. The audience screamed and cackled with a mix of terror and delight, lifting their knees high to avoid the crawling masses as the staff in attendance hastily tried to corral everyone.

(In retrospect, tossing chocolate money frivolously about probably wasn't the smartest idea we had. Nevertheless, the show must go on.)

Taking their final bows, the entire cast gathered on stage and invited the audience to join them in a closing, cheerful execution of "We Wish You A Merry Christmas." However, what was meant to be an innocent invitation gave way to a sudden onslaught of consumers and neighborhood children all charging the stage at once. In a frenzied jostle of musical talent and desire for attention, a festive free-for-all burst forth as the choir rose to their feet and intermingled with a swarm of spirited moans and beaming, drooling faces.

"*Cue the tree!*"

For the grand finale, I tugged a hidden rope attached to a wagon that ferried a six-foot twinkling Christmas tree center stage behind the ensemble. The audience oohed and ahhed. This time, unlike the beginning of the play, *every* lip was moving as the entire auditorium sang along together. In fact, the holiday spirit had so engulfed the crowd, no one seemed to mind too much when Neishi, a 240-pound Samoan consumer, climbed up on stage and began to strip.

The time was 8:15 p.m. Time to cue the house lights and send everyone home.

The crowd spilled out into the cool, crisp air of the auditorium courtyard under clear December skies. There, the once and celebrated Shepherd Hills Famous Players, sweaty and exhausted, joined the hodgepodge to sign autographs and pose for pictures. I remember clearly the faces of family members, so many proud faces; mothers gathered in their fur-collared coats like a sleuth of coifed bears, bathed in perfume and dotted with rouge and lipstick, fathers wearing neckties and after-shave. They all dressed up to come and see us perform. And drawn by their sides were their sons and daughters; consumers mingling and milling about, outfitted proudly in their costumes like fully decorated uniforms, their faces aglow.

As for me, I hung back, silent and light-headed. If I were being cheeky you could say I was pulling a Jay Gatsby; a man self-invented, throwing a magnificent party only to stand removed while observing it from afar. But that would be giving myself way too much credit. Truth is, I was simply content to watch unobtrusively the people I served – both current and from a time now past – treated to an outpouring of hugs, handshakes, kisses on the cheeks and pats on the back. I'd never felt such a sense of parental pride. It was then I glanced up at the sky and could've sworn I saw a solitary balloon skate by. But of course, there was no balloon. Still, I thought of Jackie Chuckam and wished he could've been here with us, wondering which role I might have assigned him. He would've made one hell of a Ghost of Christmas Yet To Come, instead of the ghost he was.

As small a production as it was, directing this play gave me something to cherish. For a brief, otherwise insignificant fragment of time, I felt like the teacher I'd always wanted to be. It granted me the opportunity to take each of my consumers aside one-on-one, to coach them, to motivate them to get their part just right. More valuable than any amount of skill training, I wanted them to know they weren't second-class citizens. Our little play gave them a taste of the public recognition they deserved – not *because of* their disability, but *in defiance of* it. But most of all, it felt good to see the old gang together again. It was, and always had been, small moments like these, moments I wanted to climb inside of, that gave me the greatest amount of pleasure – something I never would've gotten in a classroom. For almost twenty years I had watched each of them – Jim, Owen, Sammy, Darlene, Holly and Hughie – evolve from a hidden fortress of uncertainty tucked behind a cow pasture to a solid place in society, independent and sustained. What better reason for applause, even if that applause was only symbolic?

As the accolades continued, I felt a familiar leathery hand take hold of mine. It was Jim, pulling me with him into the fray. There he shouted with startling aplomb, *"Hey, embody – it's Steeb Gigger. Muh-my houseparent!"*

"Steve Grieger!" echoed Rebecca. "Our director!"

The emotion I felt was palpable. To a mixed strain of hoots and cheers, Owen and Sammy hoisted my arm in the air as if I'd just won the heavyweight championship of the world; winning applause along with the consumers – and *from* the consumers. Truthfully, I would've been just as content to have remained backstage, peeking through the curtain, proud and silent. But my cast wouldn't hear of it. Whether Jim had been told by Rebecca to go find me or whether it was his own spontaneous idea, I'll never know. Either way, to hear him announce me the way he did, to bestow me the same honor as the rest, moved me beyond tears.

All in all, the evening was a smashing success. With the last prop and hand-held microphone stored away, the tree and wagon tucked safely offstage, the floor swept clean of scattered, half-chewed gold foil, and the entire cast and audience on their way home to bed, I turned out the lights and securely locked the auditorium doors behind me.

At home, my head hit the pillow still abuzz, replaying the performance and its aftermath in my brain, as one final thought entered my mind:

You mean we have to do this again tomorrow *night?!*

CHAPTER 23

ACCEPTANCE

"The sins of the father are passed from generation to generation unless the chain is purposely – and purposefully – broken."
– Nebu, philosopher

"You're going to miss everything cool and die angry."
– Patton Oswalt, comedian, to a heckler

DESPITE MY EFFORTS to remain an amiable distance from my old man, one afternoon I received a phone call.

"Steve, this is your father. I have something to tell you."

I felt my grip tighten around the phone as he paused. For a brief moment I was eight years old again and stiffened obediently. It was then he said, more forcefully, "And you better listen to me and listen good!" Instantly, the phone left my ear and slammed back into the cradle. Any minute now I expected his wooden leg to come hurtling at me from halfway across the country.

I'd never had a chance to reconcile my feelings with my father before he left. I remember trying once, but it proved useless, asking questions he couldn't or wasn't willing to answer. At our last good-bye, as he packed up his car along with the Old Spice, the Kentucky Club and the bourbon, I was shut out by a wall of indifference; a thinly-veiled disappointment that I could only interpret as a personal dismissal.

CHALLENGED: A TRIBUTE

Perhaps if there had been outlets available to him such as medications or therapy or simply success, our home would've been different. I wouldn't characterize my father as a bad man, but rather a man burdened by a dark heart. His was a life that was only as full as the dreams he never realized – and for that I resented him.

And yet, the very same resentment I carried is what helped me to bond with my consumers, as I could often feel a similar sense of resentment in them. Theirs was a resentment at their own disabilities, even if they couldn't voice it or understand it. Resentment remains the one obstacle we strive to steer our way around on a daily basis. Its size and danger fluctuates with an unpredictable spite. So when it comes to how things should have been, how the world remains unfair, I remain committed to the job.

A few days later I received a vicious letter from a man who signed it "Dad." The letter claimed my mother and I were to blame for all his problems in life.

I stood frozen, clutching the letter, astounded. Then I smiled sourly, recalling something my mother used to say. She used to quip that someday Dad would find a way to blame us for two things before he died: The loss of his leg and World War II. This letter came close.

Initially, I tried to deny that he would send me something like this; that it was just a bad dream. But this was quickly replaced by realization. Then anger. Then rage. I grew livid. *How dare he?!* There was no way I was going to let the bastard get away with this, not at a point in my life when I had finally grown self-assured and proud of what I was doing.

That night I poured my heart out onto the page and pulled no punches about all we had endured. A lifetime of anguish and humiliation, of fists and shouts, of blame and victimization. I slashed my ball point across the page with precision and vengeance. For the first time in my life I understood the symbolic meaning of a poison pen letter. With each new sentence, each new outrage, I found myself systematically slaying my father. Slash by slash. Words like martyr, ogre, disgusting, cruel, vile, you-never-did-this and I'll-never-forgive-that flooded forth, punctuated by hate, hate and more hate. It was at once a long-overdue lesson plan and killing field. No more was I going to allow him to be a condemnation in my life. I denied him any further contact with me. It was a letter that could only be ended by the harsh, cruel words: *"You're dead to me now."*

I sent the letter without having to think twice. The weight of what felt like a hundred lifetimes was lifted from my shoulders. I never heard from my father again. Maybe we live in an age of psycho-babble and selfishness, but that didn't stop me from cutting myself a big slice of self-help pie and gorging without shame.

Three weeks later my father passed away.

Complications from diabetes or something. He died alone in his rental unit, in the middle of Nowhere Special, Oklahoma, on the bathroom floor with the water in the sink still running. I never told my mother about the correspondence we'd had. I've never shed a tear over my father to this day – at least not one that I'll ever admit to. And I've never felt guilty about it.

There's no worse feeling of abandonment than when you're sitting at the dinner table next to your dad as he ignores you, sleeping in the same house as he snores peacefully in the next room a thousand miles away, or when the only acknowledgement he bestows is when he reminds you you're nothing but an inconvenience, or worse, a mark of his own failure. I used to wonder why, even as an adult, I always felt like a child, years behind everyone else, socially, emotionally. Then I realized. Maybe it's because children who are victims of abuse are still waiting for their childhood to actually begin. Waiting for all those supposed joys to rain down upon them. They're still waiting for TV daddies to take them fishing or to ball games or to read them a story before bedtime and end it with a designated kiss goodnight. Still waiting for the ignorant bliss they were promised that all the *other* children seemed to have. Simply waiting their turn.

About four months later, as the Southern California landscape changed from dry dead grass to damp dead grass, I was busy catching up by phone with my sister who now lived in North Carolina with her second husband. My sister and I had never been particularly close growing up, partly because we'd never been taught what family ties were, and partly because of our age difference of five years. In the mid-sixties, while she was tip-toeing the threshold of womanhood, I was dreaming about meeting Batman and Robin. Only later in life did we both realize and appreciate the specific upbringing we'd shared and its commonality.

In our conversation I discovered that when my father was close to death, my sister had briefly re-established contact with him for personal reasons of her own. Only then did she tell me that Dad had told her he was proud.

"Proud of what?" I asked.

"You know. Proud of you, your accomplishments. Your job."

"Bullshit!" I snapped.

"No, really," she insisted. "He told me he was. He told everybody he was."

"So why the fuck didn't he ever tell *me*?"

My sister didn't have an answer.

"Bullshit," I reaffirmed. "You know Dad. That's just the last-minute rambling of a dying atheist trying to cover his ass with God."

Since that phone conversation I've thought about what my sister said many times. But there was no point in trying to revisit it. Somehow, some way, I had run afoul of my father as a child and I never knew why, nor would ever know. Still, I wanted to tell somebody that I didn't need my old man to be proud of me. All I wanted was for him not to hate me. I didn't need for him to coddle me. All I wanted was to be acknowledged. I didn't even need for him to love me. All I needed was to feel as if I mattered.

My sister never brought it up again and I didn't ask her to. I didn't want anything to complicate my bitterness. If this had been a movie, I would've no

CHALLENGED: A TRIBUTE | 225

doubt found great joy, great retribution in my father finally proclaiming his pride in me. After all, isn't that what every child wants to hear? But even I couldn't fool myself into believing such a cliché. And yet, that cliché remains a burning hole in my stomach. But only when I let it bother me. Only when I wonder if it's time to put the fire out.

Maybe one day I'll consider doing just that.

THE RETURN OF JAMES CORNELL LIVINGSTON

When I became a Q, one of the first traditions I established was to gather everyone for Thanksgiving dinner at one of my three group homes. For those consumers who didn't leave to visit their families, this usually awarded us with a group of about five or six. I'd also made it a tradition to extend the invitation to the CLP – which always afforded us the additional company of Jim Livingston.

Thanksgiving day, 2001, I arrived at the Spring Tree Apartments to pick Jim up for dinner. I found him lying on the deck of his upstairs apartment, the same spot where Owen had fallen years before. A cold panic surged thorough me. As I roused him, I noticed at least a good two-day's growth of beard on his face. His clothes were disheveled and stained, he smelled of urine, and he was clearly disoriented. After a series of questions and broken answers, I deciphered that Jim had gone to buy a newspaper two days earlier and had forgotten his key. When he arrived home, Owen had already left for the holiday with his brother. Jim found himself locked out with no one to call for help, nowhere to go, and no knowledge of how to do anything about it. I collected Jim in the condition he was in and delivered him to the group home for dinner. There, I cleaned and shaved him, found him a change of clothes, and fed him countless helpings of turkey and mashed potatoes.

The following Monday I discussed the situation with the new supervisor of the CLP, a serious-minded woman, bright-eyed and fresh out of college, with more than a passing resemblance to Michelle Montgomery than I was comfortable with. I was taken aback to discover that six months earlier Jim had been diagnosed with "early-onset" Alzheimer's disease. It all started with a slow, steady pattern of decline: not arriving for work until noon, making dinner as late as midnight, eating raw, uncooked food splashed with puddles of ketchup. Soon, simple cognitive functions such as cleaning his room or planning a grocery list were met with stubborn resistance and puzzled stares. All those ADL skills Jim had painstakingly learned by habit were now fading away. In fact, for the last few months, discussion had been battered back and forth between Jim's social worker and the ersatz Michelle over the growing concern of his overall safety in community. But it was the event on Thanksgiving that once and for all proved something conclusive needed to be done.

Though technically he was no longer my consumer, I was damned if I was going to stand by and watch Jim frog-leap into a nursing home. After some initial research, I discovered that with his new diagnosis Jim now qualified for an ICF/DD-H facility. Purely by coincidence – if coincidence is a fair assumption – I happened to have a vacancy at one of my homes, a blue and white Cape Cod-alike known as Columbia Court. The match couldn't have been more perfect or perfectly timed. The decision was an easy one. By mid-December, just in time for Christmas, James Cornell Livingston moved from his CLP apartment to Columbia Court, and back into the welcoming arms of peers and staff alike.

I immediately became an A student of the disease. I attended seminars. I bought books. I in-serviced the staff on its particular signs and symptoms. In effect, I took it upon myself to take responsibility, because no one else was as invested as I was. We learned that Alzheimer's disease is defined as *"a neurological disease in which the brain begins to calcify, characterized by loss of mental ability severe enough to interfere with normal activities of daily living."* Short term memory loss is the most common early symptom, wherein the person may be able to recall things from twenty years ago with vivid clarity, yet not be able to remember what they ate that morning for breakfast. Moreover, I was saddened to learn that people with Down syndrome – if they live long enough – are disposed to dementia, without fail. Some years ago, it was quite common for individuals with Down syndrome to die early in life. In the scheme of things their bodies are generally weaker and their physiology runs on a clock that ticks faster than others'. However, with each passing decade and each new development in modern medical treatment, people with Down syndrome have now begun to live longer. Hence, only now are we seeing the effects of dementia on this very population simply by virtue and curse of prolonged life.

Over the years I'd often grappled with the dichotomy of keeping a working relationship with the consumers separate from my personal feelings. But with Jim I couldn't help it. Not only had I come to admire him, but I'd grown to respect him as a man who endured a lifelong grind of assembly-line treatment. Jim survived a time when daily humiliations were Standard Institutional Practice, medications tasted like tin foil, psycho-analytical therapy was akin to a sledgehammer to the skull, and the concept of dignity was as foreign as clean underwear. Jim was also a man who'd been abandoned by his family, left to evolve from a simple-minded, bathroom-obsessed castaway, to an underestimated blip on a chart, to a contender for independence – all by his own order, his own course. Now, as his disease settled into place, he was to begin a passage of another sort. Whereas typical ISP goals for Jim used to include things like learning how to ride the city bus, write a check or increase his menu repertoire, progress would now be measured by a simple lack of regression. And though People First dictated that we alter the negative impact of our language, it seemed disrespectful to soft-pedal the phrasing. People First-speak be damned, Jim Livingston didn't "have" Alzheimer's, he was *afflicted.*

Watching Jim change caused me to reflect on the progression of my own life – specifically my life with the consumers at Shepherd Hills. In the CLP, Jim and I had shared a connection that emerged concurrently as we both learned a new understanding of living on our own. Now, as his mind and body prepared to evaporate, I found myself urgently struggling to keep that connection alive. Jim had once been like a brother to me, and now it was as if he'd taken on the role of an aged father. I wasn't there for my own father by choice; I will be there for Jim.

The day he moved into Columbia Court I was there to help Jim unpack. Buried at the bottom of his tattered suitcase was a crinkled plastic witch's mask. I asked Jim to put it on. With the same great care and reverence as always, he slowly fed the frayed elastic over his head and slipped the mask into place. He then raised his hands in claw-like kind, and with eerie, wicked glee, he cackled dryly with a reassuring familiarity.

"*Eeeee-hee-hee-hee-hee!*"

By 2002 the old main campus was finally vacated, sold, and ultimately razed from a sturdy edifice of brick and stucco to a single heap of ash-white rubble. All to make way for future condos. One living space sacrificed for another.

I, for one, was sad to see it go, not just for sentimental reasons, but because Shepherd Hills, with its assemblage of dorms based on functioning levels culminating in the unique Independent Training Facility, was a rare place where consumers could actually "graduate" to a better life. For those like Jim, moving progressively from unit to unit, learning skills along the way, there will never be anything else like it. What remains behind are gaps in the system. Residential placement is now determined by forcing square pegs into round holes – never mind the triangular ones.

But what holds fast are the dynamics of the job. Bottom line, working in this field can easily become one big, giant comfort zone. The surroundings become an extension of what we ourselves go home to at night. It's a job with family rooms and sofas and TVs and back yards and barbecues. The older you grow, the older the consumers grow with you – and there's undeniable comfort in that. How many jobs allow you to play table games, watch DVDs, go to Las Vegas or cook dinners with dessert? And just how many jobs allow you the chance to educate others about the concept of dignity? For God's sake, who *wouldn't* want to be paid for that?

Call me a disability snob and damn me for preaching, I don't care. People with developmental disabilities are not miscreants of society any more than they're holy innocents. They can't talk to animals, see the dead or smell gold. They're not court jesters or charity cases or objects of pity. They're *people*. They use public transportation, put money into local communities, relax at the end of the day with hobbies, hold down real jobs. They possess valid opinions and outlooks. They struggle with moral dilemmas, and surprise us with keen senses of humor. They experience the full human gamut of love, joy, anger, grief and pain. And yet, cognitive minorities remain one of the most socially and economically marginalized groups in the Unites States today. The diagnosis of "mental retardation" is perhaps the most devastating label a person can be burdened with in our society.

Admittedly, as much as we "caregivers" may strive to teach consumers to take care of themselves, there will always be a need for us to help fill in the cracks found in daily living; to provide that little extra something in order to keep their world fair. A certain amount of sheltering does go on – it's inescapable. It's ingrained into the system. Still, the people I serve are ever-lasting and never fail to impress me. They press onward with a limited ability to reason in a world without reason. They achieve greatness in the things we take for granted, in ways we cannot know.

They are my heroes.

I'm often asked why I've stayed in this line of work. What was the turning point that made me an advocate? Was it because "I care" like they told us in orientation? Because of pity like I'd felt for Clara Welch? Because of my urge to teach? More directly, because of my urge to teach a controlled audience? Because of my need for a surrogate family? Because of my father's distaste – or in spite of it? Because of his disappointment – or in spite of it? Is it morbid curiosity that keeps me going? A nagging streak of humanity? Bullish pride? Or am I ultimately just in it for the laughs?

Nah.

I do it because I like it.

I do it because I can't think of doing anything else nearly as well.

I do it because the world should be, ought to be, why-oh-why can't it be . . . *fair?*

I do it because . . .

I just do it because.

EPILOGUE

"When working with the mentally challenged, remember, the coffee cup is always half full – of tea."
– placard from Dawn Barry's office wall found in the rubble of ITF Village

A S FOR THE Notorious Nine of 1982, to this wistful QMRP they only become more faceless with each passing day. I no longer share the same affinity I had with them in the CLP, let alone the all but forgotten ITF Village. Even the original staff like Dot Lindberg and Anita Rodriguez have faded away, joining the unknown whereabouts of Dawn Barry, Irma Fritts, "Baseball" Paul, Mandy Meckel, Sissy Shithead and, of course, Michelle Montgomery. My advocacy is now assigned to paper where my best strengths lie. Ultimately, it has become the best way I can serve the consumers, something that took me half a lifetime to learn.

Meanwhile, each individual continues their journey through life in his or her own way – as best as I can know:

COLE PETERSEN. Following his breakdown and subsequent discharge, I used to wonder if Cole was locked away in some mental monkey ward, or destined to reemerge as a tortured artist of the trendy Hollywood Melrose scene. Turns out he paid his dues to both worlds. After a stint at Metropolitan State Hospital, Cole (with the help of his father's finances and management) launched a successful greeting card and ceramics Web site where he creates and sells his own original hippie-dippy artwork online. Last I checked a personalized cereal bowl was going for $39.95 – shipping and handling not included.

BILLY MATTILA. One fittingly nippy day about a year ago, I ran into Billy Mattila as he was touring a new day program in El Cajon. He had a full backwoods beard, horn-rimmed glasses, and a walking cast on his right foot. He was dressed in jeans and a white cotton shirt with a "Jesus Loves Me" pin on the lapel, and looked almost identical to his father that day he visited ITF Village. It made me want to ask Billy if he'd been in touch his father, but I thought better of it. When Billy's eyes met mine I froze briefly, a surge of that all too familiar dislike shooting through my middle. After all, this was a man I'd once fantasized about choking to death. Billy grinned, wide and scraggly, and thrust out his hand for me to shake. "HI, BUDDY," he shouted gleefully. "IT *ME*! I *MISH* YOU!" We shook hands and Billy tittered like a small child at the joyful recognition of someone from his past without any of the ill memories. Hell, to him there probably *were* no ill memories. We spoke cordially, if not inconsequentially, for a few minutes, and I had to admit it was actually nice to chat with him on that level. And those few minutes were plenty.

ALFRED FORREST "IGGY" FLYNN. I'd once classified Jim Livingston as an "also-ran." But if anyone came closer to that definition, it was Iggy Flynn. Someone who drifted in and out of my life with little impact other than the fact that I remember him fondly. He was friendly, kind-hearted, happy-go-lucky, and thought farting was the pinnacle of Modern Western comedy. Iggy, probably better than anyone, embraced and embodied "quality of living" over "quality of life."

Oddly, the whereabouts of Iggy became a mystery. Shortly after he moved into the CLP, his parents emerged, discharged him, and moved the family to an undisclosed town somewhere in Texas, where I'm confident he's found a new home to hang his ten-gallon hat.

SAMMY WHITE. After a few more years with the CLP, Sammy moved to Walla Walla, Washington, with his mother. One night he called me at home. It was 3 a.m. How he found my unlisted number I still don't know. Why he called at 3 a.m. was also puzzling. He called to ask me if I had Darlene Beaudine's new phone number. Half-asleep and cranky as hell, I told him I didn't. This wasn't good enough for Sammy. He grew angry. He accused me of purposely not wanting to help him and shouted that I was denying him his rights. At first I was stunned at his harsh tone, seeing as how I'd come to think of Sammy as a friend. Then again, only friends can share such heated misunderstandings at three in the morning. It also reminded me of the way Sammy had always sought instant gratification – all the way back to our first encounter and his tearful, snot-filled plea for five dollars. However, before I could set myself into "Sammy mode" and tactfully counsel him on the inappropriateness of his call, he hung up. I've yet to hear from him again.

DARLENE BEAUDINE. Darlene still lives and works in the community, although no longer at Chuck E. Cheese. Today Darlene works for Fuddruckers Restaurant, bussing tables and mopping restrooms where she proudly wears the uniform – and cap – of a "Fuddbuddy." Despite all her OCD quirks and fanciful dance routines, Darlene's "real job" always remained crucial to her identity as a way of making a productive contribution to society, earning her the privilege of adulthood and the respect of her peers.

CHALLENGED: A TRIBUTE   231

As to her former promiscuity, Darlene now seeks the attentions of a small, very high-functioning consumer who also holds a "real job" washing cars for a Lexus dealership. Last I heard, the two have plans to get married soon.

HOLLY AND HUGHIE LAMB. To this day Holly and Hughie remain an iconic fixture in the CLP, still married and still very much in love. Sharing their own apartment proved neither too big nor too small. It was just right. Despite the symbolic status, theirs became a dedication to the institution of marriage – never mind harboring a shared disability that society still sees as predestined to fail. But while Holly remains sharp as tack and shrewd as ever, Hughie, like Jim, has been diagnosed with "early" Alzheimer's disease. Only time will tell the path it will take, and how it will affect them as a developmentally disabled married couple.

In the meantime, Holly remains bound to her wheelchair while Hughie now relies on the aid of a 4-wheeled walker. Every once in a while I spot them in the distance as they make their way to catch the bus. Only now, Holly pushes *herself* to lead the way while Hughie trails behind, feet shuffling, wheels scraping, eternally stylish in his suit and tie.

OWEN VAN WINKLE. Owen eventually went home to live his final years with his brother. It was the one thing he'd always wanted most. Till the end, he remained the same, cantankerous old man he'd learned to play so well. On occasion, he'd speak at local skilled-nursing facilities and the odd high school sociology class about his life, wearing the same magenta sports coat, I'm sure. People loved listening to Owen – that is, people who never had to work with him. He was a natural soapbox orator, or as Michelle once observed, someone who would've made "the perfect game show host." His claim to fame remains that he lived to be the oldest-living individual with Down syndrome at the time of his death, passing away in his sleep at age seventy-nine.

JIM LIVINGSTON. As the years continue to pass I watch Jim slow down, like the last few wobbles of a spinning top. Slower . . . slower. Hour-long showers have become common, with an extra hour spent obsessively trying to comb bangs that have long since been clipped for that very reason. Neither is it unusual for Jim to fall asleep while lifting a spoonful of food to his mouth as he grows lost within his slumber and his mind continues to close.

When Jim's mother died at the age of ninety-seven, his sister appeared from a little place called Thin Air – otherwise known as Bel Air, California. She traveled down, ostensibly, to acknowledge that Jim was receiving satisfactory care. At last I had my chance. In one breath I launched into a passionate recounting of all the hardships Jim had faced in order to achieve an independence few have known, and just what a truly remarkable person her brother was. When I finally stopped talking five minutes later, I looked at the clock and discovered that, in fact, *forty minutes* had gone by. Without realizing it, I had spewed a non-stop diatribe twenty years in the making, desperate to impact upon her – upon *any*body – the life force of a consumer. Jim's sister stared at me. Her face looked like a blank wall minus the sentiment. "I see," she said. "Thank you for letting me know." Then she promptly disappeared once more from his life. Like mother, like daughter.

Over time, Jim has regressed to the point where he can no longer walk unless taken directly by the hand. Many are the evenings when I help escort him from his bed to the dinner table, the feel of his gnarled, leathery hands weightlessly gripping mine for reassurance. Standing by the side of the freeway years ago with Owen, I had mixed feelings about holding a man's hand. Now it's as instinctive as guiding a child.

Though first diagnosed with Alzheimer's in 2001, Jim remains stable yet tightly gripped by the clutches of his disease. Eyeglasses confuse him, dentures frustrate him. On occasion I'll watch him sitting at the table, coloring earnestly outside the lines or wolfing a piece of his favorite chocolate cake. That's when I smile. Other times I'll watch him from the hall, sitting alone on the edge of his bed, balancing a photo album between his knees. One by one, Jim studies the small number of photos which own the past, and as he slowly turns the pages, sometimes he begins to cry. That's when I sit next to him, put my arm around him, and gently rock him.

One day I found Jim on the bathroom floor next to the toilet. He was confused how he got there and unable to stand. 911 was immediately called. His neurologist confirmed that the cause was a series of small strokes, and the best he could assure me was that they would only continue to increase. No one wants to admit the inevitability of hospice as it hovers in the distance like a black cloud.

With each passing year, Jim's memory deteriorates a little more, mercifully taking time out to pause for a good few weeks before resuming its slow decline into the advanced stages. Each day his face withers like one of those carved apple-headed dolls we used to make as children in grade school. Each day his eyes sink farther into their sockets, disclosing bone wrapped taut by skin, as the round face of Mr. Mouth unmasks a hidden jawbone. With each passing year, at his annual meeting, his support team always comments, "This could be the year we lose him." And yet, year after year, he continues to prove us wrong. Each day I continue to test Jim's memory. I ask him, "Do you know who I am?"

Each day Jim remembers.

For a brief moment he steps out from a distant fog that shrouds an uneven landscape, into a world of harmony and hope, and his eyes become clear. "Oh!" he says with a broad and bountiful smile. "It's Steeb Gigger . . . Muh-my houseparent." It remains the warmest, most soul-satisfying thing anyone's ever said to me. Two words that define security, stability, trust and love. *Houseparent.* I can't imagine a grander title.

Back when I first started in this field it was nothing more than a way to bide my time until I could achieve the perfect life in all its fleeting glamour; the perfect woman, the perfect career, the perfect identity, the perfect peace of mind. Instead, I realized the kind of fortune that sneaks up from behind and taps you on the opposite shoulder, causing you to briefly look the other way until you finally figure out the joke.

My father once told me that when I die, the world wouldn't miss me. Whether by accident, rebellion, or a simple stroke of luck, I'm forever thankful I was able to escape that brutality and discover an entirely different life. One filled with humor and excitement and challenges. One filled with people who care for each other in every sense of the word.

My dad had it backwards. It's me who doesn't miss his world.

POSTSCRIPT

THROUGHOUT THIS BOOK the terms "mental retardation," "developmentally disabled," "client," "consumer," and their variants have been used freely. This was done purposely as a means to represent the time period in which the story takes place. On October 5, 2010, President Obama signed a law mandating Federal statutes no longer use the term "mental retardation." The replacement phrase is now "intellectual disability." In fact, many states in response to self-advocates and with an understanding of the negative impact of language have turned away from using the term "mental retardation" except for diagnostic or reporting requirements. As of this writing, the American Association for Mental Retardation has changed its name to the American Association on Intellectual and Developmental Disabilities. Even the title of my job in some regions has changed from QMRP to QDDP (Qualified Developmental Disability Professional), and I wouldn't be surprised if QIDP isn't far behind.

We can only look forward to what other new, progressive, provocative, and "special" terminology the future may bring.

ACKNOWLEDGEMENTS

IN AUGUST 2005, three colleagues and I spoke at the National QDDP Conference (NAQ) in Las Vegas, Nevada, where we presented a breakout session titled "Blunders, Botches, Screw-Ups and Oops–Learning from Our Mistakes." It was a high-spirited panel discussion, sharing our stories and focusing on the humorous side of caring for people with developmental disabilities; a tribute to their individual idiosyncrasies vs. our own good intentions and over-zealous stumbles. It was from that presentation *Challenged:A Tribute* evolved.

First and foremost, I would like to thank the Home of Guiding Hands *en masse*, residents and staff alike. Working there has not only taught me a sense of perspective and priority, but it has given me a life's calling. To all the real life special individuals represented here by the Notorious Nine (plus Iggy), I owe them thirty years' worth of thanks. To all the colleagues I saw come and go, I miss you and thank you for your life lessons.

Specific to HGH, a special nod is owed to Mark Klaus, Executive Director, for his stoic professionalism and support, Karen Cook, Development Director, for her warm, wholehearted praise, and Mary Moser-Cooper, Early Childhood Development Director, for her humor and insight. Together their combined appraisal granted me the sense of authentication I needed.

What can I say about Toni Gallagher? Toni is an amazing woman, someone I both envy and admire as she is the only person I know to combine five otherwise pretty cool lives into one extraordinary life. Though Toni and I remain in touch on an occasional basis (active author-producer-world traveler that she is), still, when I needed her input, she was there for me. Toni's enthusiasm, suggestions and focus helped spark ideas I never would've thought of otherwise. Thank you, beautiful Toni, for your creativity, your kindness, and your generosity.

And then there's the masterful David Hines, fellow author and lifelong friend, who helped guide the book from its humble beginnings to its finished state. Ever since Dave graciously agreed to edit my first book *Baked-Off: Memoirs of a Pillsbury Bake-Off Junkie* in 2008, he has become my go-to guy. The earliest drafts of *Challenged* were really not much more than a collection of anecdotes – and with that I foolishly thought my work was done. It was Dave who nagged me incessantly to unleash the emotional ties *behind* each story, and thus inspired me to flesh out something personal, accessible, and (dare I say) meaningful. Thanks to Dave, *Challenged* ultimately became a story about family. Dave, I am indebted to you. This book simply would not exist without you. (I hope you agree that's a good thing.)

Though all the characters in this book retain a special place in my heart, I would most like to thank the *real* Jim Livingston. Jim passed away on February 14, 2010, Valentine's Day. He slipped away peacefully in his sleep, finally succumbing to the effects of Alzheimer's Disease. Jim taught me the true meaning of "never say never." His story, perhaps more than anyone's, remains the most inspiring: he really was abandoned as a baby, and he really did work his way up through the system to grab the brass ring of independence. But what I remember most fondly about Jim are the things he loved (besides, of course, his chocolate cake). He loved to dance, curse the Padres, act silly to get laughs, and mimic all things iconic that captivated him: The Beatles, Cowboys and Indians, Darth Vader, King Tut, and The Wicked Witch of the West. He was one of the funniest, sweetest and most trusting friends I'll ever have. I miss him terribly.

And finally to my mother, Theda, whose ever-lasting love and gentleness provided the bedrock I needed to steady myself through a childhood of self-doubt, and whose encouragement gave me direction and confidence to succeed as an adult. Sadly, she was taken from me on September 22, 2001. Though her passing occurred during the chronological storyline of *Challenged*, I ultimately chose not to include that element in the book. Her story deserves it own special consideration, which I carry with me always. I love you too, Mom.

ALSO BY THE AUTHOR

BAKED-OFF!
Memoirs of a Pillsbury Bake-Off Junkie

Is it possible to bake your way to a million dollars in just one day?
Embracing everyone from the humblest home cook to the loftiest armchair
gourmet, *BAKED-OFF!* delivers a toothy view from the Pillsbury Bake-Off®
competition floor as it follows one man's hilarious quest to win the Holy Grail
of cooking contests and its million dollar grand prize. At turns both heartfelt and
ruthless, *BAKED-OFF!* stirs up a deft blend of pop-culture commentary, expose,
recipes and romance. Join foodie Steve Grieger for a candid peek inside a national
institution as he carries us from neophyte fascination to full-blown obsession.

2009 Culinary Scene Literary Award – Best Memoir
2009 San Diego East County Writers' Conference – Best New Author

Available online from
xlibris.com, amazon.com, bn.com,
or from your local bookstore

Made in the USA
Monee, IL
11 August 2023

40857595R00142